Using Your PC,
Second Edition

Baffled by computer–ad technospeak? Here's all you need to know!

❶ 100MHz 486DX4 CPU

Let's start from the back. *CPU* stands for Central Processing Unit—the brains of your computer. 486DX4 tells you how "big" that brain is—the higher the number, the more powerful the processor. 100MHz tells you how fast that CPU runs.

❷ RAM

(random-access memory) temporarily holds data and program instructions that the CPU is currently using. You need at least 8M (megabytes) to run Windows programs efficiently.

❸ Hard drive

serves as the main storage facility for your programs, files, and data. A 520M hard drive should provide enough space for home and business uses.

❹ Floppy drive

records and plays back information from floppy disks. Use floppy disks to transport your work from computer to computer.

❺ Local bus graphics

help your computer work faster by speeding up the video display.

- ❶ Intel **100 MHz 486DX4 CPU**
- ❷ 8M of **RAM** upgradable to 96M — ❸
- 520M **hard drive**, 12 ms average access time
- ❹ 1.44M high-density **floppy drive**
- **Local bus graphics** — ❺ ❻
- Quad-speed **CD-ROM**, 16-bit **sound card, speakers** ❼

❻ CD-ROM

(compact disc, read-only memory)—the disk drive that transfers information stored on CD to the computer. With CD-ROM, your computer can display powerful programs like encyclopedias, full-motion video, and stereo sounds.

Multimedia System!

Great for home or office applications

Comes with popular software packages

- ◆ 14" .28 dot pitch color **SVGA monitor**, 1024 x 768 **resolution**
- ◆ 14.4 Kbps internal **data/fax modem**
- ◆ 101-key keyboard and **mouse**
- ◆ Includes **Windows 95**
- ◆ Free **application software**: Microsoft Works, Microsoft Money, Encarta '95, various games

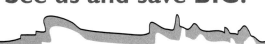

See us and save BIG!

❼ Speakers and sound card

allow your computer to play music and digital sound effects.

201 W. 103rd Street
Indianapolis, IN 46290
(317) 581-3500
Copyright© 1996 Que Corporation

❽ SVGA (SuperVGA) monitor

has the highest resolution and can display the most colors on the screen of any monitor type.

❾ Resolution

is the number of horizontal and vertical dots (pixels) that your monitor can display. The higher the numbers, the crisper the image. A 1024 × 768 display is best for games, drafting, and desktop publishing software.

❿ Data/Fax modem

lets you send and receive data or faxes through standard telephone lines. 14.4 Kbps is the minimum speed you should have for accessing the Internet. The bigger the number, the faster the modem.

⓫ Mouse

is used to give instructions to your computer and to move objects around on the screen. You'll need a mouse to use Windows 95.

⓬ Windows 95

is system software. It performs all the complicated tasks of running and maintaining your computer.

⓭ Application software

is the collection of programs you use to get your work done.

Using

Your PC, Second Edition

Using

Your PC, Second Edition

— Michael O'Mara and Gerry Routledge —

Using Your PC, Second Edition

Library of Congress Catalog Number: 95-71757

ISBN: 0-7897-0637-7

97   96   95   6   5   4   3   2   1

Interpretation of the printing code: The rightmost double-digit number is the year of the book's printing; the rightmost single-digit number, the number of the book's printing. For example, a printing code of 95-1 shows that the first printing of the book occurred in 1995.

All terms mentioned in this book that are known to be trademarks or service marks have been appropriately capitalized. Que cannot attest to the accuracy of this information. Use of a term in this book should not be regarded as affecting the validity of any trademark or service mark.

Screen reproductions in this book were created using Collage Plus from Inner Media, Inc., Hollis, NH.

Composed in *ITC Century*, *ITC Highlander*, and *MCPdigital* by Que Corporation.

Credits

President
Roland Elgey

Vice President and Publisher
Marie Butler-Knight

Associate Publisher
Don Roche, Jr.

Publishing Director
Brad Koch

Editorial Services Director
Elizabeth Keaffaber

Director of Marketing
Lynn E. Zingraf

Managing Editor
Michael Cunningham

Title Manager
Kathie-Jo Arnoff

Senior Series Editor
Chris Nelson

Acquisitions Editor
Deborah Abshier

Product Director
Robin Drake

Editor
Lynn Northrup

**Assistant Product
Marketing Manager**
Kim Margolius

Technical Editor
David Shinn

Technical Specialist
Nadeem Muhammed

Acquisitions Assistant
Tracy M. Williams

Editorial Assistant
Carmen Krikorian

Book Designer
Ruth Harvey

Cover Designer
Dan Armstrong

Production Team
Anne Dickerson
Chad Dressler
Trey Frank
Jason Hand
John Hulse
Stephanie Layton
Michelle Lee
Kaylene Riemen
Bobbi Satterfield
Michael Thomas
Chris Van Camp
Kelly Warner
Jody York

Indexer
Mary Jane Frisby

About the Authors

 **Michael O'Mara** has been helping others learn to use computers and software for nearly ten years, first in a corporate setting, and then as a staff author with The Cobb Group, where he wrote innumerable articles about leading computer software programs and served as Editor-in-Chief of several monthly software journals. Now a full-time freelance writer, he has co-authored or contributed to other Que books, including *Using DOS; Using Windows 3.11;* and *Special Edition, Using CompuServe.*

 **Gerry Routledge** is a Canadian computer consultant who has been teaching and writing about computers "since binary had only one number." He specializes in PC technical support seminars for non-technical personnel and has written several books over the years, including Que's *Using DOS* and the first edition of *Using Your PC.* Gerry is the owner of Routledge Computer Services in Montreal, Quebec.

Acknowledgments

It takes a lot of people to produce a book like this. Many of them are behind the scenes, and their names only appear on the credits page. The reader never knows how hard these folks worked to get this book on the shelf. We owe them *all* a lot of thanks—but we want to mention a few people in particular:

Product Director Robin "Whackmaster" Drake kept the technical level and page count on track, while guaranteeing we got *most* of what we wanted.

Editor Lynn Northrup pulled all the pieces together, while making sure the text was smooth, readable, and technically consistent.

Technical Editor David Shinn provided crucial technical assistance. His expertise helped ensure this book's usefulness and broad appeal.

The production staff got the pages laid out, proofread, and shipped in record time. We couldn't have done it without them.

We'd like to hear from you!

As part of our continuing effort to produce books of the highest possible quality, Que would like to hear your comments. To stay competitive, we *really* want you, as a computer book reader and user, to let us know what you like or dislike most about this book or other Que products.

You can mail comments, ideas, or suggestions for improving future editions to the address below, or send us a fax at (317) 581-4663. For the on-line inclined, Macmillan Computer Publishing has a forum on CompuServe (type **GO QUEBOOKS** at any prompt) through which our staff and authors are available for questions and comments. The address of our Internet site is **http://www.mcp.com** (World Wide Web).

In addition to exploring our forum, please feel free to contact me personally to discuss your opinions of this book: on CompuServe, I'm at 72002,2515 and on the Internet, I'm **rdrake@que.mcp.com.**

Thanks in advance—your comments will help us to continue publishing the best books available on computer topics in today's market.

Robin Drake
Product Development Specialist
Que Corporation
201 W. 103rd Street
Indianapolis, Indiana 46290
USA

Contents at a Glance

Connecting Your PC to the Rest of the World 301

Appendixes 345

Table of Contents

Inside the box
see page 11

The PC's comfy— now what about me?

see page 24

Know your system unit
see page 37

4 What Exactly Is a CPU?

5 Understanding Memory

*What's all
this about
memory?
This
chapter
gives you
the scoop.*

*It says I'm
out of
memory!
What does
that
mean?*

see page 72

6 What You Need to Know about Monitors

7 Disks and Disk Drives

*A type-
writer and
then some!*

see page 96

How to use
a wild card

see page 121

Part II: Getting Comfortable with Windows 95

10 Getting Started with Windows 95

Are you new
to Windows
95? This
is your
chapter!

*What's in
this folder?*

see page 156

Part III: You Need Software!

13 Word Processing Makes Your Written Work Look Good

How to jazz up those boring documents see page 183

14 Crunch Numbers with Spreadsheets

*Having fun
with your
PC*

see page 237

Part IV: Other Equipment to Buy for Your PC

19 Printers and Scanners

23 Bulletin Boards and On-Line Services

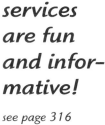

*Finding
the cool
stuff*

see page 336

Part VI: Appendixes

A What to Do When You Need Help

Need help?
Check this
appendix
for answers
to your
questions

B What's on the CD?

This CD's
packed with
features!

What if I have Windows 3.1, 3.11, or Windows for Workgroups?

C What If I Have an Earlier Version of Windows?

Copying, moving, and deleting files

see page 416

Introduction

Computers used to be run by scientists or people who worked for the government. These folks wore white lab coats and didn't seem to speak plain English. In those days, most people were a little in awe of computers and felt intimidated by them. In general, you just avoided computers then. You didn't have to use them, and you didn't have to care about how they worked.

Times have changed! These days, computers are on your desk, in the ATM where you get cash, even in your *car*. You can't avoid them. In fact, you probably already know more about computers than you ever thought you would. And you need to know more.

That's why we put together *Using Your PC*, Second Edition. It's for people just like you, people who use computers and need someplace to go—quickly—when a question pops up. This book assumes that you've already mastered the *really* hard things in life, like raising kids, running a business, killing crabgrass, cooking a soufflé, and maybe even programming a VCR. You're probably an experienced computer user but not a computer *expert*—nor do you want to be.

What makes this book different?

You don't need an advanced degree in engineering or computer science to read this book. In the pages that follow, every topic from the parts of a computer to finding out about the so-called information superhighway is covered in plain English. We tell you just what you need to know without all the technical mumbo-jumbo, the zillion ways to do the same thing, the mass of nonessential details. After all, you're not studying for a degree in computer science—you're trying to get some work done! You can think of this volume as the ultimate "quick-answer" book for anyone who uses a computer—at work, at home, or at school.

How do I use this book?

Using Your PC, Second Edition isn't a textbook. You don't have to start at page 1 and read all the way to the end. It's not a mystery novel either, so if you want to skip to the last chapter first, help yourself.

You'll probably be surprised at some of the things you can do with a computer. That's why, if you have the time, it's worth flipping through the chapters, looking at the headings, and searching out the references to the things you do at work. The people who published this book went to a lot of trouble to make sure that those interesting ideas would leap off the page and catch your attention as you browse. (And it shouldn't take that long—after all, this isn't one of those 1200-page monster books that helps you build up your biceps every time you lift it.)

This book will come in especially handy when you have a big job to do or need to know something and you're not sure where to begin.

How this book is put together

For easy reference, the text is divided into six major parts. These parts are listed below with a brief summary of their contents.

Part I: What Is All This Stuff?

Chapters 1 through 9 give you a look into what makes up a computer. Illustrations show which piece of your computer is which, and what plugs in where. We explain what a CPU is and how it works, what a disk drive is for, what the heck DOS is, and why you should care about any of this. You even get a crash course on how to set up your computer.

Part II: Getting Comfortable with Windows 95

If you bought a new computer recently, it probably came with Windows 95 installed. Chapters 10 through 12 cover Windows 95: how to work the Windows desktop, find your way around your computer's filing system, and start those other software programs that let a PC do so many interesting things. Chapter 12 even shows you how to personalize your Windows 95 PC with your own screen colors.

Part III: You Need Software!

Computers aren't really very useful without a good collection of software, so Chapters 13 through 18 provide a fast introduction to some of the major programs. Do you crunch numbers? Read Chapter 14 to learn about popular spreadsheet programs. Do you need to communicate with other computers over a modem? Explore the world of communications programs in Chapter 18. Other chapters in this section provide details on word processing, databases, the popular software suites—even educational programs and games!

Part IV: Other Equipment to Buy for Your PC

Printer. CD-ROM. Scanner. Multimedia. Modem. Do you know what all this stuff is? They're the special gadgets you can add to your computer to make it more productive, or just more fun. Chapters 19 through 21 provide the details on what each of these items is good for. You'll even find out what to look for when you go shopping.

Part V: Connecting Your PC to the Rest of the World

There's a wealth of information you can access with your computer just by connecting it to some sort of network. And it doesn't have to be expensive or even very complicated. Chapters 22 through 24 give you your options, discussing everything from e-mail and CompuServe to the Internet and the information superhighway.

Part VI: Appendixes

Sooner or later, you will have a problem or question about using Windows 95 or your computer. Appendix A provides a push in the right direction, with instructions on how and where to get help when you need it.

You may have noticed that this book contains a CD-ROM in the back. It's full of fun, interesting, and useful software and information. Appendix B shows what the programs look like, and gives you some details on each program to help you decide whether you want to try it.

If your computer doesn't have Windows 95 installed on it, you're probably using an earlier version of Windows. Appendix C explains some of the major differences between Windows 95 and earlier versions, and shows you how to perform everyday tasks using an earlier version.

And, of course, the Index helps you find your way around the book. You already know how to use that!

Information that's easy to understand

This book contains a number of special elements and conventions to help you find information quickly—or skip material you don't want to read right now.

TIP   **Tips either point out information often overlooked in the** documentation or help you use your PC more efficiently. Some tips help you solve or avoid problems.

CAUTION   **Cautions alert you to potentially troublesome situations or** activities. In general, the text will warn you of things you need to avoid doing.

Q&A   ***What are Q&A notes?***

Cast in the form of questions and answers, these notes provide you with advice on ways to avoid or solve common problems.

  Plain English, please!

These notes explain the meanings of technical **terms** or computer **jargon.**

Sidebars are interesting nuggets of information

Sidebars provide interesting but nonessential reading—side-alley trips you can take when you're not at the computer or when you just want to take a break from the regular text. Here you'll find more technical details, funny stories, personal anecdotes, or interesting background information.

Watch for different typefaces. Stuff in a `special typeface` indicates what you see on your screen. **Bold** indicates new terms that you need to know or text that we want you to type. Every once in a while, you'll see <u>underlined</u> letters in Windows commands; pressing these letters is a faster way to use the commands.

Need more information? Try these other books

This book gives you a lot of information about how your PC works and how you can use it. As you become more comfortable with your computer, you may need a more complete reference book on DOS, Windows, or other subjects. Que has books on a large variety of subjects and in a wide range of series for different users. Here are some you may find interesting and useful:

- *Computers Illustrated*
- *Upgrading Your PC Illustrated*
- *MS-DOS 6.2 QuickStart*
- *Using DOS*
- *Using MS-DOS 6.2*, Special Edition
- *Windows QuickStart*, 3.11 Edition
- *Using Windows 95*
- *Windows 95 Visual Quick Reference*
- *Special Edition Using Windows 95*
- *Using the Internet*
- *Using CompuServe*
- *Que's Computer User's Dictionary*, 6th Edition

Que also publishes multiple books on most major software products, including Microsoft Office, WordPerfect, NetWare, Lotus 1-2-3, and others. For more information on purchasing Que books, call toll-free 1-800-428-5331.

Part I: What Is All This Stuff?

1

The Pieces and How They Fit

● **In this chapter:**

- **Computers are full of gadgets**

- **What do all these pieces do?**

- **What's the difference between software and hardware?**

- **System software is different from application software**

- **What types of computers are there?**

This chapter explains how the parts of your PC work and why you have them. It's much easier than taking one apart (and potentially less expensive). . . . . ➤

Afew years ago, I showed an older lady how to take apart a personal computer (or PC) and put it back together again. As each part came out of the box, we discussed its purpose and set it aside. Then she put it all back together again. She did this to overcome a fear of PCs. She had been a typist for 25 years and her typewriter had just been replaced with a computer. Being an overly sensitive man, her boss had said to learn it or retire.

I don't recommend that anybody start taking their PC apart. Margaret was a special case who couldn't learn about it until she knew it wouldn't bite her. Instead, just read this chapter. Once you know the pieces of the puzzle, all other PC concepts in this book will be easier to understand.

That big box is where the action is

You might want to think of your PC's main box, or **system unit**, as an orchestra pit filled with different musical instruments. Here's the best part of this analogy: *you* get to be the conductor. All the instruments in your orchestra work together to convert your directions (or **input**) into a new musical masterpiece (or **output**). No one part is more important than another. They all depend on each other in some way.

 Plain English, please!

Input is information, or data, that flows into your computer. **Output** is information that flows out of the computer after the computer has done something to it in some way. If you ask a computer to add two and two, for example, the twos are input. Whatever answer comes out is output. The whole point of having a computer is to turn input into output.

Here's the list of instruments you'll generally find in the PC orchestra:

- A floppy drive or drives
- A hard drive
- Expansion slots
- A power supply
- A motherboard
- Memory
- A CPU

Inside the box

Expansion slots
Expansion slots allow you to add adapter cards
that add capabilities to your computer. Speakers,
CD–ROM drives, and telephone wires all plug into
devices that sit in these slots.

Memory chips
These computer chips hold programs
and data while you're using them. Since
they turn off when the PC is turned off,
we use the disk drives as permanent
storage.

Power supply
The power supply converts
electricity from the wall into
lower voltages that are more
suitable for the computer. It
also has a fan that helps keep
all the parts cool.

Motherboard
Every computer has a
motherboard, which
holds most of the
electronics that make
a computer work.

CPU
The letters stand for Central
Processing Unit. This is a computer
chip that lives on the motherboard
and controls what goes on inside
the computer.

Floppy drives
This is where floppy disks are
shuttled in and out. The drives
record and play back information from the floppy disks,
using them as a storage
location.

Hard drive
Contains a non–removable disk
that stores information you use a
lot. The hard drive is faster and
holds more information than a
floppy disk, so it serves as the
main storage facility.

The disks go in the floppy disk drives

The floppy drive (see fig. 1.1) works like a tape recorder, except that you use a magnetic floppy disk instead of magnetic tape. Any work that you do can be **saved** onto a **floppy disk** (often just called a **disk**). Later, it can be **read** or played back into the computer so you can work on it some more.

Floppy disks are most often used to carry information from computer to computer. They're also handy for making **backup copies** of information stored on the hard disk.

Fig. 1.1
Disk drives hold floppy disks, which carry information from computer to computer.

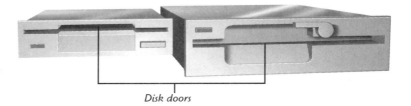

Disk doors

The hard disk is for permanent storage

The hard drive contains a **hard disk** that is mounted permanently inside the computer. Think of the hard disk as a really big floppy disk that you can never misplace. You need a hard disk because it's a *permanent* place to store your work. Any letters you type are held in computer memory while you work on them, but that just fades away (taking your work with it) every time the PC is turned off. By saving your work to disk, you can always get it back again. All the information that you need on floppy drives and hard disks is stored in Chapter 7.

What's a motherboard?

Your computer's **motherboard** is simply the "Mother of all Boards" in the PC. It's the biggest circuit board in the box and everything else connects into it in some way. On the motherboard is your computer's memory (sort of an electronic scratch pad) where most of the work gets done. The CPU chip also plugs in there. It performs calculations and directs traffic as information flows from component to component. Chapters 4 and 5 will demystify CPUs and computer memory.

Why do I need expansion slots?

Your computer's expansion slots are designed to accept special plug-in **adapter cards** that add to the PC's features. Almost anything that you can attach to a PC must connect to an **adapter card** that plugs into one of the expansion slots. For example, your computer probably has adapter cards that provide connections for the printer, the monitor, and the mouse. Without the **video adapter** sitting in an expansion slot, there'd be no place to plug your monitor into the PC! Collectively, the expansion slots are usually called the **bus**, and we take it for a ride in Chapter 3.

The monitor: a window into your computer

Besides being the most obvious part of a PC, the monitor is also your main source of output information from the computer. If you type something wrong, you can see the mistake on the screen. You can correct it, too—and make any other editorial or layout changes before finally sending a job to the printer.

Messages that pop up on the screen give you feedback about whether or not a command was successful. The PC will even use the screen to tell you when it's not feeling well. See Chapter 6 for details on picking the best monitor.

You know what the keyboard is for

Just as the monitor is the PC's standard output device, the keyboard is your usual input device. Obviously, you type with it—using about 26 of the hundred-odd keys that are found there. The rest of the keys are used for giving commands, editing work, or moving around on the screen.

The far right of the keyboard consists of a **numeric keypad** where people who like calculators can enter numbers. The numbers across the top of the keyboard will do the same thing if you are more comfortable typing numbers like a typist. Maybe we don't need all these keys after all. Get the whole story on keyboards in Chapter 8.

Think of the mouse as an electronic hand

Using a mouse is like using a remote-control hand to move things around on your screen. As you push the mouse around on your desktop, the pointer on your screen duplicates those movements. Pressing the buttons on the mouse makes the pointer press buttons on the screen. You can use it to select from **menus** of commands—and to draw pictures, too.

The printer takes your data from computer to paper

Every year, someone says that the paperless office is coming. But every year, the sales of printers skyrocket as we strive to produce fancier, bigger reports in less time than before. There's just something very reassuring about holding a printed report in your hand. You can pay anywhere from $100 to $10,000 for a computer printer today, and the choices are constantly increasing. Thankfully, the costs are decreasing as well. Chapter 19 explains the different models and capabilities.

Speakers, modems, and other luxuries

I went to a car dealership last month and was overwhelmed by all the expensive options that were available. Quadraphonic sound, electric seats, cruise control, a compact disc player, and a built-in cellular phone nearly tempted me—until I saw the price tag. I settled for the standard model.

Just like car dealerships, computer stores will offer **multimedia** computers that include all the bells and whistles. For those of us with more modest needs (and wallets), more basic models are available without all the options. Unlike a car, though, you can economically **upgrade** an existing computer by buying bits and pieces whenever you can afford them. (Ever try to buy air conditioning for a ten-year-old Chevy?)

Some of the options that you can add to your system are also pretty useful. Others are just plain fun. Either way, get the store to install your new purchase for you. They'll probably do it for free if you ask.

Speakers and a sound card, for example, allow your computer to play digital sound effects and music. And if you're going to go "hi-fi," you better get a CD-ROM player, too. Besides using it to read through that digital encyclopedia, you can play your favorite stereo CD at the same time. These are the most common **multimedia devices**, and we tell all in Chapter 20.

If you're stranded on the shoulder of the information superhighway, get into the fast lane with a high-speed **modem** that connects your computer to the phone lines. Modems let your computer chat with (or scream at!) other computers that are equipped with modems. With the right programs and about three months of experience, you'll be burning up the wires. Modems and communication are explained in Chapters 21 to 24.

As long as we're talking about burning up the wires, are you protected against lightning strikes and power surges? Buy your computer a surge suppressor (see Chapter 2). And how about an ergonomic chair to protect your back (see Chapter 2)?

The soft side of computing

All the stuff we've talked about so far is called **hardware**—the computer equipment that you can actually touch, drop, and break. **Software**, on the other hand, consists of the programs that you load into your computer, and this is a primary concept for all users to understand. Software can't be seen or touched by humans because it is simply a set of instructions for the computer to follow.

Wait a minute here. A disk would be software then, right? Sorry. A disk is strictly storage. It's a way to store software—just like a CD stores music. Instructions on the CD tell the CD player what sounds to make through the speakers. Software on a disk tells the computer what to show on the screen or print on the printer.

There are two kinds of software: **system software** and **application software**. System software performs your computer's housekeeping chores and keeps everything running smoothly. Application software is the stuff you use to get real work done. Windows 95 and DOS are examples of system software, while a word processor like Microsoft Word is an example of application software.

 TIP   In this book, and elsewhere in the world, application software is generally just called a **program**.

Software that works with the hardware

Without *some* kind of software, your computer would be little more than an expensive paperweight. Fortunately, something called an **operating system** (another word for system software) keeps tabs on your computer hardware and makes all the components work in unison. When you first turn on your computer, it's the operating system that makes all those panel lights blink and gets everything going.

Unlike most programs that you deal with, you don't have to give any commands to load the operating system into the computer. This is done automatically whenever the machine is turned on. Once the operating system is on the screen, you can start using whatever program you want to work with that day.

All operating systems are not created equal

For many years, **DOS** (it rhymes with *moss*) was the only choice for an operating system if you had an IBM-compatible PC. DOS stands for **Disk Operating System**. DOS has many limitations and it isn't powerful enough to run the newest application programs. In addition, commands have to be entered at the keyboard as a complex series of keywords.

GUIs (short for **graphical user interface**, but pronounce it *gooey*) make an operating system easier to understand and use. The most common PC GUIs are Windows 3.1 and Windows 95. Windows 3.1 was the first really popular GUI and is installed on most computers that are between two and five years old. Windows 95 is probably the operating system on your computer if you bought it in, well, 1995.

Windows 3.1 is not *really* an operating system because DOS is still hidden back there somewhere. It pretties up DOS with a lot of graphics, push-buttons, and pop-up messages. It's sort of an operating system with lipstick, matching pumps, and a handbag. Windows 95 is a true operating system on its own and it doesn't need DOS (or DOS's limitations) to do its thing. No matter which GUI you have running your computer, it's always easiest if you use a mouse.

To give you some idea of how helpful a GUI operating system can be, take a look at figure 1.2, which shows a DOS screen after turning on the computer. Not much to look at. No hints about what to do, either. Now look at figure 1.3, which shows the same computer with Windows 95. Now we're getting somewhere!

Fig. 1.2
This is how DOS looks: kind of boring, with few clues on what to do next.

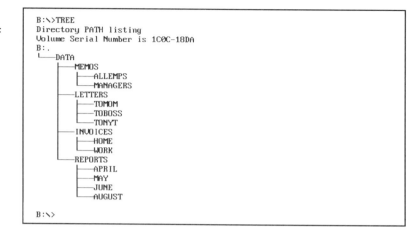

```
B:\>TREE
Directory PATH listing
Volume Serial Number is 1C0C-18DA
B:.
└──DATA
    ├───MEMOS
    │   ├──ALLEMPS
    │   └──MANAGERS
    ├───LETTERS
    │   ├──TOMOM
    │   ├──TOBOSS
    │   └──TONYT
    ├───INVOICES
    │   ├──HOME
    │   └──WORK
    └───REPORTS
        ├──APRIL
        ├──MAY
        ├──JUNE
        └──AUGUST

B:\>
```

Fig. 1.3
GUIs are easier and more fun to use than DOS and certainly easier to look at.

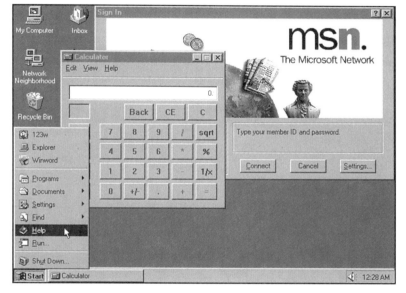

Software that works with you

If your computer had nothing more than system software, it would be about as useful as a horse with two legs. Sure, you could make the disk drives spin or the monitor light up, but that's not exactly useful work. Luckily, the world has programmers who create programs—such as word processors, spreadsheets, and games—that let you do interesting things with your computer. You might say that you talk to the program and it talks to the operating system for you.

Here are some typical programs you may already know about:

- Microsoft Word—a word processor

- Lotus 1-2-3—a spreadsheet program

- ProComm Plus—a communications program

- Paint Shop Pro—a graphics program

- Wing Commander—a game

- Math Blaster—an educational game

- Quicken—a home-finance program

So where do I store all these programs?

A computer disk is not unlike a tiny filing cabinet that stores programs and data and organizes the information so that you can get it back anytime (see fig. 1.4). What's really cool is how much information they can hold. A floppy disk can easily hold the equivalent of 1,000 typewritten pages. A hard disk can hold 400 times that or more!

Fig. 1.4
Think of the computer disk as a filing cabinet that stores and organizes information.

Later in this book, you'll learn the details of how disks work. But, for now, be aware that there are several kinds of disks, including floppy disks, hard disks, and CD-ROMs. All of them perform the same function: they provide a safe place for you to keep information until you need to use it.

Memory that forgets faster than you do

Just having a disk full of software isn't really enough to start using a computer. To use the software, you have to load it into your computer's memory. What's computer memory? Technically, it's a row of microchips on your computer's motherboard (see fig. 1.5). But from a practical viewpoint, it's more like an electronic desktop where you do your work. Just as you have to open a filing cabinet and spread your files out on your desk to start working, you get copies of your software, letters, and memos from your disk and put them into memory. That's when you can see them on the screen and start working with them. For complete information about your computer's memory, check out Chapter 5.

Computers need memory because it works very fast with your programs and data—much faster than any disk. Disks, however, have a big advantage over memory: the information on a disk stays there until you erase it. The computer's memory gets blanked out the instant you turn off your computer. Good thing your brain doesn't work that way! You'd sure learn to hate mornings.

Fig. 1.5
Your computer's memory is made up of microchips.

Types of computers

In this book, we talk mostly about desktop computers, which are, of course, the kind of computer that you usually see sitting on a desk. But other types of computers work similarly:

- **Laptop computers** weigh only around ten pounds. In spite of their light weight, they include a full (although sometimes smaller) keyboard, hard drive, floppy drive, and built-in screen.

- **Notebook computers** (see fig. 1.6) are a lot like laptop computers, but are even smaller, weighing only about six or seven pounds. Still, like a laptop, a notebook computer comes with a full keyboard, floppy drive, screen, and hard drive.

Fig. 1.6
Notebook computers
are light and easy to
carry around.

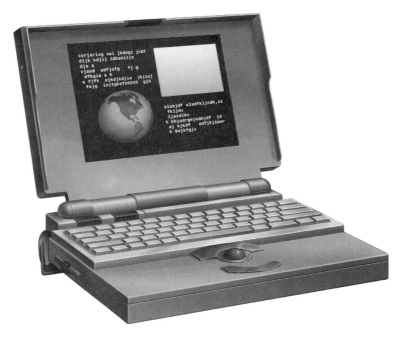

- **Palmtop computers** are the smallest of the lot but, surprisingly, often feature built-in applications like simple word processors, databases, and spreadsheets. Their tiny keyboards, however, make typing about as easy as building a ship in a bottle.

The First Day at Home: How to Hook It All Up

● **In this chapter:**

- **Choosing a location for your equipment**

- **But I want to be comfortable, too!**

- **Taking everything out of the boxes**

- **What are all these gadgets? Hooking it up**

You're just itching to rip open the boxes and see what's inside. This chapter shows you how to do it and gets you hooked up right the first time! . . . . ❯

C
ongratulations! You're the proud owner of a brand-new, bouncing baby PC! Like any new parent, you probably took extra care bringing your bundle (or more likely, bundles) of joy home. You started up slowly at every intersection, and you went around manhole covers so the PC wouldn't get bumped and bruised. Don't feel silly—everybody does it!

Choosing a good place for your PC to live

It's important to make sure that your PC gets settled in someplace appropriate (see fig. 2.1). You can add years to your computer's life by setting the system up carefully, or subtract years by setting it up poorly.

Fig. 2.1
Careful planning of the system's location makes your work more productive and also protects the PC.

Task lighting

Dedicated electrical outlets

Phone jacks for modem and network access

Adjustable seating

Surge suppressor

Ergonomic keyboard and mouse trays

Avoid vibration, please

Choose a table or desk that's sturdy and won't break under the weight of the PC, monitor, pizza crusts, and all the other things that tend to accumulate in work areas.

CAUTION **Never place your computer on one of those little wheeled tables.** You'll be too tempted to roll it around the room now and then, looking for the ideal spot. Assuming that the PC doesn't fall apart completely, the vibration could loosen components, or even severely damage them. For the same reason, avoid placing the PC on a filing cabinet. The shock created when you slide heavy drawers open and closed can be rough on the PC's internal components.

If you bought a printer with your system, it's wise to keep it on a different surface than the computer. Many printers shake around a lot. Invest a few extra dollars and buy a separate printer stand.

Lots of fresh air

Your PC needs air, and lots of it. Be sure that you leave at least three inches of space all around the main box. A tiny little fan in there has the enormous task of sucking cool air through all the slots and vents to keep the machine from burning up, but the fan needs access to air outside the box.

 TIP **Check periodically to make sure the fan is running and not** blocked with dust. If the machine is ever quieter than usual, make sure the fan is still running. If it isn't, save your work immediately, shut down your computer, and seek help from a computer professional.

The monitor needs as much fresh air as the computer itself. There are little slots along the top and back of most monitors to aid in cooling the electronics. Avoid covering them with books and other clutter.

 Plain English, please!

The **monitor** is the part of your computer system that looks like a TV.

 Q&A *Since ventilation is so important, would it be good to put the PC near a window?*

No. Sunshine causes heat problems, too. I know of an office that had three PCs which locked up and died every afternoon at 2:00, but always worked fine the next morning. When Daylight Savings Time arrived, the three PCs began stopping at 3:00. As soon as the company bought window blinds, the problem went away.

Out of the traffic patterns

Try to place the PC away from main traffic lanes, because people carelessly knock plugs out of outlets, loosen cables, spill drinks, and lean on keyboards.

After you locate a spot with less traffic, it's time to plan how you'll route the **cables** for your system. You have at least two power cords, as well as a cable from the computer to the printer. If your system includes a **modem** (see Chapter 21 to find out what to do with your modem), you have telephone wires running around, too. All the cables and wires should be placed behind the desk or wherever they won't be kicked, tripped over, or pulled.

The electronics in your PC are pretty sensitive—even the slightest loss of power or a power surge can render your system useless! For less than ten bucks you can buy a power strip with surge protection, an on/off switch (so you don't have to flip a bunch of switches every time you turn your system on and off), and several outlets. When you're ready to hook everything up, be sure that the power strip isn't anyplace where you can kick it.

 TIP   **Rather than just pushing an armload of wires over the back of the** desk, coil the extra-long cables into neat loops, then secure the loops with twist ties to keep the cables tidy.

The PC's comfy—now what about me?

Ergonomics is a field concerned with the study of human characteristics in order to design things that will be more useful to humans. An ergonomic work environment is one that lets you work fast, work smart, and stay comfortable and avoid injury while doing it.

The most common problem affecting people who use computers for a living is a disorder called **repetitive strain injury**. The most common repetitive strain injury is **carpal tunnel syndrome**, which is a painful nerve disorder caused by a buildup of tissue in the nerve channels of the hand and wrist. You can get it by typing for long periods of time with your wrists and hands at the wrong angle.

The information in the following table might help you to fend off computer-related pain.

Problem	Prescription
Most desktops are not the right height for comfortable typing.	Look into a sliding keyboard tray that pulls out from under the desk.
Back pain can be caused by marathon typing sessions.	Spend some money on a good chair that is fully adjustable.
Your arms and wrists get tired during a long typing session.	Your high school typing teacher lied to you. You're allowed to rest your wrists on something. Office supply stores sell special pads that help keep your wrists at the right angle.
The early design of the desktop was wrong and nobody has bothered to fix it.	Place the monitor on the computer desk so that your eyes are level with the top of the screen. This helps avoid back pain.
Too much time spent sitting still causes problems.	Take a break every hour or so and move around to circulate the blood. Don't forget to flex your fingers and twiddle your thumbs.

Emptying the cartons

You're standing in the middle of the floor with a collection of different-sized boxes around your feet. Where do you start? First, identify as many things as possible by the markings on the cartons. Monitors and printers come in large boxes and are usually clearly marked by the manufacturer. Another big box (which may also be clearly marked if you bought a "name-brand" PC) contains the computer's system unit.

 Plain English, please!

The main part of the computer, where all of the "thinking" occurs, is called the **system unit**. This usually looks like a flat, rectangular box.

As long as you're examining the boxes, look around for the packing slip. It should contain a complete list of the items shipped to you—use this as a checklist to make sure you got everything you paid for.

Always start by unpacking the system unit since it's the central point of the system.

TIP **A small knife will come in handy now, but make sure you cut the** tape on the boxes and not the cardboard. If there's something wrong with the system and you have to send it back, you may find that the warranty insists on "original packaging." Consider saving the original boxes in a storage closet or garage for the next time you move.

Once the box is open, lift out the system unit and place it on the desk, the floor, or wherever you plan to use it.

Don't push the system unit all the way against the wall just yet, though. You still have lots of wires to connect to the back, so turn the back to face you, and leave yourself room to work. If there's a plastic bag around the system unit, remove it now.

Take the monitor out of its box and place the monitor beside the system unit. Again, if there's a plastic bag, take it off. Some monitors come with a separate swivel base that snaps onto the bottom of the monitor. If you have one of these, turn the monitor over and snap the base on now. There may be a diagram in the box that explains how all the little tabs and slots fit together.

The keyboard might have been packed with the system unit, or might be in its own flat box. Either way, remove the packaging and place the keyboard wherever you intend to use it, in front of the system unit or the monitor. You can pull the mouse out of its box now too, and place it near the keyboard.

If you bought a printer, open its box now, and place the printer wherever you like. Leave any other boxes aside for now. They contain cables and manuals that you'll use in a minute. Now that you're ready to connect all the pieces, take a moment to set up the system unit, monitor, keyboard, and mouse in a useful relationship to each other (see fig. 2.2).

How to unpack those big cartons

The easiest way to get a bulky item out of the box might affectionately be called the "Newton method." Open the top flaps all the way and gently roll the carton over so that the opening is facing the floor. The box can be lifted off easily, as gravity keeps the contents of the box pressed down against the floor.

The other advantage to this method is that you get a good look at all the Styrofoam. Be sure to check for hidden holes stuffed with goodies, because power cords and manuals are sometimes hidden in slots in the foam.

Fig. 2.2
Everything's out of the boxes now! As soon as you connect a few plugs and turn a few screws, you'll have a fully connected, working system.

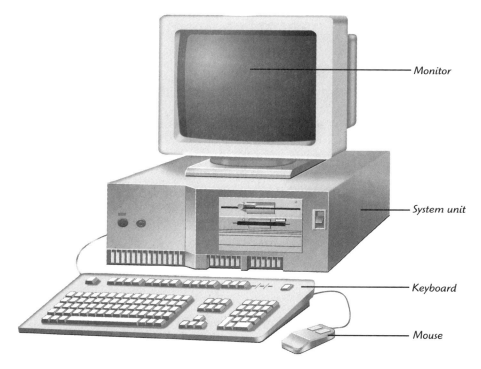

Monitor

System unit

Keyboard

Mouse

Wrestling with cables

There are two ways to hook up a computer. You can wade right in, plug things together wherever the plugs will fit, close your eyes, and flip the big switch. Or you can read this section carefully.

Tiny tool time

Start by arming yourself with a few useful tools:

- A small Phillips screwdriver (the kind with the cross-shaped head)

- A small standard screwdriver (the kind with the flat head)

- A pair of long-nosed pliers (optional, but handy when you need to hold something)

Plugging in

Now is a good time to open any remaining boxes and bags. You'll probably find power wires and a few other cables used to connect the printer or the modem. Your computer and monitor probably have power wires that are not attached to the units. It's okay to plug these into the back of the units now, but not into the wall!

CAUTION **Don't turn on the power until everything is connected properly.** Since it's often difficult to tell by looking at a power switch whether it is on or off, don't allow any power into the unit until you're ready. Let the wires dangle, or unplug the power strip if you have one.

Monitors and computers usually use the same kind of power cord, so it doesn't matter if you accidentally swap them. On the back of the monitor, there's a male three-prong plug that one end of the cord fits onto. A similar power supply plug is on the back of the PC.

You should have one leftover wire coming out of the monitor. This is the cable that connects the monitor to the PC. We'll find a place for that one later.

Attaching the printer

The printer is pretty easy to figure out, so you can attach the cable for this right away, if you want. One benefit of hooking up the printer cable first is that it reduces the possibilities of connecting something to the wrong spot in the system unit later on.

Q&A *My printer came with another small box. What do I do with it?*

Depending on the type of printer you bought, this is probably the ink cartridge. Dot–matrix printers use a ribbon, inkjet printers use bottles of liquid ink, and a laser printer uses a toner cartridge. They all do the same thing and without them, your printer won't work. Check the manual that came with the printer to make sure you insert the cartridge correctly.

The printer cable is probably heavy, gray, and about six feet long. One end has a D-shaped connector with 25 pins. This will go to the PC's **parallel port**. The other end has a strange-looking connector that could be male or female depending on your outlook (see fig. 2.3). This end attaches to the printer, and instead of being held by screws, is secured by two clips that snap into place.

Fig. 2.3
The printer cable is the easiest to connect because there is usually only one possible combination of plugs.

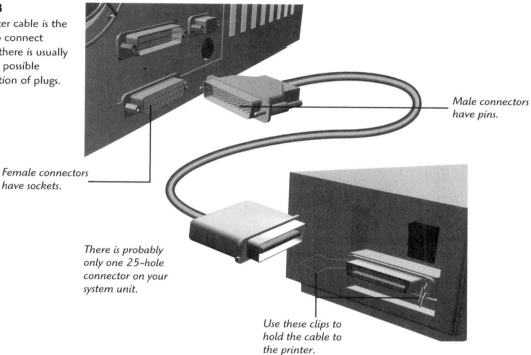

Male connectors have pins.

Female connectors have sockets.

There is probably only one 25–hole connector on your system unit.

Use these clips to hold the cable to the printer.

66 *Plain English, please!*

The 25–pin female connector on the PC is called a **parallel port**. This port is sometimes referred to as LPT1 (you have to pronounce each letter in LPT1, because trying to say it as a word really makes you spit like a camel). 99

Since the plugs are D-shaped, there is only one way that they will fit. The end that connects to the PC may have little twisty knobs that screw onto the plug, or it may have tiny screws. If it has knobs, turn them by hand. If it has screws, use the screwdriver to screw them in, but not too tightly. Someday you may need to remove them.

What are all the other connection sites for?

The remaining connection locations on the back of your system unit are for the keyboard, monitor, mouse, and other things you might want to buy in the future. We'll do the simplest things first and then see what's left over.

The keyboard is pretty easy to figure out. The only thing to watch for is that some PCs have a mouse port that looks identical to the keyboard port. A little sign over each port should show a picture of a mouse or a keyboard or should be labeled with the word "mouse" or "keyboard." If your computer doesn't have these two plugs side by side, your job is even easier—just look for the only round hole in the back. Once you've located the keyboard port, hold the keyboard connector against it while rotating slowly. The connector is round, but only goes in at one spot (sometimes this is found by lining up arrows like those on an aspirin bottle). Push it in gently until it's snug.

The monitor is the last major part to connect. Look on the back of the PC for a small D-shaped connector with 15 holes in three rows (see fig. 2.4). This is called the **video port**.

Fig. 2.4
The video port often is located off by itself at one end of the computer.

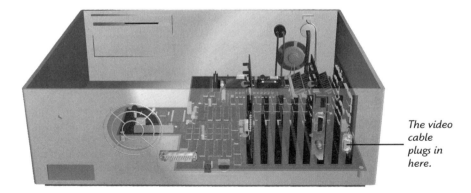

The video cable plugs in here.

 **CAUTION** **Don't get confused. Besides the video port, your PC may have a** port with 15 holes in *two* rows, which is where you could plug in a joystick if you bought one to play games with.

Remember the monitor cable we left hanging a while ago? Now it's time to connect that cable to the PC. Attach the monitor's cable to the port shown in figure 2.4. Secure the cable to the PC by turning the little screws. Remember not to screw them in too tightly.

You sometimes see an extra black plug on the back of the PC that looks like the power plug, but is female. This is typically used to provide power to a monochrome monitor from the PC, but few companies use it. Your monitor probably doesn't have the right type of connector. (Of course, if the monitor's cable *does* fit, then by all means, plug it in.)

These wires are too short

The unfortunate truth about **tower PCs** (the ones that stand on end) is that they look great on the floor, but the wires for the mouse, keyboard, and monitor are usually designed for desktop systems. They are rarely the right length to reach behind a box that's sitting four feet away on the floor. This throws your ergonomic planning out the window as you double over across the desk to reach the keyboard.

Luckily, most computer stores and business centers sell extension cords for common computer devices, including the keyboard, mouse, monitor, and printer. For a complete set, expect to pay about $30 or $40.

 CAUTION **Keep one thing in mind when buying a printer extension: never** allow the cable to exceed 20 feet. That's a reliable cable length for error-free printing. After 20 feet, the signals from the PC start to get mixed up and fade away before they reach the printer.

Finishing up

As mentioned earlier in this chapter, some computers have a special mouse port that resembles the keyboard connector. They are always marked to distinguish one from the other, so if you have that kind of connector, just attach it the same way you did the keyboard—use a gentle twisting motion until you feel it slip into place. Then push gently.

If your PC doesn't have any round ports left and you do have a mouse, it's probably a serial mouse that connects to a serial port. Look for a 9-pin male connector on the PC that matches the 9-pin female connector at the end of the mouse's "tail" (see fig. 2.5). If your PC only has a 25-pin male connection on the back, you may need a 9-to-25-pin adapter. This adapter is often included with your mouse, but you can buy one for a couple of dollars.

Fig. 2.5
A 9-pin serial port is
very common for the
mouse connector.

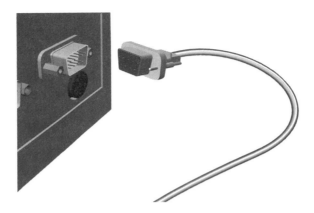

I bought a modem—I think

If you decided that your computer should talk to other computers in the
outside world, you probably got a modem. Modems come in two styles and
therefore may have either of two types of connections. They can be **internal**
(inside the case of the PC) or **external**, where they sit on the desktop (see
Chapter 21 for more information on modems).

Internal modems are the easiest to hook up because they're already part of
the PC. Look for two telephone plugs in the back of the PC, near the other
connectors. Now, look around on the floor for a telephone wire that has one
of those clear plastic telephone plugs at each end. One end goes into the wall
telephone outlet and the other goes into the hole on the back of the PC,
marked "Line." Still have one telephone jack in the back of your PC? Plug
your phone into it so you can talk, too. After plugging in the telephone, you
should hear a dial tone when you lift the receiver.

TIP **If you don't have two jacks on your PC, you can buy an adapter**
(called a **line splitter**) so that you can switch between using your modem
and your phone without having to plug and unplug them each time you
want to switch.

External modems have a couple of extra connections to make. If you have
one of these, you still hook it to the wall with a telephone wire and attach a
regular phone, so make those connections first. The next two connections
you must make, however, are to connect the modem to the computer, and
then to provide electricity to the modem.

To connect the modem to the PC, look around for a gray cable that resembles the printer cable. It should be a **serial cable** with a 25-pin male connector at one end and a 25-hole female connector at the other. The male connector goes into the modem and the female connector goes into the remaining 25-pin port on the PC.

 Q&A *I don't have a 25-pin anything left on the back of my system!*

Serial ports on PCs come in two sizes (9-pin and 25-pin) for no apparent reason. Most manufacturers cover all the bases by providing one plug of each type, but not always. If you're stuck at the end of all your connections with one large plug and one small hole, you can buy an adapter in most computer stores for less than $5.

Your last modem connection brings electricity from the wall. You can't have too many power cables left, so look around. Many modems use a little black transformer. Plug 'er in and you're set.

I still have some speakers here!

If you purchased a multimedia PC, then you probably got a pair of small speakers and maybe even a microphone. There's most likely a CD-ROM drive built in to the computer too, but you don't have to hook it up. You only have to plug the speakers and the microphone into the connections for your **sound card** in the back of the PC.

This can get pretty messy, so read carefully. In my experience, the little round holes for the jacks on the sound card are rarely marked and there are probably four of them. When in doubt, *read the manual*. Look around for the booklet describing the connections. If you plug something in wrong here, you might damage the sound card when you turn on the power.

You want to connect only one of your speakers to the hole labeled *line out* or *speaker out*. The second speaker connects to the first speaker like a long chain. If you received a microphone, plug that into the hole labeled *mic in*. The microphone might have come with a little holder that you're supposed to stick to the side of your monitor. Test the angle and position before mounting the holder. You don't want to work with that thing poking you in the eye, and the sticky backing is usually permanent.

Looking for cardboard

As a final step, look into the slots on the front of the PC to see if any little cardboard tabs are sticking out. These are often used to protect the disk drives from damage during transit, and must be removed before use. If you don't see anything poking out of the front of the PC, you're okay.

 CAUTION **Never attempt to pull out the cardboard disk drive protectors** without releasing them from the drive. After you flip open the latch or push the button on the drive to release them, they should come out easily, or with at most a little wiggling.

3

Inside and Outside the Box

● In this chapter:

- ● What are all those buttons and things on the front of my computer?

- ● Basics you need to know about disk drives

- ● Adding parts to your computer might be easier than you think

- ● How to look after your motherboard

- ● Where does a computer's power really come from?

With a few simple tools and some basic instruction, novices can open the computer case and noodle around, even if they've never changed the oil in a car. . . . . ❯

Most people have a stereo system somewhere at home. And most stereos have several components—a receiver, tape deck, CD player, and speakers—connected with a bunch of wires. Your computer system is a lot like that stereo setup, with different components and wires going everywhere. Just as a receiver is the central part of a stereo system, the **system unit** (that big gray box) is the central part of a computer system. Everything that goes in and out of your computer goes in and out of the system unit.

 Plain English, please!

People call the main computer box the **system unit** because it contains all the key components of the computer system. You may also hear it referred to as the CPU, which stands for central processing unit. The CPU contains the electronic chip, called the **microprocessor**, that does the bulk of the actual "computing" for the PC.

So, tell me about the system unit

Like the front of your stereo receiver, the front of your system unit has buttons and switches that you use to control the computer. If you can run your stereo, you sure won't have any trouble running your computer. Look over the illustration on the next page to see what the front of the system unit does.

 Q&A *My computer doesn't look anything like the one in the picture. Are they the same?*

Computers aren't all alike on the outside, but they generally all work the same way. Your system unit may not have all the bells and whistles or may have something extra. Check the documentation that came with your computer if you have any trouble identifying what's on your system unit.

Working on a computer isn't like brain surgery

Some kinds of repair work require highly specialized skills. Brain surgery is a good example. Radio repair is another (remember the "no user-serviceable parts" sticker?). But repairing your system or adding circuit boards doesn't take the special training of a brain surgeon or radio repair person.

Know your system unit

Here's an introduction to the buttons and lights found on the typical system unit. Being familiar with these can help you identify when the system unit's working correctly.

No, the **key switch** isn't an ignition that you turn to start the PC's engine, though you wouldn't be the first person to try. It's actually a lock to keep people from using your computer. (Most people rarely use this lock.)

Press the **reset button** when you want to restart your computer without turning it off.

The **turbo light** comes on when the turbo button is on (pressed in) to show that your computer is running at its fastest speed.

The **CD-ROM drive** has a little drawer that slides out when you press the button on the front.

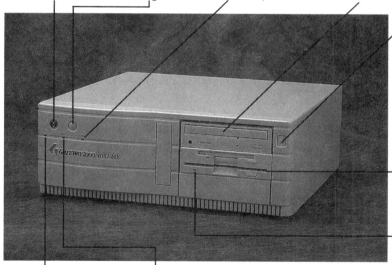

Press the **power switch** to turn on the system unit, but don't expect components like your monitor and printer to come on, too. They each have their own power switch.

From the front, a **floppy disk drive** looks like a slot with some sort of button or lever.

A **floppy disk light** indicates when the floppy disk drive is reading or writing information.

Of course, the **power light** shows that your computer is on.

The **hard disk light** comes on when your hard disk is busy reading or writing data.

Your system may also have a **turbo button**, which changes your computer's speed. When the button is pressed in, your computer runs fastest. Hint: Leave it in all the time, unless you're the type who would always opt for the stairs over the elevator in the Empire State Building!

Look at the back of your system unit (see fig. 3.1). See those slots filled with little metal plates? Those are the cover plates for the expansion slots, where you can add expansion cards to your computer to make it do things like produce digitized sound effects and talk to other computers over phone lines.

 Plain English, please!

A basic PC comes with limited capabilities. Usually, it can send information to a monitor and a printer and can deal with a mouse. To add more features to your computer, you have to add circuit boards to slots in the motherboard, so that the sockets for the card show at the back of the system unit. The circuit boards you add are called **expansion cards**. Examples include sound cards and internal modems (to learn more about sound cards and modems, respectively, see Chapters 20 and 21).

Fig. 3.1
Your computer's expansion slots are definitely user-serviceable. The circuit boards you put in these slots give your computer extra capabilities.

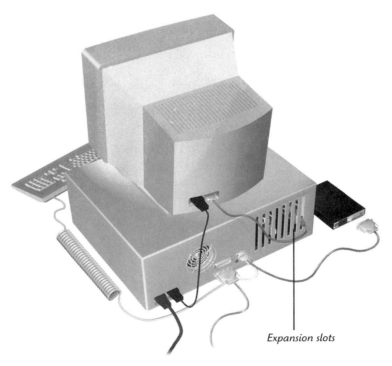

Expansion slots

To get at those slots, you have to take the cover off your system unit. To do so on the typical system unit, you unscrew a half-dozen screws around the back of the computer and slide the cover toward the front of the computer. When you've slid the cover all the way forward, lift it vertically off the system. Then you can add an expansion card simply by pressing the card gently into one of the slot receptacles on the motherboard (see fig. 3.2). You can find more specific instructions for installing cards into expansion slots by reviewing the instructions that come with the card.

Fig. 3.2
Your PC can get new power from expansion cards that you place in the PC's expansion slots.

What else do I need to know about adding stuff to my computer?

You should give some thought to expansion slots when you buy your computer. If you're buying a basic system unit with only a hard drive and a floppy drive but think you'll add other components like a CD-ROM drive later, make sure you buy a system unit with five to seven expansion slots to give yourself ample room to grow.

You also need to give some thought to your warranty before you open your computer to

upgrade it. For some systems, especially laptop units, opening the case voids the warranty, which is something you never want to do. To avoid the void, postpone your upgrade until the warranty expires. Or check with the manufacturer to see if the upgrade can be performed by a licensed dealer (this'll cost you, depending on what you're having done).

CAUTION **Electrostatic discharge (ESD) is one of the biggest killers of** electronic components. There is enough ESD in the human body to destroy not only a circuit board, but all of the components that you touch while you are inside the system unit. Your local computer retailer probably sells a variety of devices you can use to ground yourself to prevent ESD damage. Be sure to use a grounding device, such as an antistatic wrist strap, before touching anything inside your computer.

Spinning a disk

Cassettes and compact discs (CDs) store the music that you play with your stereo. Without a tape or CD, your cassette deck or CD player remains silent. Every computer has to have at least one floppy disk drive so you can copy information between computers, as well as install new software. Within the system unit, there's also a hard disk drive. This drive stores the operating system software that lets you control your computer. It also stores the different programs that you use to perform computing tasks. Let's take a closer look at drives.

Disk drives from the outside in

The outside of a floppy disk drive has only a few distinguishing features: the disk slot, the disk activity light, and the disk door button or latch. The disk slot is, of course, where you insert the disk. On a 5¼-inch floppy drive (see fig. 3.3), you have to turn the drive-door latch in order to insert or remove disks. For a 3½-inch floppy drive (see fig. 3.4), you simply insert the disk and press it gently to place it in the drive; you press the drive button to eject the disk.

CAUTION **Never remove a disk from a drive while the drive's light is on.** If you do, information on the disk might be damaged.

Fig. 3.3
A 5¹/₄-inch disk drive
has a drive-door latch
and a very wide slot for
the disk.

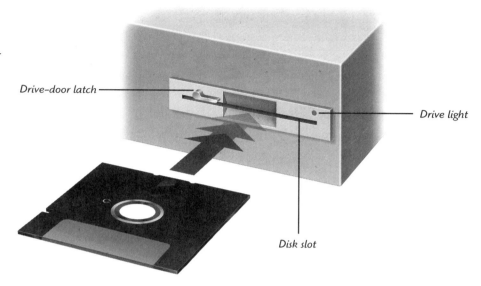

Drive-door latch

Drive light

Disk slot

Fig. 3.4
A 3¹/₂-inch disk drive is
the most popular type
of drive these days.
When you get a new
computer, make sure it
has one of these!

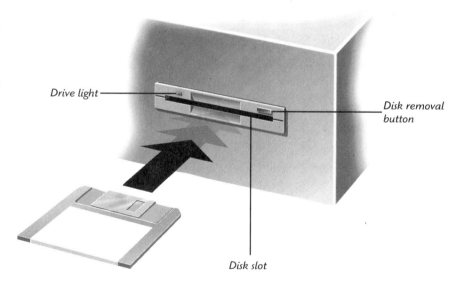

Drive light

Disk removal
button

Disk slot

The hard disk drive lives within your computer and you'll probably never see it unless you open the case. It has a light that tells you when it's reading and writing information. Observing this light tells you when your computer is trying to do its job.

Disk drives from the inside out

If you understand the way a cassette recorder works, you have a jump on understanding disk drives.

A cassette recorder reads and writes information (usually music) by running a magnetic tape over the recorder's record and play heads. A disk drive reads and writes information in a similar way, but instead of using record and play heads, a disk drive has read and write heads—different names for almost the same thing.

Because a computer needs to rapidly read information stored in many different locations (that is, in different files), disk drives record information on a spinning magnetic disk. The read and write heads move across the spinning disk (see fig. 3.5), rapidly reading and writing information as needed.

Fig. 3.5
A floppy disk drive works somewhat like a cassette recorder, recording information on a magnetic disk.

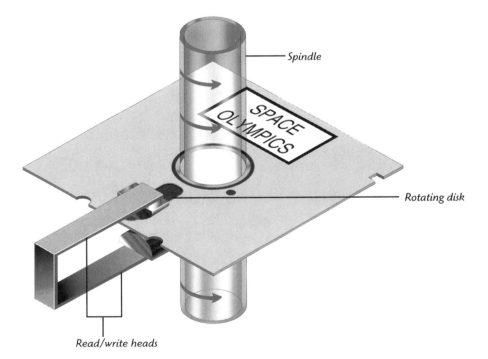

Spindle

SPACE OLYMPICS

Rotating disk

Read/write heads

Floppy disks contain a single, flexible magnetic disk **platter** (a round, flexible plastic disk) enclosed within a plastic case. Hard disk drives, whether external or built-in, contain several rigid disk platters, providing plenty of storage room.

To CD-ROM, or not to CD-ROM

More and more often, software comes on **CD-ROMs** (see fig. 3.6) rather than on floppy disks. This is because a single CD-ROM can hold more information than 500 floppy disks and more than many hard disk drives. If you consider that some software packages (especially games) come packed with 20 or more floppy disks, you know why software publishers are anxious to switch to CD-ROMs.

 Plain English, please!

> CD-ROM stands for **compact disc, read-only memory**. CD-ROMs are small, silvery disks that are read by the CD-ROM drive using a laser. They are called "read-only" because you can't change the data on them—your computer can only read and copy the data on them. **"**

Although most software can still be purchased on floppy disks, it won't be long before CD-ROMs dominate. For this reason, you should consider adding a CD-ROM drive to your computer as soon as possible. Otherwise, you may not be able to install all the software you want. See Chapter 20 for more information about CD-ROM software and CD-ROM drives.

Fig. 3.6
CD-ROMs can store more information than a $1/2$-gigabyte hard drive. CD-ROMs are ideal for multimedia information because fancy graphics, digital video, and sound take lots of storage space.

All roads lead to the motherboard

Your entire computer boils down to one circuit board called the **motherboard**. All the components of your computer—disk drives, modems, sound cards, and printers—end up attached to the motherboard in one way or another. Just like the expression "all roads lead to Rome," all roads in your computer lead to the motherboard.

The motherboard is the largest green circuit board inside the system unit, usually lying flat in the bottom of the case. The motherboard holds the brains and memory of your computer and, via slots on the board, connects with all peripheral equipment (such as a printer) that's part of your system.

Finding the CPU

If all roads lead to Rome, they also lead to Rome's Senate. And, as surely as the Senate ruled Rome, your **CPU** rules your computer. Nothing happens until the CPU decrees it should happen.

The CPU (central processing unit), also known as the **processor** or **microprocessor**, determines the speed and capabilities of your computer and is the most important part on the motherboard. If you look at a motherboard (see fig. 3.7), you'll discover that the CPU is usually the biggest chip on the board. The CPU processes and computes data (you can learn all about CPUs by reading Chapter 4).

Fig. 3.7
Your computer's motherboard holds the CPU, where your computer makes most of its decisions.

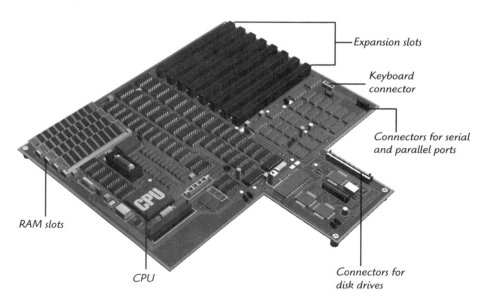

Expansion slots

Keyboard connector

Connectors for serial and parallel ports

RAM slots

CPU

Connectors for disk drives

Oops! I forgot where I put the memory

Your computer's memory is also on the motherboard. The **RAM** is easy to find because it's a bunch of small chips on little circuit boards that plug into the motherboard (see fig. 3.8).

 Plain English, please!

> **Random–Access Memory** (RAM) temporarily holds data and program instructions that the CPU is currently working with. Using RAM makes your PC operate faster because the CPU doesn't continually have to say, "Excuse me, what program was I executing?" or "I'm sorry. Where is that file located? I need it from the disk again." The more RAM your PC has, the more tasks it can juggle for you.

Fig. 3.8
Your computer's memory comes on little circuit boards that plug into the motherboard's RAM slots.

The total memory in your computer depends on the size and number of memory chips you have. To run today's heavy-duty programs, you need a computer with at least 4M of memory, but 8M or 16M is better.

A slot machine where you can't lose

The motherboard offers **slots** where you insert cards, including expansion cards for adding new components to your PC (refer to figure 3.2 to see what a slot looks like). Most PCs come with some slots already filled. For example, your monitor attaches to a video card that's plugged into one slot. The remaining slots are for adding sound cards and other types of cards, as described earlier in this chapter.

Lots of other things that nobody cares about

Ancient Rome was a big city, with lots of buildings where the city's business was conducted. Your PC's motherboard is also like a small city. Instead of buildings, though, it's filled with computer chips and other electronic parts that help conduct the computer's business. Outside of the CPU, memory, and expansion slots, however, there's not much else of interest to anyone except a computer technician. You're off the hook!

Riding the bus

Roads that led to Rome were made of stone. The roads in your PC, called the **bus**, are made of thin metal conductors, which are like thin wires hidden within the motherboard. Your CPU uses these metal roads to shuttle information between the parts of your PC. You don't need to do anything with your PC's bus. It's just nice to know it's there.

All roads have speed limits, and the same is true of your PC's bus, which has a limit to how fast it can transfer information. Obviously, the faster the bus, the faster the PC can work. Modern **Pentium** computers usually come with motherboards featuring the **PCI bus**. This is the fastest bus around.

The local power company

Your computer has its own power company, called a **power supply**. Of course, the power supply isn't a big building filled with spinning turbines. Instead, it's a large rectangular box inside your computer's system unit (see fig. 3.9).

Fig. 3.9
Who shut off the
lights? Your computer's
power supply provides
power to the com-
puter and its many
components.

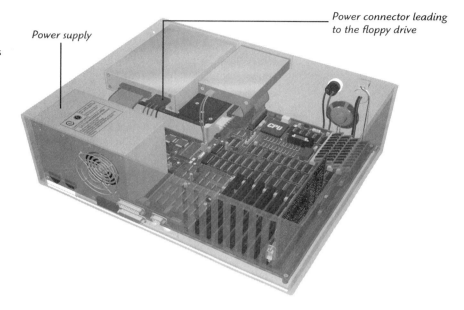

Power supply

Power connector leading
to the floppy drive

All your computer's internal components connect to the power supply in one
way or another, usually by way of a bundle of wires leading from the power
supply to each component. These wire bundles end in a plug that is pushed
into the component.

Because the power supply just transfers power, it leaves your computer
subject to power fluctuations and spikes from your power lines. As you
learned in Chapter 2, you need to plug your computer into a surge protector
to protect its circuitry; don't forget this inexpensive piece of protection for
your computer.

What Exactly Is a CPU?

● **In this chapter:**

- **What's the CPU, and what does it do?**

- **What do the CPU model numbers mean?**

- **You might have heard about the math coprocessor**

- **SX, DX, SL—which is best?**

- **And then there's the Power PC**

- **Can I add something to my system to speed it up?**

Most people are surprised when I tell them a CPU is not much more than an adding machine. Despite rumors to the contrary, it's not really a brain. . . . . ▶

The real workhorse behind any computer is the CPU. CPU stands for central processing unit, which is a holdover from the 1950s, when computers less powerful than your average PC filled entire buildings.

Obviously, computers are much smaller today and a zillion times more powerful, but the name stuck just the same. The CPU now takes the form of a tiny electronic chip within the system unit, and is often referred to as the **microprocessor** or **processor**.

If you really want to read the gory details, this chapter thrashes the topic around in a little more detail.

What does the CPU do?

The CPU, shown in figure 4.1, is kind of like a traffic cop with a calculator in his hip pocket. Information is constantly flowing back and forth between the various parts of the PC and the CPU. The CPU stands in the middle, deciding what goes where. One of the CPU's jobs, then, is the *control* of information flow. When you type at the keyboard, the CPU receives every keystroke and redirects it to the right place. When you print a letter, the CPU takes the characters from the screen or the disk and sends them streaming through the cable that connects your computer to your printer.

Every once in a while, the CPU notices that some of the data flowing by is actually a command to perform a mathematical calculation. It stops the traffic for a second, pulls out its calculator, and adds up the next two numbers going by (or divides them, multiplies them—whatever). Then it returns to its traffic-control duties.

It's a good thing that CPUs are very fast, because if there was nobody directing the traffic while the cop was off crunching numbers, there would be a heck of a mess! The operating speed of the CPU is the major factor in determining the **power** of the computer.

Fig. 4.1
The CPU *is the computer chip that controls all the information flowing between the other components, and calculates numbers when required.*

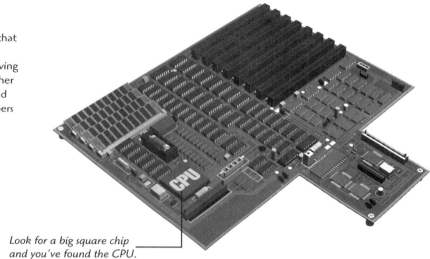

Look for a big square chip and you've found the CPU.

A sort-of-technical discussion of what the CPU does

The traffic-cop analogy holds true for every computer in the world, but the story raises a couple of questions:

- Where is this mysterious "right place" where the CPU redirects information?

- What gives the CPU the command to stop controlling and start calculating?

The "right place" is the computer's electronic memory, or **RAM**. The "commander" that directs the CPU (and is the real brains behind the outfit) is the software program that's also in memory. Chapter 5 has more information about memory, and Chapter 1 has everything you need to know about how software controls the hardware.

The CPU has to work very closely with memory because the most powerful CPU around can only juggle about eight characters at one time (granted, it juggles VERY quickly!). The RAM in your computer constantly cycles through millions of characters that may need the CPU's attention. In order to process the characters stored in RAM, the CPU must move data to and from RAM at an incredible pace. The faster the CPU, and the more efficiently it moves data to and from RAM, the more processing power in the computer.

The CPU gets its orders from the software program that is also loaded into the computer's memory. Some of the information being shuttled around by the CPU takes the form of **program commands** that tell the CPU what to do with particular pieces of data. In fact, if the CPU was not constantly being instructed how to do things, it wouldn't do anything at all.

CPUs have not only gotten faster over the years, they have become capable of handling data in bigger chunks. They can work with more memory than ever before, and they now have small amounts of extremely fast memory built right in to help them move information to and from RAM.

How CPUs are named, and what that name tells you

The CPUs in all IBM and IBM-compatible computers have been invented by Intel Corporation, or copied by those who duplicate, or clone, Intel CPUs. Intel named all but their newest CPUs (the Pentium and the P6) with model numbers—boring, but a good way to tell one from another.

 Q&A   *What do you mean by IBM-compatible?*

IBM-compatible computers are computers designed to function identically to actual IBM systems. These systems are largely based on IBM's original design, although many IBM compatibles offer unique features that set them apart from IBM computers.

Intel did have some logic to its numbering system. The first two numbers are always "80"—and since these numbers are always there, most people leave them off when describing a CPU. For example, the 80486 CPU is often referred to as just a "486" (pronounced *four eighty-six*).

A good rule of thumb is that the higher the number, the more powerful the CPU (that is, a computer with an 80486 CPU will be faster than a computer with an 80386 CPU).

There's a good chance that this is all you really need to know, but if you want to know more about the capabilities of *your* CPU, read the rest of this section.

The Stone Age: the 8088

Pronounced *eighty eighty-eight*, this was Intel Corporation's first commercially successful CPU. It also had a cousin known as the 8086. They are practically useless today, because software programs need more power than the 8088 can pump out. Strictly stone knives and bear skins technology. If you have one, sell it to someone you hate.

 TIP **Computers that use 286 or 8088 CPUs today don't even have a** resale value. You'll be hard-pressed to find someone willing to pay for one. Why not consider donating these old machines to schools or charitable organizations?

The 20th century: the 80286

Intel and IBM started the computing equivalent to the Industrial Revolution when the 80286 was installed in the first **IBM AT**. (**AT** stood for Advanced Technology, which is kind of funny by today's standards. But in the early 1980s, this was a desktop machine for power users only!) Although CPUs have been improved since then, most modern IBM-compatible computers are descendants of this computer. At twice the speed of the 8088 and with a potential of 16 times the allowable memory, this was the first power-user machine. Today, though, software programs are too big and require more power than the 286 can dish out. It's sad to see an old champion put out to pasture.

The trial run: the 80386

If the 286 was the Model T of CPUs, the 386 is a '65 Cadillac. Big, fast, and smooth with lots of goodies under the hood that only an engineer would appreciate. This CPU is the absolute minimum if you want to run modern operating systems (see Chapter 2 if you don't know what an operating system is) like anything named *Windows* or IBM's *OS/2*. Even games and educational software usually suggest "at least a 386" to make programs run smoothly.

Q&A *Just how much memory is a CPU allowed to use?*

The various CPU models have limits on how much memory they can really use. We call this the *maximum addressable memory*. The 8088, for example, only had enough internal circuitry to talk to, or *address*, one million characters of memory. The 286 could address 16 million characters if needed. Later CPUs address much more than that.

Understand that **maximum addressable memory** is not a reference to how much memory is in a PC. It is a technical specification for how much you could put in a PC, and that is defined by the type of CPU.

The real thing: the 80486

Although technically, this chip is really a 386 with a supercharger, it is fast enough to last a couple more years on the market. Graphical presentations and large calculations, both of which need a lot of processing power, really barrel along on these systems. Intel would like to aim this CPU at the home market so that it can sell Pentiums and P6s in the workplace.

Pentium? I was just getting used to numbers!

The **Pentium** was supposed to be called the 80586, but Intel realized that other manufacturers were copying their designs and selling '86 clones. They tried to protect themselves behind copyrights, but a judge determined that numbers can't be owned by anybody. So the name was changed to Pentium. Whatever it's called, it's today's most common *muscle-CPU*. If your PC has a Pentium processor, you'll be able to run all the software likely to be written in the next five years.

How do I know how fast my computer is?

You already know that each subsequent improvement in CPUs made the CPU more powerful. Basically, every new model is able to handle more data in a single operation than "last year's" model could. The speed with which the CPU performs those operations is measured in megahertz, or millions of cycles per second. CPUs are sold by model and speed. A 486DX-50 runs at 50 megahertz. This is a faster machine than a 486DX-33, but not as fast as a 486DX-66 or a Pentium-90.

The new kid on the block: the P6

Intel has announced the newest member of its CPU family and called it the **P6**. (What? We're back to numbers again?) The P6 is actually made up of two chips in one package and has lots of goodies that make even the mighty Pentium seem slow. At this time, the P6 is being aimed at the high-end corporate market and is a little pricey for home use.

What's a math coprocessor?

Since day one, Intel has offered a **math coprocessor** chip as an option to anybody who thought they needed one. Its purpose is simple. The CPU must always stop controlling the flow of information whenever it has to crunch some numbers. It stands to reason that having an assistant who specializes in mathematics would make for a pretty efficient team. Essentially, the traffic cop can put away his calculator and direct traffic all the time, because he has a certified public accountant standing beside him.

Intel uses model numbers that end in a "7" to designate the various math coprocessors it sells. The models are matched to specific CPUs, so an 80286 CPU requires an 80287 math coprocessor, a 386 requires a 387, and so on.

If your CPU is an 80486DX, Pentium, or P6, you got a math coprocessor as standard equipment. These models have the math coprocessor built right into the chip. You couldn't take it out if you tried.

Do I need one?

You will definitely benefit from the speed enhancements as long as your usual work requires a great deal of mathematics. Applications that rely heavily on calculations are spreadsheets, graphics programs, and computer-aided design (CAD) programs. That last one is computerese for drafting. (See Part III of this book for more complete descriptions of software.)

Since most people use graphical-based operating systems these days, all the recent chips from Intel have the math coprocessors built in.

What do the DX and SX mean?

The 386 and 486 lines of CPUs are sold in two trim levels, just like cars. Think of DX as the deluxe model and SX as a sporty entry-level model that moves a little slower. The 386SX, for example, is considered to be too slow for Windows 3.1 and the 486SX is too slow for Windows 95.

What's SL?

There is yet another type of 486 chip on the market and it carries the designation *SL*. This is a low-power-consumption version that is intended for laptop computers to extend their battery life. It is used in desktop models sometimes, under the banner "environmentally friendly." Just like the SX models, these chips are usually a little slower than their fully powered DX cousins.

What's a Power PC?

Depending on what happens in the marketplace, it may be your next CPU. (That's right, it's actually a CPU and not a PC at all.) For years, consumers have been complaining that Apple and IBM machines can't communicate or run each other's software because their internal designs are so different. The two companies finally got together, and with the help of Motorola, designed what they hope to be the CPU of the future. Theoretically, if IBM makes a new computer using this chip, and Apple does the same, everybody will be happily sending information back and forth with no worries.

The Power PC is actually faster and cheaper than Intel's Pentium. The only thing hurting the Power PC's popularity is that Intel has 15 years worth of software programs written specifically for its chips. This head start gives the '86 family a bit of a cushion while Intel tries to convince people of the speed advantages of the newest P6. Competition in this industry is fast and furious indeed!

Can my PC be upgraded?

This is a common question that can't be answered easily. It depends on what you start with and what type of PC you want to have when you're done. For this discussion, we'll assume that you want to upgrade a 486 to a Pentium, and anything else to a 486DX.

- If you still have an 8088-based PC, the answer is no. Too many parts have to be switched to make it a worthwhile investment.

- 286s and 386SXs can theoretically be upgraded to 486s, but you have to buy a completely new motherboard. Total cost is between $300 and $1000.

- A 386DX can be upgraded to a 486DX by simply replacing the CPU chip. One company makes this upgrade kit, which sells for about $300. But the performance may not be worth the cost.

- Many 486 computer manufacturers have advertised their PCs as "Pentium-upgradable." You simply buy a new CPU chip and you're off to the races—sort of. Design differences between the 486 and the Pentium mean that this chip is more like a Pentium SX. Again, the performance may not be cost-effective.

A final note: the other parts of the computer are being improved as quickly as the CPU. Hard disks, memory, and video get bigger and better all the time. Spending your money on a CPU upgrade may be like dropping a Corvette engine into a Volkswagen. If you really want to live on the cutting edge of technology, you should consider selling your old system and using the money for a down payment on an entirely new PC.

5

Understanding Memory

● **In this chapter:**

- **What's memory, and why do I need to know about it?**

- **What's the difference between RAM, ROM, and disk space?**

- **There are all kinds of memory**

- **Where's the memory in my computer?**

- **How much memory does my computer have? How do I find out? And how much memory do I need?**

- **Solution to memory problems**

Ever had to "cram" for a test—only to forget everything the next day? Your computer's memory works the same way. . ➤

What is memory, anyway? To understand what memory is, think of your computer's memory as a desktop where you work. Files, letters, and reports can't be read if they are still in a desk drawer or filing cabinet, right? You have to open them on your desk before they can be used. When you're finished with a document, you can put it away again, clearing off your desk for the next project.

If you've just typed a letter to Mom and you can see it on the screen of your word processing application, then both the letter and the word processor are in memory right now. Unless the information you're working on is in memory, along with the application that knows how to do it, you can't do anything with a computer.

CAUTION   **When you finish typing, don't just turn off your computer! A** computer isn't a typewriter. When your letter or whatever is finished, you have to *save* the stuff you typed to disk. If you just turn off the machine, you turned off your letter, too—and it's gone! See the section "You can't trust your memory" for details.

Why does everyone keep harping on memory?

Quite simply, you need it to make the whole system work, and if you want to keep the system working, you should learn about a few of its quirks:

- If you don't have enough memory, the system runs slow or won't run at all.

- If you have too much, you wasted precious dollars you could have spent elsewhere.

- If it's not set up correctly, some programs won't load.

- If you (or the power company) turn off the electricity, it forgets everything you did with it—forever.

There is no doubt that memory issues in a PC can be confusing at first glance. But simple common sense and an understanding of the facts will avoid a lot of frustration down the road.

You can't trust your memory

The computer's memory isn't permanent, any more than yours is. You have to write down important information that you need to know later, right? (Was that *555-1291* or *555-1921*?) So does your computer. And just like you're going to record your thoughts on paper, tape, or sticky yellow notes, the computer can record the information you enter on paper (as a printout), tape, or disk.

Electronic memory is okay for short periods...

Your computer's memory is electronic. It's formed from rows of little microchips. Microchips push electrons around, electrons come from electricity, and electricity comes from Niagara Falls. (Well, mine does, anyway.) If something happens to Niagara Falls or to any of the wires between there and the back of your computer—Poof! Instant amnesia. Any work that hasn't been saved to disk is lost forever.

...but magnetic storage is the long-term solution

Because the information in memory is so susceptible to the whims of the power company, disk drives become the place for long-term storage. They store data magnetically, rather than electronically. You're probably familiar with this concept from cassettes or videotapes. You may not understand how it works, but you know that you can record Jay Leno, take the tape out of the machine, and you've got Jay on file forever. Your computer works the same way, but generally you store the stuff you type on magnetic disks instead of tapes.

 TIP **Don't stick your floppy disks to the sides of filing cabinets with** refrigerator magnets; exposure to magnets will erase any disk.

Q&A *Where's that file I was working on yesterday?*

If you think you've lost a file, and the computer was turned off sometime between then and now, there's a good chance that you forgot to save your work to disk.

To prevent this problem in the future, remember that memory needs electricity to hold information and disks don't. Before you throw the big switch at the end of the day, use the program's command to save the file to disk. For example, in most Windows-based programs, you can just choose the Save command from the File menu.

Even my software programs need memory?

When you buy software programs—for word processing, accounting, design, graphics, and so on—they come on floppy disks or maybe a CD. They may get installed onto your computer's hard disk so you can get to them quickly, but they don't do their work there. Remember, all programs are kept on disk, so they're safe when the computer is turned off. When you're ready to use a program, your computer must copy it into its memory—computer people call this **loading** a program into memory. In this case, **load** and **copy** mean the same thing.

Bits and bytes defined

Despite what you may see on the screen, the CPU and the RAM of your computer only recognize two things—1s and 0s. How these two digits get converted into letters, numbers, and pictures is where bits and bytes come in.

The 1s and 0s are arranged in a kind of Morse code, where different combinations represent the various letters of the alphabet. These groups of 1s and 0s are called **bytes** (pronounced *bites*). A byte is therefore one character. The little 1s and 0s in each byte had to be called something too, so they were called **bits**. A byte is always made up of eight bits.

Where is the memory?

If you ever look inside a computer while someone is working on it, you'll see the memory sitting right there in nice straight rows of identical chips. From outside the computer, you can't *see* the memory, but you can see what it *does*.

The next two sections describe the major types of memory on your computer—**RAM** and **ROM**. Later sections describe how memory is subdivided even further—into conventional memory, upper memory, and so on.

What are RAM and ROM?

When computer jocks discuss computer memory, they generally talk about RAM, which is an acronym for **random-access memory**. RAM (pronounce it like the male sheep) actually describes the kind of chips used to make up the computer's memory, but most people just use "RAM" and "memory" interchangeably.

The term *random access* means that the microprocessor doesn't have to search through every character in memory when it needs only a certain piece of information. It goes directly to data that it needs and reads it. Computers are so fast because they use this random-access method to push information around inside the memory chips.

ROM stands for **read-only memory**. The term *read-only* means you can't write anything onto that chip. A ROM is a chip that contains a simple program or set of instructions; in a computer's case, the instructions that start your computer when you turn on the power.

Will you or anyone you know ever have to actually do something with ROM? Probably not. It's installed at the factory and just quietly does its job.

What's the difference between RAM and ROM?

Punch in a bunch of numbers on your calculator and then turn the switch off and on again. The numbers disappeared because they were in the calculator's RAM memory. But every time you turn the calculator back on, it still knows how to add and subtract. That knowledge is stored in a program built into the ROM, and can't be forgotten by the calculator. The numbers that you enter exist only in temporary memory—RAM. After you get the result, you don't care about the numbers anymore, so they're erased from memory.

There is no difference between a calculator and a computer when you're discussing memory—except of course for the size (or **capacity**) of that memory. A calculator can hold about eight numbers before it shows you that little "E" on the display. With a computer, you can type pages and pages of meaningful text and will probably run out of things to say long before you run out of memory.

SIMMs are simple

In most desktop computers, you can add more memory if you want or need it. If you're thinking about doing this, you need to add a new term to your computer vocabulary: **SIMM**. (It stands for **Single In-Line Memory Module**, but you don't really need to know that.) In a SIMM setup, the memory chips are permanently attached to little circuit boards about three inches long. They just plug right into empty slots on your computer's motherboard. That's really about all you need to know about SIMMs, except what they look like (see fig. 5.1).

Bytes, kilobytes, and megabytes

In computerese, a byte is exactly one character. The word "byte," for example, is four bytes long. The byte is the basis for all measures dealing with the computer, but as computers have increased in power, we now talk in **kilobytes** (each kilobyte is roughly 1,000 bytes), **megabytes** (roughly 1,000,000 bytes), and **gigabytes** (roughly 1,000,000,000 bytes). The abbreviation for kilobytes is **K**. Therefore, 640K is about 640,000 bytes. Megabytes shortens to **meg** or **Mb** or just **M**. Gigabytes is usually shortened to **gig** or **Gb**.

You might see an ad for computers with the phrase, "1.4M floppy, 1.2Gb HD." This computer has one floppy drive that accepts 1,400,000-byte floppy disks and a hard disk that holds just over 1 billion bytes. Remember to pronounce it right! Say, "One point four meg" and "one point two gig" or everyone will think you're a dummy.

Fig. 5.1
SIMMs consist of many chips mounted on a single card. They can be changed and upgraded quickly.

CAUTION **Don't just go out to the discount office supply warehouse and** pick a couple SIMMs off the shelf. You just can't stick any old SIMM in any old computer. Leave this to a qualified person who can tell you what you have and what you need. And NEVER try to install them yourself!

Extended? Expanded?

Like the science-fiction writers of the fifties who dreamed of going to the moon and beyond, programmers and technical support personnel look up to the skies and dream of a day when there will be just plain *memory*. Until that day arrives (and it *is* coming), we'll have to accept the fact that the memory inside our PCs gets categorized into a confusing mishmash of names that sound alike and describe very little.

Think of memory as being stacked much like the floors in a high-rise building. The first 640 floors (640K) of RAM are **conventional**. The floors between 640 and 1024 (1M) are called **upper memory**, and any floors above 1024 are called **extended memory**. Figure 5.2 helps put it in perspective.

Fig. 5.2
When memory is installed in a new computer, the first 640 kilobytes to go in are called conventional. The next 384 kilobytes are called upper memory, and anything after that is called extended.

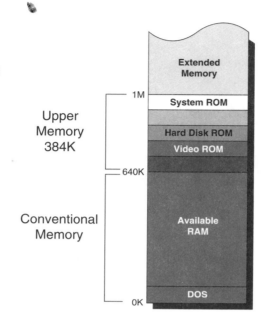

 Q&A *I use Windows 95. Do I really have to know about all these kinds of memory?*

If your computer uses Windows 95 or OS/2, most of these memory types will be invisible to you, although technically they're still there. When you use an older DOS–based program with one of these operating systems, whatever types of memory the program needs will automatically be provided.

Conventional memory

When DOS was written for machines with Intel 8088 processors, the programmers limited the amount of RAM memory the microprocessor could use to 640K: "Yes, that's right! Our new operating system can take advantage of all your computer's memory, right up to 640,000 bytes! Nobody will EVER need all that, but this baby is built for the future!"

Unfortunately, we outgrew that "infinite limit" two or three years into the PC's childhood, and DOS is still the operating system installed on most of the PCs ever sold. It's still around because some of the most popular software packages need DOS to work. No matter how many mega-gobs of memory your system really has, if you ask DOS to count up the bytes, it will say you have 640K of conventional memory.

Upper memory

Actually, early computers *could* use a little more memory than 640K—up to one full megabyte of memory. Remember that your computer has more than just RAM for memory—it also has ROM. Years ago, somebody made the arbitrary decision that the megabyte of potential memory for the 8088 processor should be broken down into 640K of conventional memory where it could talk to RAM, and another 384K of upper memory for ROM. Add the two numbers together and you get 1024K, or 1 megabyte. (See the following sidebar if you don't follow this math.)

Simply put, when the processor is talking to RAM, it's moving things around in conventional memory. When it's reading from ROM, it's working in the 384K upper-memory area.

Expanded memory

Expanded memory was invented to work around the 640K limitation of the old 8088/DOS combination. As desktop computing gained in popularity, people began seeing unpleasant messages on their screens, like Out of memory. It became obvious that the bottomless 640K was more shallow than anyone had ever imagined. Lotus (the 1-2-3 company) was forced to sit down with Microsoft (the DOS company) and Intel (the chip company). Together, they hammered out a solution using hardware and software. The result actually fooled the processor and DOS into using more memory than either of them thought they could.

TIP **If you use an older XT-type of computer or DOS-based business** program (for example, Lotus 1-2-3 Version 2.3 or WordPerfect 5.1), your system might already have or could benefit from expanded memory. Ask your favorite computer consultant.

If you only use more recent software such as that written for Windows or OS/2, you probably don't need it.

Extended memory

Is your computer an 80286 or an 80386SX? It can talk to 16 megabytes of memory if you have it. 80386, 80486, or Pentium? You can use four gigabytes (that's billions of bytes). Any memory installed over one megabyte is classified as extended memory. This kind of memory is easier and faster for a processor to use than expanded memory. Plus there's a lot less chanting and wand-waving.

Since all of the latest computers can use extended memory, the people who write programs have begun to insist that you get some. Windows and OS/2 *love* extended memory. In fact, they can't live without extended memory, and the more the better.

Virtual memory

Just as *virtual reality* isn't really reality, *virtual memory* isn't really memory. It's actually a big file (sometimes called a swap file) on your computer's hard disk. Newer operating systems like Windows 3.1 and Windows 95 will automatically create these files and store extra data in them when the electronic memory (RAM) is filling up. Virtual memory helps to avoid Out of memory error messages.

The one problem with virtual memory is its lack of speed. Any disk is, after all, *much* slower than RAM. If your computer seems slow and the hard disk light is always on, you probably need to buy more RAM.

 TIP **Today's programs need lots of memory if you want them to run** without any problems. The more you have, the more likely it is that you'll be able to do all the things you want, when you want. So aim for eight megabytes or more of RAM.

Why does a 360K floppy disk hold 368,640 bytes?

No matter how smart they seem, computers are only capable of seeing things as "on" or "off." Computers represent "on" with a number 1 and "off" with a 0. That's it. Two numbers. So how do they get anything done? They just put a bunch of 0s and 1s together into strings that represent any number or character the computer needs.

All this counting by twos forces us humans to make weird adjustments when we deal with computer memory. If you take the number 2 and keep doubling it (2, 4, 8, 16, and so on), you

arrive at 1024, which is the closest you can get to 1,000. Somebody years ago decided that this would be a good unit of measurement and called it a kilobyte even though it's not really a **kilo-**anything. So a K is really 1024.

The 360K floppy disk? Get out your calculator and do the math: 360 times 1024 is 368,640.

And, a megabyte is actually 1,048,576 bytes. Don't worry about it. Just remember that **kilo** is a thousand and **mega** is a million.

How much memory do I have on my computer?

There are a few ways to find out this number. The easiest is to watch the screen right after you turn on the main switch. It helps to make sure that the screen is turned on and warmed up before turning on the computer. Most computers go through an internal diagnostic procedure that verifies the memory installed in the system by counting the bytes. (Sometimes this is accompanied by a nifty ticking sound.) The highest number reached before the screen goes blank and the operating system loads is how many kilobytes of memory you have. Just round it off, divide by one thousand, and say "Meg." The computer I'm typing on counts to 16384, then wipes it out and does other stuff. My laptop counts to 8192 and then goes blank. The first is a sixteen-megabyte machine. The second has eight megabytes.

Okay, some computer models don't do it. Nobody knows why. For these machines, you have to ask the computer to report the amount of memory.

Checking your memory with Windows 95

Windows 95 knows all about your computer's components and will tell you what's there. Point to the icon named My Computer and press the *right* mouse button. (That's called **right-clicking**.) Click Properties in the pop-up menu. A window called System Properties appears. It contains, among other things, the amount of RAM installed in your PC and the CPU type (see fig. 5.3).

Fig. 5.3
The System Properties window tells you about the devices in your computer. Click the Cancel button to close the window when you're finished.

Checking your memory with DOS

If your PC uses DOS or Windows 3.1, you'll have to give a DOS command to count up your memory. (See Chapter 9 of this book for more on DOS.) At the DOS prompt, follow these steps:

1 Type **MEM** and press the Enter key. A report should appear on the screen.

Q&A *I got an error message when I typed MEM!*

If you don't have DOS 5 or higher, you'll see the message Bad command or filename. Skip the rest of this procedure.

2 Write down the numbers for Total Conventional Memory and Total Extended Memory (or XMS).

3 Add the two numbers together and round them off to the nearest million. That's how much RAM is installed in your computer. Some versions of DOS make the addition unnecessary. Simply look at the first number next to Total Memory!

If you can't use MEM, there are diagnostic software utilities that do the job very well, but they are far beyond the scope of this book. Ask around at your office or among your friends. Somewhere, you'll come across someone with the know-how and the willingness to help.

 Plain English, please!

MEM is a DOS command that you type at the keyboard when the DOS prompt is visible on the screen. It provides a report about how much memory is in your system and how much is currently being used by programs. Most DOS commands are just shortened versions of longer words. See Chapter 9 for other examples.

How much memory do I need?

The type of work that you do and the kinds of software that you do it with determine your memory needs. If you only work with DOS and a few software applications that were written for it, you might be quite happy with 640K. Lotus 1-2-3 Version 2.3 and WordPerfect 5.1 are examples of DOS applications that are quite content sitting in that little space we call conventional memory. You *might* want to look into obtaining some expanded memory (see the preceding section), but this depends entirely on how big your documents and spreadsheets are. If everything seems to be running smoothly, don't worry about it.

GUIs are memory hogs

If your computer runs one of the **graphical user interfaces (GUIs)** like Windows 95, Windows 3.1, or OS/2, buy as much memory as you can reasonably afford without going into bankruptcy. These operating systems have lots of pretty colors and lots of little pictures that you grab with your mouse and drag around the screen. This takes loads of memory just to display, and you're not even doing any work yet.

Remember how you're supposed to think of your computer's memory as a desktop? Windows puts so many nifty gadgets and tools on your desk that you don't have any room left for your work unless you get a larger desk.

 TIP **When you buy software, the side of the box usually says how much** RAM the program needs. Don't believe this for a minute. These are always *minimum* requirements. Windows 95 and OS/2 only run efficiently with 8M or more of RAM, although Windows 3.1 can probably get by with 4M.

The programs that you buy to run with Windows generally need more memory than their DOS cousins. How many programs you use at the same time also has an influence on how much memory you should have. If you use only a word processor or a spreadsheet most of the time, and if your documents are not the size of *War and Peace*, the memory amounts suggested above are probably fine. If you use two or more programs at once, and cut and paste numbers between them, you'll probably need twice that amount to hold the programs and all their data.

If you are doing any work with computer graphics (that's pictures, page layouts, and so on), you'll probably need 16M of RAM. This is particularly true if you have a scanner attached to your system and you are scanning photographs (see Chapter 19 for information about scanners).

Managing your memory

The various types of memory, how they relate to each other, and how they get massaged by different kinds of software is called **memory management**. Only in the world of DOS could such a thing even be possible. Remember that we're discussing an operating system that was written around 1980, then added to and patched up here and there over the years.

The concept behind memory management is to try and free up as much conventional memory as possible by moving smaller programs out and putting them into other types of memory, such as upper or extended. You know already that having lots of memory is a good thing (the bigger the desk, the more work you can do). But since DOS can't work with more than 640K of memory, the size of the desk is fixed from the start. The only thing you can do is clean it off a bit.

What does it mean, Out of memory?!

You probably have too much information in there for the memory to hold. Save your work, exit the software, and then restart the computer. If it happens again while you're working on the same job, you probably do need more memory. Work with smaller documents until you can get someone to install it for you. This might also be a symptom of needing to get your memory managed a bit.

I get errors when I run Windows programs

With Windows 3.1, these errors were typically called General Protection Faults. In Windows 95, they appear far less often because Windows 95 does a better job of managing memory (and it's only a memory management problem most of the time). Write down what you were doing when you saw the message, exit the software, and then try again. If it happens again, especially with the same window open, you might need to update some of your programs to newer versions.

Uh oh—I got a parity error

The parity error happens when a special parity chip tattles on RAM and tells the CPU that memory is not giving it the right information. If you've never seen a parity error, it's because memory chips are pretty dependable. If you do get one, try turning off the PC, waiting thirty seconds, and then turning it on again. You lost all your work anyway, so turning it off won't hurt. (Humming a funeral dirge at this point is appropriate.) If the error occurs again, or if the system won't start at all, you've got a serious problem that needs under-the-hood servicing.

If parity errors only occur once in a while, then the problem might be something *external* to the PC that you can fix yourself. The following table might help you pinpoint the problem. If not, you've got a hardware problem and you need to take the PC in for service.

Possible cause	Try this
Static electricity	Raise the humidity or buy a special static mat from the computer store.
Power surges and spikes	Invest in a good-quality surge suppression outlet (see Chapter 2).
Other devices on the same circuit	Take the Mr. Coffee, the electric fan, and the laser printer off the same extension cord and plug them in somewhere else.

6

What You Need to Know about Monitors

● In this chapter:

- What kind of monitor do I need?

- Graphics modes and graphics adapter cards

- What types of graphics can my computer display?

- What do resolution and memory have to do with graphics?

- I'd like my computer to show more colors

- What's a screen saver?

Although it looks like a TV, you'd have a hard time watching HBO on your computer's monitor. But without it, you and your computer won't have much to say to each other . . . . ➤

A waggish friend and former office mate once put an old pair of TV antennas on top of her computer's monitor to make it look, as she put it, "really retro"—like one of those funky black-and-white TV sets from the 1950s. Your computer's **monitor** (also known as the **screen** or **display**) looks a lot like a TV and functions in much the same way. Just don't try channel surfing on it!

Besides being the most obvious part of a PC, the monitor is also your main source of output from the computer. Whether you're playing a game, typing a sales report, or managing the files on your disks, you need your screen to see what you're doing. Because so much of your time is spent staring at your monitor, it pays to have one that won't make you go blind.

What are my choices?

When you're ready to buy a monitor for your PC, you have lots of choices: everything from old-fashioned black and white to photographic-quality color. Because the picture on the monitor also depends on your computer's graphics abilities, you need to know what kind of graphics adapter your computer uses. The **graphics adapter** is a board that plugs into one of the expansion slots. It must be the same type as the monitor you select, so sometimes buying a new monitor means buying a new graphics adapter, too.

If you're in the market for video, here are some points to consider:

- The minimum you should settle for is called **VGA**, or in technospeak, Video Graphics Array. If you settle for less and get **EGA** (Enhanced Graphics Adapter) or the really horrible **CGA** (Color Graphics Adapter), you'll have a hard time with much of the modern software that likes brilliant colors and fine resolution.

- If you plan to use your PC for graphic design, photographic work, or drafting, you want a state-of-the-art display. Go with a **SVGA** (SuperVGA) system, which has higher resolution and can show even more colors (up to 16.7 million!) than VGA. Most new computers come with SVGA as standard equipment.

We'll tell you a lot more about this stuff in the sections that follow.

What do "graphics modes" have to do with my monitor?

Here's the lowdown: personal computers display information in various **graphics modes**. Just think of a graphics mode as a way of drawing information on the screen. The simplest graphics mode is text-only (see fig. 6.1) and allows only two colors, black and white.

Fig. 6.1
The simplest displays show only text, which can get real boring real fast. They are "DOS only" displays that can never work with any version of Windows.

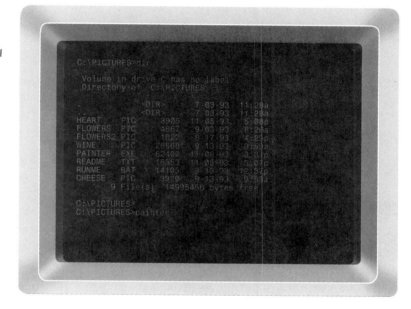

The most sophisticated graphics modes can display everything from two-color text to photographic-quality pictures containing hundreds (or even millions) of colors (see fig. 6.2).

Fig. 6.2
The best monitors can show pictures with almost as much detail as a photograph. When called upon, they also show the old two-color text screens with ease.

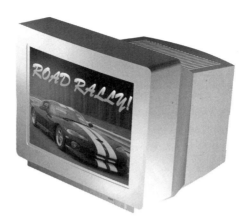

TIP   **Monitors can be real energy hogs, especially if they're left on all** the time. "Green" monitors, also called Energy Star monitors, are a little more environment-friendly because they conserve electricity. These displays know when they're not being used, and even while still on, can cut their power consumption considerably.

Monitors and adapter cards: a matching game

For your computer to be able to display a specific graphics mode, both the computer and the monitor have to be able to handle it.

The computer's end of things is handled by something called a **video adapter card**, which plugs into the motherboard. In order for everything to work right, the monitor and the video adapter card have to match. If you have a terrific monitor but only a so-so adapter card, you're going to get a so-so picture. The reverse is true, too.

When you buy a new computer system, it comes configured with a matching video adapter card and monitor. Most today can operate in VGA and SVGA (see table 6.1). The information in this chapter will be useful if you have an older computer and want to upgrade the video, or if you're considering buying a specialized or oversized monitor with your new system.

Table 6.1   Graphics adapters from A to Z

Acronym	Meaning	Type	Comments
MDA	Monochrome Display Adapter	Black and white	Limited to displaying text. A museum piece by today's standards.
CGA	Color Graphics Adapter	Color	Allows "chunky" (ugly, that is) graphics in only four colors. This display standard has all but disappeared. Don't bother.
HGC	Hercules Graphics Card	Black and white	Allows both text and graphics that are a lot less "chunky" than CGA. Still, it's out of date.
EGA	Enhanced Graphics Adapter	Color	Can show 16 colors at a time with less "chunky" lines. A little better than CGA but also obsolete. Again, don't bother.
MCGA	Multi-Color Graphics Array	Color	A lot like EGA, but with the ability to show 256 colors at a time. Never caught on, though, and is pretty much extinct.
VGA	Video Graphics Array	Color	The reigning king, although it's losing ground to SVGA. This adapter gives detailed graphics with up to 256 colors. A nice choice for most folks.
SVGA	Super Video Graphics Array	Color	The current cutting edge, allowing even more detailed graphics than VGA with *many* more colors. If you plan to use your PC for graphic design, photographic work, or drafting, you'll want this kind of adapter.

Q&A *I have some software that doesn't display in color. Do I need a monochrome screen?*

In most cases, the better adapter cards can handle all graphics modes from text-only up to the maximum ability of the card. For example, a VGA card can show MDA, CGA, EGA, and VGA images. For that reason, an SVGA adapter card can handle just about any graphics mode in existence. This capability ensures that the adapter can display older software that displays in a particular mode.

What makes for a good picture on my screen?

A lot of things work together to determine how great the picture on your monitor looks. You know now that the two pieces of important hardware are the monitor and the video adapter card. But what, specifically, are the important characteristics of these two pieces of hardware? Here's a list:

- Resolution

- Number of colors

- Memory

- Speed

What is screen resolution?

The image on a monitor is made of rows of tiny dots. The number of dots that a monitor or adapter card can display horizontally and vertically on the screen is called **resolution**.

On a VGA display, for example, the best resolution is 640×480, which means the picture can have at most 640 dots across and 480 dots down. An SVGA monitor and adapter can easily achieve 1024×768. There are two reasons why a high resolution may be desirable. First, you get much finer detail of graphics images like photographs or blueprints. Second, if your screen is cluttered with lots of objects, you can spread them out more and see the "big picture" (see figs. 6.3 and 6.4).

Fig. 6.3

This Windows 95 desktop shows three applications opened using 640×480 resolution. It is almost impossible to work in this mess!

Fig. 6.4

Here are the same three applications using a screen resolution of 1024×768. Higher resolutions let you see more of the screen (even if it seems like you're looking down from the top of a building).

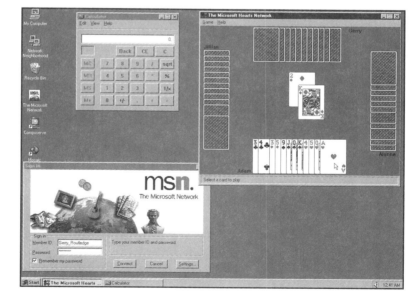

TIP **Make sure your display can handle at least 640×480 resolution,** because so many software packages demand it. Any less, and you'll be forced to run software from the Stone Age.

Q&A *My monitor's documentation talks about "pitch"— is this a baseball thing?*

No, you can put away your cleats. Remember those commercials where a TV manufacturer claimed to have surrounded all the colored dots on the screen with a black background? Well, the distance between the dots is called the **dot pitch**. The closer the dots, the better the picture. If the dot pitch is too big, everything seems fuzzy. Some of the best monitors have a dot pitch of .28mm (millimeters) or less, which is great for SVGA displays. For regular VGA, you can probably get by with a dot pitch of .31mm. When buying a new monitor, make sure the dot pitch isn't over .31mm.

How many colors are enough?

Another factor that controls the richness and realism of a display is the number of colors that can be shown at one time. Imagine da Vinci or Michelangelo trying to paint a scene with only a few colors in his palette. The minimum number of colors needed to show detailed graphics these days is 256. If you want to work with photographs, you'll probably need a monitor and adapter that can handle 16.7 million colors. (This is known as **true color**. Crayolas were never like this!) So if you have an older graphics adapter that can't display at least 256 colors, consider upgrading your video.

How much video memory do I need?

Your graphics adapter card even has its own RAM memory, so it can construct graphical images without hogging the main memory used by the system. Generally, the greater the resolution and the more colors displayed, the more memory needed to construct an image.

A good SVGA adapter card carries at least 1M of memory on board. Any less, and you may have to run at lower resolutions when you want lots of colors (or fewer colors when you want high resolutions).

Do I need a fast adapter card?

Adapter cards are a lot like little computers whose specialty is graphics. Just like computers, different adapter cards work at different speeds. Even a fast computer will appear to work (yawn) slowly if the video adapter doesn't have enough muscle. Fast adapter cards, on the other hand, generate images… well, faster. If you're using a graphical operating system like Windows 95, a speedy adapter card is a *must*. Fast adapters for this type of work are often called **video accelerators**.

CAUTION **Beware of monitors that use interlacing to generate their displays.** Some monitor manufacturers try to make cheap, slow monitors achieve high resolutions by using this technique. The result is a barely perceptible flicker that causes headaches and eyestrain.

 Plain English, please!

An **interlaced** monitor displays every second line of the screen image in one pass, then it goes back and fills in the lines it missed on a second pass. Some monitors will only begin interlacing when used at very high resolutions. (This makes them almost useless at those resolutions.) Other really cheap monitors will interlace the display at *all* resolutions. Either way, be sure to check the documentation that comes with the monitor and choose the **non-interlaced** variety whenever you can.

How can I soup up my display?

The more you have to wait for your computer to draw all those little pictures and windows, the less work you're going to get done. Even if you upgrade your system to have a really fast processor, a slow video card still limits how fast you can get anything done.

One way some PCs get faster graphic displays is by using something called a **local bus**. It's a special circuit in the motherboard that gives a computer's CPU direct access to the graphics hardware. This special connection really zaps graphics information through the computer, although you need a **local bus video adapter** to take advantage of it. You can't just go out and upgrade your system to local bus—it has to be there in the motherboard already. If your system doesn't already have it, buying an accelerator board is the best way to improve graphics performance.

Many people choose to speed up their computer's graphics by buying a video accelerator. Although they sound like an option you can just add on, they're really complete video-card replacements. Accelerator boards, which are used mostly with graphical operating systems like Windows 95, are fine-tuned for graphics tasks, and make your system sizzle when it comes to redrawing the display.

Accelerator boards can cost as much as $1,000. The good news is that you don't need to plunk down that much cash to improve your Windows graphics speed. A typical graphics accelerator board costs less than $200. Buy the best board that you can afford, but don't go *over*board. You don't need to buy a top-of-the-line board unless you'll be doing a lot of sophisticated graphics work or want top-quality multimedia capabilities.

Hanging a virtual "out to lunch" sign on your monitor

In the old days, if you left your monitor on and idle too long, the image got burned into the screen. From that point on, whenever you used the monitor, you could see this ghost-like phosphor image in the background. (Next time you visit your local ATM, look closely at its screen and you'll see what I mean.) To avoid the burn-in problem, clever programmers created **screen savers**, which blacked out the screen whenever the computer was not being used.

Today's color monitors don't burn-in like the old days, but screen savers are as popular as ever. That's because screen savers no longer just turn off the screen; they do all sorts of clever things like show cartoons or draw fantastic designs. You can even get screen savers based on a favorite movie or computer game.

Commercial screen savers cost money, of course. You can expect to pay between $20 and $40 for such graphics extravaganzas. However, there are lots of free screen savers floating around, many of which are clever enough to warrant a look. The Windows 95 operating system comes with its own built-in screen savers. You can find other free screen savers on BBSs or on-line services. (If you don't know about this on-line stuff, see Chapter 23.)

7

Disks and Disk Drives

● **In this chapter:**

- I have two different slots for disks in my computer. What's the difference?

- How to tell which disks are high density and which are double density

- I'm trying to copy stuff on a disk, but it won't let me

- A hard disk can hold as many as 500 floppy disks—or more!

If you've ever seen a 5¼-inch disk, you'll know why they call them "floppies" . . . . ➤

n Chapter 5, we explained how the computer's memory is where all the real action takes place. We also explained that electronic memory is temporary at best. Every time you turn off the power—poof! The fact is that the only safe place for permanent storage of information is on a disk.

Disks are the computer equivalent of filing cabinets. And just like filing cabinets, they're actually pretty easy to use, especially if you take a few minutes to become familiar with how they work. This chapter gives you tips on how to use your floppy disks, drives, and hard disk effectively.

What's the difference between these disk drives?

You could say that floppy drives are your computer's shipping and receiving department. The disks you stick into the drive are like packages that deliver information to the computer and carry information out from your computer. Without floppy-disk drives, you'd have a hard time transferring information from one computer to another (unless you are connected to a network, but we'll talk about that in Chapter 22).

Computer technology improves and changes constantly. And disk drive technology is a big part of those changes. Every few years, someone invents a new and better disk drive that needs new and better disks.

You'll run into many varieties of disks and drives. Luckily, only two characteristics determine the type of drive you have:

- The physical size of the disk that the drive can accommodate

- How much information can be stored on the disk

Sizing up a floppy

The physical size of a floppy disk is either $3^1/_2$ inches across or $5^1/_4$ inches across. The larger $5^1/_4$-inch disks have been around a lot longer, but they don't work as well. They're easier to damage, they don't hold as much information, and they're bulkier to carry around. Since $3^1/_2$-inch disks are so much better, they took over the floppy disk market pretty rapidly. Today, $5^1/_4$-inch disks are being phased out fast; most new computers don't even have a 5¼-inch drive and soon they'll be almost impossible to find.

How much can they hold?

Like most things in computing, the capacity of a disk is measured in kilobytes (K) or megabytes (M). (If you don't understand these terms, go back and read Chapter 5.) And just to make things difficult, here's another term for you. A disk's capacity is determined by its **density**, which is how much information can be packed into one place on the disk.

If this density stuff is making *you* feel a little dense, think about it like luggage. There's a big difference between a hard-sided suitcase and a paper bag. Even if they're about the same size, you can always get a lot more in a suitcase because you can pack the clothes in tighter. Disks are like that, too. Some disks—**high-density disks**—are better at cramming more information into the same amount of space (and you don't have to sit on them to close them).

For quick reference, the following table lists the various types of disks and their capacities.

Disk size	Type	Capacity
5¼-inch	Double density	360K
5¼-inch	High density	1.2M
3½-inch	Double density	720K
3½-inch	High density	1.44M

Which kind do I need?

Which disks you can use depends on your drive. A high-density drive can handle any disk that will fit into it. A double-density drive can never handle high-density disks. If you have the oldest type of drive, a 5¼-inch double density, my suggestion is to replace it with a 3½-inch, high-density disk drive.

Every so often, somebody sends me a 5¼-inch disk, so I have both sizes of drives installed in my home PC. Both drives are high density, so I can read any kind of disk that comes across my desk.

TIP   **If you have a lot of information stored on 5^1/$_4$-inch disks, you** should transfer that information onto 3^1/$_2$-inch disks as soon as you can. Since 5^1/$_4$-inch disks are becoming obsolete, most of your coworkers can't read them now, and you won't be able to access them if you get a new computer that doesn't have a 5^1/$_4$-inch drive. As a bonus, you'll need fewer disks to hold the same information because high-density 3^1/$_2$-inch disks have the greatest capacities.

Although it's easy to tell the size of a drive by the width of the slot and by whether it has a lever (5^1/$_4$-inch) or button (3^1/$_2$-inch), drives aren't labeled with their densities. If you don't know what density your drive is, check the documentation that came with your drive or computer. Of course you could always insert a disk that you *know* is high density and try to read it. If it works, you have a high-density drive!

Which disk is which?

Now that you know which disks you can use, how can you tell the disks apart? With 3^1/$_2$-inch disks, telling a double-density disk from a high-density disk is as easy as separating roses from mushrooms.

Here's the trick: look at the corners of the disk. If there's a hole in each corner, you have a high-density disk (see fig. 7.1). If there's only one hole, it's a double-density disk. Many high-density disks also have an "HD" stamped in one corner.

Figuring out 5^1/$_4$-inch disks is a lot tougher. One way to tell a double-density 5^1/$_4$-inch disk from a high-density disk is to read the label. If there is no label, try looking at the hole in the middle of the disk. If there's a narrow metal ring around the hole like the one shown in figure 7.2, it's a double-density disk.

Fig. 7.1
This little disk packs a lot of wallop! It holds over 1.44M.

So does this.

This hole means it's a high-density disk.

Fig. 7.2
A double-density 5¹/₄-inch disk has a narrow band around the hole. High-density disks don't.

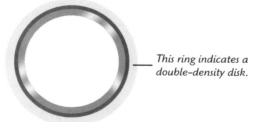

This ring indicates a double-density disk.

Getting ready to use your disks

Before you can use a new disk, you have to format it. **Formatting** prepares the disk's surface to hold information. When you format a disk, the disk drive marks off magnetic tracks on the disk—tracks that are a lot like the grooves on a record, except grooves on a record hold music, and the tracks on a disk hold programs and data. Until you create these tracks, you can't use the disk.

No matter what operating system you use, formatting a disk is pretty simple. Windows 95 users can read all about it in Chapter 11. DOS users get the scoop in Chapter 9.

 TIP   **Many disks sold today are preformatted by the manufacturer. If** you're about to do something that requires a lot of disks, such as backing up your system, buy preformatted disks. The time savings is well worth the small extra cost.

Write-protect your disks if you want to avoid accidents

How does your VCR know that it can tape over your recording of last week's *Seinfeld*, but it can't tape over that copy of *Pinocchio* you bought for the kids? Prerecorded movie tapes are usually **write-protected**. This write-protection makes it impossible to erase what's already there or write over it with something new. On video tapes, there's a plastic tab you can knock out to create a hole. This tells the VCR's "feelers" that it can't use this tape to record. Of course, it's not really permanent—if you want to tape over it later, you can fool the VCR by putting a piece of Scotch tape over the hole.

On 3½-inch computer disks, it works nearly the same. If the hole in the disk is covered, the computer knows it's okay to write to the disk. If it feels a hole, it knows it can't write to that disk. With 5¼-inch disks, it's just the opposite; a covered hole means don't write, an open hole means it's okay to write.

Most software programs you buy will come on write-protected disks (just as prerecorded videos are write-protected). You can also protect the disks that you use yourself (see the next section for details).

Q&A *If a disk is write-protected, can I still use it?*

Just like a protected VCR tape, you can still read from a protected floppy disk. You can copy files or run programs from the disk. You just can't change anything that's already on it.

How do I know if my disk is write-protected?

To check the write-protection of a 3½-inch disk, turn it over so you can see the round, silver disk hub on the back. Look for the notch in the upper-left corner (like you see in fig. 7.3). If the little black switch is pushed up, the hole below it is exposed. This means that protection is on. If the black switch is pushed down to cover the hole, the write-protection is off.

To check a 5¼-inch disk, face the disk toward you and look for a square notch on the right side. If you can see the notch, it means the disk is not write-protected. To turn protection on, cover the notch with a sticker or piece of tape, as shown in the figure. To turn protection off, carefully peel off the sticker.

Like any other kind of switch, you can turn a disk's write-protection on and off as many times as you want.

TIP Usually, a box of new 5¼-inch disks includes several small stickers you can use to write-protect the disks.

This disk is not write-protected.

This disk is write-protected.

Fig. 7.3
Write-protect a floppy
disk to keep from
accidentally formatting
it or changing the
information it contains.

Taking care of your disks

Now that you know a little about floppy disks
and how they work, you may be wondering how
safe your data is on a floppy disk. The truth is that
$3^{1}/_{2}$-inch disks are fairly robust, thanks to their stiff
plastic shells. Still, there are many ways disks can
be damaged. Here are some ways you can keep
your disks out of harm's way:

- Keep disks away from all magnetic fields,
  including paper clip dispensers and electronic equipment like speakers, TVs,
  amplifiers, and telephones (yes, even
  telephones contain magnets).

- The metal detector in airport security gates
  can affect floppy disks. It's better to hand

the disks to the security attendant for
manual inspection than to have them
scanned by the device.

- Store your disks in some sort of disk file box
  that protects them from dust.

- Never get a disk wet, expose it to direct
  sunlight, or toss it on a heater vent. Don't
  leave them in the car in any weather. Cold
  is just as bad as heat.

- Never insert or remove a disk from a drive
  when the drive's "busy" light is on.

Q&A *Why do I have trouble with other people's disks?*

Just like a stereo cassette player, disk drives have heads that must be aligned for the drive to work properly. When a drive's heads become misaligned, you'll suddenly find that disks formatted on another machine or your older disks don't work anymore. Unfortunately, this isn't a problem that you can fix yourself. A trip to the repair shop is a solution. Often, it's cheaper to replace the drive.

Of course, the problem might also be caused by mixing disk densities. If all your friends have high-density drives and yours is only double density, you will never be able to read those disks.

What about the hard disk?

If a floppy drive is your computer's shipping and receiving department, the hard drive is the information warehouse. You use floppy disks to transfer information into and out of your computer. Sometimes, the information on a floppy disk goes directly into your computer's memory. But usually the information ends up on your computer's hard drive, which is located inside your computer's system unit.

Since you really don't want to open up your computer to see what the hard drive looks like, you can see a picture of one in figure 7.4. From a technical aspect, a hard drive works about the same as a floppy drive. The main difference is that the hard disk never leaves the inside of the computer (it also isn't floppy).

The big advantage of a hard disk is how much information it can hold—often more than would fit on *500* floppy disks! This massive storage makes a hard disk great for storing information you use a lot. Also, hard drives work much faster than floppy drives, so you don't have to wait as long.

Because you can pile so much information onto a hard drive, it's easy to end up with an electronic mess—tons of stuff crammed in and no convenient way to reach in and grab just one item if you need it. See Chapter 11 for advice on organizing your hard drive so that you can locate anything you want, whenever you want it.

Fig. 7.4
The hard drive is
hidden inside the
system unit.

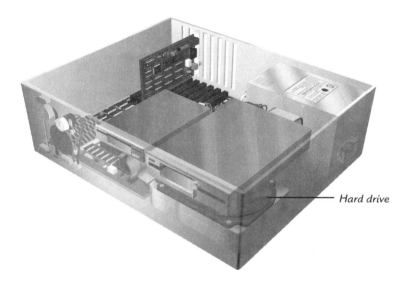

Hard drive

Of Mice and Keyboards

● **In this chapter:**

- **Your computer keyboard is different from your old typewriter keyboard**

- **What are these strange keys like Ctrl and F10?**

- **Restarting with Ctrl+Alt+Del**

- **The mouse doesn't work like your TV remote control**

- **This thing doesn't look like a mouse at all!**

About the only thing your computer can't do is teach you how to type. Well, actually, it can even do that if you have the right software! . . . . ➤

Until computers learn to read our minds, you'll need a reliable way to get information from your head into the computer. Any gadget you use for this purpose is known as an **input device**. The two most common devices are the **keyboard**, which almost anyone would recognize, and the **mouse**, which is newer to the computing world but an invaluable tool nonetheless. If you're not familiar with these devices, this chapter tells you everything you need to know.

A typewriter and then some!

They might look vaguely similar, but don't be fooled! Your computer's keyboard is a lot more than just a typewriter. Sure, you can type on a computer keyboard, but you can also use it to give commands to your computer, complete a series of tedious tasks in just a few keystrokes, and more.

Even though computers are much more sophisticated than typewriters, the bulk of the keys on your computer's keyboard look and act much like typewriter keys—producing letters, numbers, and symbols. It's the extra keys that make the difference.

The 10-key pad

If you work with numbers frequently, you know that typing numbers on a typewriter is a pain in the neck (or the hand) compared to punching them in on a calculator. They're located on the top row and out of comfortable reach. Fortunately, keyboard designers realized this and added a **numeric keypad** to the standard set of keys.

My keyboard is bent!

You probably have one of the newer **ergonomic keyboards** that are designed to place your hands and wrists in a more comfortable (and less injury-prone) position. The Microsoft Natural Keyboard is a common example of this style.

Although they look funny, ergonomic keyboards contain all the same keys as the regular kind. They may even contain a few extra keys that give you special shortcuts to Windows commands. Chapter 2 has more information on ergonomic keyboards and other nice things you can do for your body.

The numeric keypad works just like a 10-key calculator, all the way down to the + and – keys. Generally, the only difference is that the multiply key is * instead of ×, and the division key is / instead of ÷. So, if you're a speed demon on a calculator, you should have no problems using the numeric keypad.

Q&A ***When I press the keys on my numeric keypad, they're acting like arrow keys. What's going on here?***

In the upper-left corner of the numeric keypad, look for a key labeled Num Lock. If Num Lock is on (usually indicated by a little light on or above the key), the keypad keys work like numbers. When it's off, they work like arrow keys (you'll learn more about arrow keys in a minute).

Other special keys

Your computer's keyboard also features a group of keys that are unique to computers. Most of these keys are found sandwiched between the regular keyboard and the numeric keypad. They have strange names like Scroll Lock, Home, End, and Insert. How these keys work often depends on the software you're using. Table 8.1 shows their most common uses.

Table 8.1   Keys labeled with words

Key	Use
Insert	Switches between Insert and Overtype modes (see the explanation after this table)
Delete	Deletes the character to the right of the cursor
Home	Moves to the beginning of a line
End	Moves to the end of a line
Page Up	Moves one page up towards the beginning of the file
Page Down	Moves one page down towards the end of the file
Print Screen	Sends the on-screen image to either the printer or the Windows Clipboard
Scroll Lock	Controls scrolling of the screen in some programs
Pause/Break	Stops screen from scrolling, or, when used with the Ctrl key, stops a DOS command
Num Lock	Switches the numeric keypad on and off
Esc	Usually cancels a command

One of the great things about computers, as opposed to typewriters, is that you can type, edit, and erase your data right up to the second before you print your words out on paper.

Insert mode and **Overtype mode** are the greatest thing since sliced bread. When you're in Insert mode, you can start typing in the middle of a line you already wrote, and the existing characters are "pushed" to the right—you don't have to write over what you already have. In Overtype mode, the new characters replace the old characters automatically. Think of it as an automatic eraser.

What's with all these arrow keys?

When you type on a typewriter, you have to roll the paper up and down and use the space key to position the carriage wherever you want on a page. Making a minor correction after you've already removed the paper from the machine is almost impossible because you can never get the characters to line up properly again.

No more! A computer doesn't have a carriage, so there's no problem with alignment. If you want to make a correction, you just use the arrow keys to position the blinking cursor where you want to make a correction and start typing!

There are several groups of keys on the keyboard that enable you to move the cursor around:

- The first set is to the bottom right of the regular keys. Each of these keys is marked with an arrow that shows which way the cursor moves when you press that key.

- The numeric keypad also has a set of arrow keys that you can use to move the cursor. But to use them, you have to make sure that the Num Lock key is off. (If you press the arrow keys on the number pad and get numbers on the screen, the Num Lock key is still on.)

- If you look at the keyboard, you'll notice that there are at least ten different keys that display some sort of arrow. (My keyboard has 13!) Luckily, most of them have words on them that explain their purpose. Shift, Backspace, Enter, and Tab have arrows on them, but they don't move the cursor around; they work just as they do on a typewriter.

Ctrl and Alt don't work?

The other keys are pretty straightforward, but two special ones, Ctrl (pronounced *control*) and Alt (pronounced just as it looks) aren't so obvious. Ctrl and Alt don't work by themselves. You use them in combination with other keys (usually a letter key) to give commands to programs. Sometimes you even hold down a couple of keys at the same time, like Ctrl and Shift, or Ctrl and Alt.

If you're in Word for Windows, for example, and you hold down the Ctrl key and press *I*, Word puts the letters you type next in *italics*. (By the way, press Ctrl and *I* again to turn this off!)

 TIP **You learned earlier that you can restart your computer by pressing** the Reset button on the front of the system unit. DOS users have been doing it another way for years: hold down Ctrl+Alt, and then press the Delete key. Be sure that you are at the DOS prompt when you do this.

If you use Windows 95 or Windows 3.1, this key combination will close the program that is currently running in memory. Either way, be careful! The "three-fingered salute" erases whatever you have on the screen and is used mostly to restart the PC when something goes wrong.

F is for function

There's one more group of keys I haven't discussed yet. You'll find these keys either at the top or to the far left of your keyboard (maybe both). They're easy to find, because they're marked F1, F2, F3, and so on, up to at least F10 and possibly as high as F12.

The F in these keys' names stands for *function*, so they're usually referred to as **function keys**. How the function keys work depends solely on the program you're running. Since programs all do different things, the function keys work differently as well. Usually, they're used for shortcuts or common tasks. Function key F1, for example, usually calls up Help screens to guide you through unfamiliar tasks.

When you examine the pull-down menus used by your programs, you'll probably find that many common commands have keyboard shortcuts listed next to them. Most people prefer to use at least some of these shortcuts because your hands don't have to leave the keyboard.

Q&A ***The screen says*** `Press any key to continue.` ***My keyboard doesn't have an Any key. What should I do?***

Lots of people get confused by this message. It literally means any key! The PC just needs to know you're ready to go on; just touch anything on the keyboard (except Shift, Caps Lock, Ctrl, or Alt) when you're ready.

A mouse is a very handy gadget

These days, having a computer without a mouse is like playing golf without any clubs. You can probably kick or throw the ball along the course and eventually get it in the hole, but it sure is a lot more work!

Your mouse is like a remote control. It lets you manipulate objects on the screen almost as if you had a robotic arm inside the monitor working for you. The mouse is particularly handy at pressing on-screen buttons and selecting from menus.

Although you can control Windows from your keyboard, you probably wouldn't want to. It often takes two, three, even four or five keystrokes to accomplish what you can do with one click of the mouse.

Anatomy of a mouse

A mouse is really not much more than a box with a ball sticking out the bottom and a cord sticking out the end (the tail?). When you move the mouse around your desk, the ball (called the **tracking ball**) rolls and sends a signal to the computer. The computer uses this signal to make the on-screen **mouse pointer** move across the screen in the same direction. Turn your mouse over and look at the bottom to see what I mean. You can roll the tracking ball around with your finger and watch the pointer move to get the idea.

On top of the mouse are buttons. The average, garden-variety mouse has two buttons, but some have three. You use the buttons to activate objects on-screen. (On a three-button mouse, the middle button is either not used, or is given a special purpose by some programs. You can ignore the middle button for now and concentrate on the other two.)

So what do I do with it?

Using a mouse takes some getting used to, but once you master it, you'll never want to be without one.

Here's what you do with a mouse:

 TIP **These instructions assume you are right-handed. If you're left-handed,** reverse all these instructions (but you Southpaws are used to that anyway, right?).

1 Put the mouse on the right side of the computer, near the keyboard. It needs to sit on a flat, clean surface. A **mouse pad** is recommended.

2 Lay your hand loosely on top of the mouse, placing your index finger on the left button and your middle finger on the right button. Don't grip the mouse too hard! Your hand should rest comfortably on the mouse's back.

3 Roll the mouse around on the mouse pad. As you do, watch the screen. The mouse pointer should roll the same way the mouse does.

4 Roll until the pointer is over a piece of text or some other thing on the screen, like an icon or menu name.

5 Now click one of the mouse buttons. Which button you click and how many times you click it depends on the program you're using and what you want to do. Some tasks you can do are listed in table 8.2.

Table 8.2 Using the mouse buttons

Action	How to do it
Point	Roll the mouse until the on-screen mouse pointer is over a screen object.
Click	Press and release the left mouse button.
Right-click	Press and release the right mouse button.
Double-click	Click the left button twice very quickly.
Drag	Point to an object, press and hold down the left mouse button, and move the mouse.
Right-drag	Just like dragging above, but hold down the right mouse button.
Drop	After dragging an object, release the mouse button to drop the object where you like.

Right-clicking and right-dragging are common functions in Windows 95. Other operating systems rely mostly on the left button only. You may need to practice these actions to get them down, but it won't take long before your mouse is almost as easy to use as your own hand.

 Plain English, please!

A **mouse pad** is a little "rug" you put under the mouse to give the tracking ball better traction. It's usually made of soft rubber or plastic. A mouse rolls better on the somewhat rough surface of a mouse pad, just like tires work better on dry pavement than on ice. 🙰🙰

When a mouse is not a mouse— other pointing devices

Ever tried using a PC and a mouse on one of those little folding airplane tables? As computers become smaller and more portable, manufacturers are constantly looking for ways to save space. Instead of a mouse, some computers use other types of pointing devices, such a **trackball** (which is basically a mouse turned upside down). Figure 8.1 shows a typical trackball installed in a laptop computer.

Fig. 8.1
Trackballs are handy on laptop computers because they need less room to operate. Roll the ball with your thumb to position the pointer and then click one of the buttons.

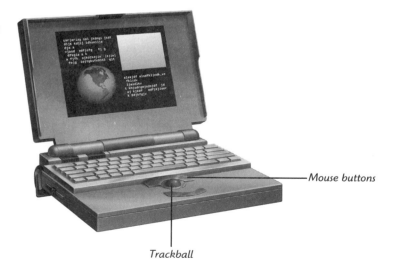

Mouse buttons

Trackball

Another common rodent replacement is the "pencil eraser" style of pointing device that is integrated right into the keyboard. This really is about the size and shape of a pencil eraser and it responds to gentle sideways pressure by moving the mouse pointer across the screen. When it's time to click a mouse button, you'll find them at the bottom of the keyboard, near the space bar.

Some of the newest laptop PCs use a touch-sensitive pad that resembles a tiny blackboard or slate. You can move the pointer around the screen by tracing small circles on the pad with your fingertip. Need to click the button? Just tap the pad with your finger when the pointer is in position.

Typical mouse problems and solutions

- Why is my mouse pointer so jumpy?

If you find that your mouse pointer moves erratically even though you're rolling the mouse smoothly, you've probably got dirty rollers (not you, your mouse).

Turn your mouse over and pop off the little door that holds the tracking ball in place. (Look for little arrows to tell you which direction to twist or push.) Remove the ball and look inside the mouse. You'll see two rollers that the ball rolls against. Hint: Those stripes on the rollers are greasy dirt! To clean the rollers, use alcohol and a Q-Tip. Sometimes it helps to blow a puff of air inside the box, too, to remove any dust. In bad cases, you can try scraping the crud off the rollers with your fingernail.

- I think this mouse is dead!

First, check that the mouse is plugged into the back of your computer. You can't expect to use an unplugged mouse any more than you can use a car without a battery.

If the mouse is plugged in, try restarting your computer and watching the screen as the various start-up programs run. Often some sort of mouse-related message appears. If you don't see such a message, your **mouse driver** (the program that makes it run) may not be loading or the computer may think you have a different kind of mouse than is really installed. Ask a computer guru for help with this. Finally, make sure that the program you're using takes advantage of a mouse. Many of the older DOS programs don't.

What Does DOS Do?

● **In this chapter:**

- **How to find out what's on a disk**

- **What are directories and why do I need them?**

- **DOS commands that copy, move, and delete files**

- **I didn't mean to delete *that* file!**

- **How to format a floppy disk**

- **Oops! Can I UNformat a floppy disk?**

If you've used a PC in the last few years, you've been using DOS whether you knew it or not! . . . . ➤

Do you have a computer guru—someone you can call for help when you're having a problem? When gurus get you out of trouble, they usually mutter to themselves and type much too fast for the eye to see. Then they jump up, warn you not to do it again, and walk away quickly before you can ask what you did wrong.

Know this about computer gurus:

- They all act like this.

- They do it on purpose.

- Their knowledge is based on a good understanding of DOS.

Since the first PCs began to appear, DOS has been the underlying operating system that made them work. Sure, the popularity of Windows and Windows 95 has made DOS less essential for the average user, but it's still running on 80% of the world's machines. The fact is that Windows 3.11 hides DOS from you, but when it's time to print or work with a file, the chances are that DOS is doing most of the real work in the background. Even in Windows 95, there's still some remnants of the old DOS world. People who yearn for the "good old days" can open a DOS window and type their commands the old-fashioned way.

People may tell you that DOS is complicated, cold, and unfriendly. I prefer to think of it as coolly efficient. Even experienced Windows users often drop back to good old DOS because many file operations are faster there. You name it—it prints, runs software, and basically keeps everything running smoothly in the background. Besides, if you're not running a graphical user interface like Windows, DOS is the only choice you have. So make the best of it. The good news is that handling files and disks with DOS is pretty easy. Honestly!

 TIP **The next time a Windows 95 user tells you that his machine is** easier to use and more intuitive, just answer, "Oh yeah? How come you have to press the Start button to stop your PC?"

What's on this disk?

Since **DOS** stands for **Disk Operating System**, it stands to reason that it must be pretty good at, well, operating the disks in your PC. But disks aren't the only thing that DOS understands. It also does a bang-up job of managing your filing system for you. In Chapter 11, we discuss how all the information that is ever placed on a disk is actually grouped into **files**. A file can be a letter that you've typed, a picture you've drawn—whatever.

In your office, you wouldn't take all your files and just throw them into a big room for safekeeping. You'd organize them into filing cabinets, individual drawers, and possibly sort them even more by grouping them in special folders. DOS allows you to do pretty much the same thing by placing your computer files in **directories**. (In Windows 95, directories are now called **folders**, but they're exactly the same thing.)

Directories are simply a way to group your files on a disk so you can find them more easily. (Imagine wandering into that room full of loose files and looking for last month's sales report.) You can assign a label or name for every directory on your disk so that you'll know what types of files each contains. Most of the time, you create your own directories and name them yourself. Sometimes, software packages that are installed on your hard disk will create their own files and directories. When this happens, you don't usually get to choose the names (and it's best if you don't try to change them).

Want to see the files and directories on your disk? Try DOS's DIR (short for *directory*) command. Of course, your PC will have to be turned on first. Once it's warmed up, your monitor will display something like figure 9.1, the cold and unfriendly DOS prompt. The prompt is the C:\ with the flashing cursor beside it. This means, "Hey! I'm ready! Type a command!" but takes up a lot less space on the screen. (I told you DOS was efficient.)

All set? Type **DIR** and press the Enter key to send your command to DOS. When you do, you'll see many rows of information fly up your screen like the credits at the end of a movie (see fig. 9.2). This information is actually the listing of files and directories on your hard disk. There may be only a few lines, or hundreds, depending on what you have on your hard drive.

Fig. 9.1
When you first turn on your computer, you usually end up at the DOS prompt.

```
C:\>
```

TIP **It doesn't matter whether you type DOS commands in capital** letters or lowercase. DOS knows what you really mean even if you miX iT uP!

Fig. 9.2
The DIR command tells DOS to show you the names of the files on the current disk drive.

```
C:\>DIR

 Volume in drive C is HARDDISK
 Volume Serial Number is 1CAF-AAF9
 Directory of C:\

DOS          <DIR>      06-05-93   2:17p
WINWORD      <DIR>      01-30-94   2:48p
INFO         <DIR>      07-22-93   2:57p
UTILS        <DIR>      06-05-93   3:08p
WORD         <DIR>      06-05-93   3:09p
WINDOWS      <DIR>      06-05-93   3:18p
AMOUSE       <DIR>      03-22-94   2:52p
COMMAND  COM    52925 03-10-93   6:00a
MOUSE    SYS    34581 10-04-90   3:09p
WINA20   386     9349 03-10-93   6:00a
CONFIG   SYS      239 05-15-95   9:23p
AUTOEXEC BAT      270 05-15-95   9:39p
        12 file(s)       97364 bytes
                      22415360 bytes free

C:\>
```

Entries in the list that have the word <DIR> after them are directories. Remember that directories are like file folders because they hold files. After each directory's name is the date and time that the directory was originally created.

Anything in the list that doesn't have <DIR> after it *must be a file*. (Files and directories are the only things you can ever have on a disk.) After each file name is the size of the file measured in bytes and the date and time that the file was created. After the list, DOS displays the number of files (including directories) that appear in the list, as well as how much disk space those files consume. The amount of free, or unused, space on the disk is also shown.

Q&A *I use Windows and can't get to the DOS prompt!*

Whether you use Windows 3.11 or Windows 95, there's a good chance that the DOS prompt has been hidden from you. The way to get back to DOS is different for each version of Windows, but it's easy just the same.

Windows 3.11 users will need to exit Windows. From the Program Manager menu, choose File, Exit and click the OK button. DOS appears after a few seconds.

Windows 95 users will have to restart the machine in MS–DOS mode. Click the Start button and choose Shutdown. In the dialog box, select the button marked Restart the computer in MS-DOS mode? Then click the Yes button. The computer will perform a normal shutdown and then restart showing only a DOS screen. (There is no special command to turn off the PC when you are working in DOS. As long as you see the DOS prompt, you can simply turn off the switch.)

The list is too long for one screen

If your directory listing is too long and scrolls by too fast for you to read it, there is no way to go back up and see the lines you missed. There are a couple of other things you can do, though, and they're both better than typing DIR over and over again quickly.

To stop the screen from scrolling out of view, enter the command as **DIR / P**. This forces DOS to pause every time the screen fills up. When you want to see the next screenful, just press the Enter key.

You can also get a wide display of the directory listing by entering the command as **DIR / W**. This displays the file names in five columns across the screen. (You won't see the sizes or dates and times anymore, but do you really care?) Any time you follow a DOS command-word with a slash and a single letter, that's called using a **command switch**. It's a way of modifying the command's actions in some small way.

Every drive has a name

When you first start your computer, the **active drive** (the one you're working on) is usually C:, which is your hard drive. This means any commands you give will affect that drive automatically. The active drive is also called the **default drive**. You can easily see which is the default drive by looking at the DOS prompt. The prompt in figure 9.1 shows that C: (the hard drive) is the default or active drive.

To work with another drive, you just have to know its name—and that's as simple as ABC. No kidding! The first floppy drive in your system is given the name A: and if you have a second floppy drive, it is named B:. You know already that your hard drive is named C:. If you have a CD-ROM drive, it will probably be named D: (although just about any other letter is also possible).

To look at the files on a different disk, you can change the default drive. Just type the drive's letter followed immediately by a colon. (Think of the colon as DOS's way of knowing that you're telling it about a disk drive. Forget the colon and DOS won't know what you mean.) For example, to change to drive A, type **A:** at the DOS prompt and then press Enter. If you get the message `Bad command or filename`, don't panic. You probably forgot to type the colon right after the letter. (Did you type a semicolon by mistake, or leave a

What are these files named CONFIG and AUTOEXEC?

When you first look at the list of files on your hard disk, many of the file names will seem to be in some kind of foreign language (and you know that *you* didn't put them there). Most of these files are **startup files** used by your PC's operating system when you first turn on the machine. They are very important and should never be modified or erased unless you really know what you're doing.

Your startup files contain information about your PC that the operating system needs to know. If

you have a CD-ROM, for example, there are probably a few references to that device sprinkled liberally throughout the startup files. Other things that may depend heavily on these files are the mouse, your monitor, sound cards, and speakers.

So where are the files that you've been saving to the hard disk in the past? They're stored safely in directories and we'll examine them more closely in the section, "Directories are like file folders."

space between the characters?) Try again. When you get it right, your computer switches to drive A and the DOS prompt will look something like this:

```
A:\
```

You can now type **DIR** to see the files and directories on your floppy disk (see fig. 9.3). Hint: The /P switch works here too, just in case the list is too long for one screen.

Fig. 9.3

In this illustration, the user has made drive A the active drive, then used the DIR command to see what's on the disk in drive A.

```
C:\>a:

A:\>dir

 Volume in drive A has no label
 Directory of A:\

LETTERS         <DIR>         10-05-95    3:14a
REPORTS         <DIR>         10-05-95    3:14a
ARTICLES        <DIR>         10-05-95    3:15a
        3 file(s)                  0 bytes
                        727,040 bytes free

A:\>
```

You can change to any drive in your system, as long as you know its letter. You can even go back to drive C: whenever you want. With floppy drives and CD-ROMs, make sure you have the correct type of disk inserted before you try to access them. Otherwise you'll get an error message.

Q&A ***DOS is telling me my drive's not ready. Now what?***

Whenever you try to switch to a drive that doesn't contain a floppy disk, you'll see this:

```
Not ready error reading drive A

Abort, Retry, Fail?
```

To fix the problem, insert a floppy disk into the drive and then press R for retry. If you don't have a floppy disk handy, press F, which stands for Fail. You'll get this message:

```
Current drive is no longer valid>
```

It sounds pretty horrible, but DOS is really asking you to type the letter of a drive that contains a disk. Your hard drive always has a disk, so try that one. Type **C:** and press Enter. There you go. You're valid again!

Directories are like file folders

In order to work with the files that are stored in your directories, you have to be able to open the directories and look at their contents. (It's really just like opening a file folder.) You can also make new directories to suit your personal filing system, or remove old ones you no longer need.

Change to the directory you want

DOS's command for opening directories is CD (short for *change directory*). To open any directory, just type **CD** followed by the directory's name. Need an example? Suppose you used the DIR command on drive A and got the listing shown in figure 9.3 in the preceding section. In that example, there's a directory on A: named LETTERS. To open it, you would type **CD LETTERS** and press Enter. Your DOS prompt would change to this:

        A:\LETTERS>

You could then type **DIR** again to see what files are located in that directory. You might see something like figure 9.4. As you can see, the LETTERS directory contains not only a few files, but also another directory named OLDLETS. Think of this as a file folder within a file folder. It just gives you a more exact way of organizing your work.

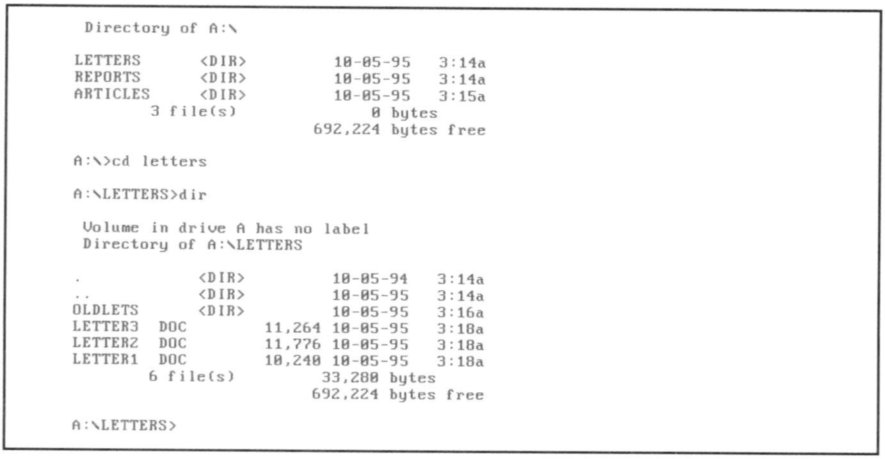

Fig. 9.4

In this illustration, we've opened the LETTERS directory and then typed DIR to see the contents of that directory.

```
    Directory of A:\

    LETTERS    <DIR>           10-05-95    3:14a
    REPORTS    <DIR>           10-05-95    3:14a
    ARTICLES   <DIR>           10-05-95    3:15a
          3 file(s)                  0 bytes
                           692,224 bytes free


    A:\>cd letters

    A:\LETTERS>dir

      Volume in drive A has no label
      Directory of A:\LETTERS

    .           <DIR>           10-05-94    3:14a
    ..          <DIR>           10-05-95    3:14a
    OLDLETS     <DIR>           10-05-95    3:16a
    LETTER3  DOC        11,264  10-05-95    3:18a
    LETTER2  DOC        11,776  10-05-95    3:18a
    LETTER1  DOC        10,240  10-05-95    3:18a
          6 file(s)             33,280 bytes
                           692,224 bytes free

    A:\LETTERS>
```

At this point, you could open the OLDLETS directory by typing **CD OLDLETS**. Your DOS prompt would change to

```
A:\LETTERS\OLDLETS>
```

This prompt shows that you are inside the OLDLETS directory, which is itself inside the LETTERS directory, which is located on drive A.

Q&A *I don't get any kind of error message, but my DOS prompt doesn't show the directory name.*

No problem. Type the mystical DOS command **PROMPT pg** and press Enter. If the directory name suddenly appears, ask your computer guru to set your PC to do it automatically all the time.

Q&A *How do I deal with the message* `Invalid directory`*?*

You get this message when the directory you typed either doesn't exist, or isn't visible from the directory you're in. (In the example, you can't change to LETTERS if you're not on drive A, and you can't change to OLDLETS if you're not already in LETTERS.) Use the DIR command to make sure you're trying to change to a directory that really exists.

How do I get out of this directory?

If you start using the CD command to move around the directory structure of a disk, you might want to know how to get back out and close all those open folders. No matter how many folders you have opened, or how many commands you typed to get there, it only takes one command to close everything:

```
CD \
```

This takes you right back up to the top, something DOS users refer to as returning to the **root directory**. Essentially, it's like closing all the folders, putting them back where they belong, and closing the file drawer. Now you can start all over again and explore another branch of directories.

TIP The backslash (\) might be located anywhere on your keyboard, depending on the manufacturer's whim. Don't confuse it with the **forward slash** (/) that's located on the same key as the question mark. The forward slash is used for DOS command switches. (Remember the /P from the DIR command?)

Making your own directories

When you're ready to try making your own directory for your files, you can use the MD command (short for *make directory*). Suppose you want to create a directory named MYSTUFF. Just type **MD MYSTUFF** and press Enter. You now have your own computerized folder for holding your work. You can see the new directory when you type **DIR**, and you can change to it by typing **CD MYSTUFF**. Naturally, typing **CD ** will bring you back out again.

Directory names follow the same conventions as file names. Stick to eight characters or less, using any letters or numbers, and avoid using punctuation characters. Most of them are illegal. Don't worry about it—if you try to create a directory name that DOS doesn't like, you'll know about it right away because of the error message.

How to get rid of an old directory

Just as you might find yourself cleaning out your filing cabinets every year or so, you'll probably want to clean out any old directories you no longer require. DOS provides a way to do this using the RD command (short for *remove directory*). If you want to remove the MYSTUFF directory, first make sure that you can see it when you type the **DIR** command. Then type **RD MYSTUFF**.

DOS won't allow you to remove directories if they still contain files. (This has prevented many accidents over the years.) If a directory contains files, you'll have to move or delete them first. We'll show you how to do that later on in this chapter.

Q&A *I tried to remove a directory, but I got the message* `Invalid path, not directory, or directory not empty.`

This means that you're trying to remove a directory that doesn't exist (can you see it with the DIR command?), or one that still contains files. Double-check the directory name, make sure it's empty and try again.

Keep your files neat and tidy

At this point, you've managed to look at a disk's contents and probably moved around within the directory structure. You may even have tried creating a directory and deleting it again. The computer's still working, right? Now it's time to learn the commands that affect the files you store in the directory system.

Share your files by copying them

One of the great things about disk-based information is that it's easy to copy. You can think of it as a sort of digital cloning. You'd copy a file for one of two reasons: you either want to share your information with a friend or coworker, or you want to make a **backup copy** of an important file. (After all, anything can get lost or damaged—even in a computer.)

To copy a file, you use the DOS COPY command. COPY needs two additional things typed on the same line when you use it. You have to say *what* you want to copy and *where* you want the copy to appear. The *what* is a file name and the *where* can be either a drive or a directory.

Suppose you had a file named README.TXT in the DOS directory of your hard disk that you wanted to copy to a disk in drive A. You'd follow these steps:

1 Place an empty formatted floppy disk in drive A.

2 Type **C:** and press Enter. This command ensures that drive C is the current drive. If you *know* that it is, you could skip this step.

3 Type **CD ** and press Enter. This makes sure you're at the root directory.

4 Type **CD DOS** and press Enter. This opens the DOS directory.

5 Type **COPY README.TXT A:** and press Enter. (Leave a space after COPY and a space after TXT.) DOS copies the file to drive A as requested.

In the COPY command in step 5, the what-to-copy part of the command is separated from the where-to-put-it part with a space. If you forget any of the spaces, or mix up the order of the parts, DOS will give you an error message like `File not found`, or `Bad command or filename`. Misspelling any of the words gives the same result. Check the file name and your typing, then try again.

Q&A *Why do I have to type a period in README.TXT?*

A file name is composed of two parts: the **first name**, which can be between one and eight characters in length, and the three-character **extension**. When you look at a file listing with the DIR command, you see the two parts of the name separated into two columns. Take another look at figure 9.2 to see what I mean.

When you tell DOS to work with a file, you have to use the whole name, including the extension. The trouble is that DOS uses spaces to separate the parts of the command lines into *what* and *where* sections. If you used a space to separate the file name from the extension too, you'd have too many spaces in the command and DOS would get very confused. For this reason, programmers decided years ago that we should type a period to tell DOS when we've stopped typing the file name and when we've started the extension.

This **eight-dot-three** file name idea is the same in Windows too, so it's important to know.

Delete old files you don't need

The longer you live in a house, the more junk you collect in your closets. Likewise, the more you use your computer, the more junky files you collect on your hard disk. Every so often, you'll be forced to do a little spring cleaning to delete files that have outlived their usefulness. When this happens, you'll be glad that the DOS DEL command is so easy to use.

For example, to delete the file README.TXT from the floppy disk in drive A (copied in the preceding section), you would follow these steps:

1 Type **A:** and press Enter. This makes A: the active drive.

2 Type **DEL README.TXT** and press Enter.

That's it! DOS doesn't even tell you that the command worked, but it did. If you use the DIR command to check the file list on the disk, you'll see that README.TXT has definitely disappeared. (Now if only spring-cleaning the closets was this easy.)

CAUTION **Never delete a file if you don't know its purpose! You wouldn't** be the first to turn a PC into a doorstop by erasing important files like CONFIG.SYS or AUTOEXEC.BAT!

Oops! I deleted the wrong file!

Sooner or later, you're going to delete a file and then immediately wish you hadn't. At such times, it's good to know that DOS can probably bring the deleted file back for you by way of the UNDELETE command. This command is only available in version 5 of DOS or later. Since it's so useful, you should consider upgrading if the command doesn't work on your system.

Suppose you just deleted a file called PROG.EXE from the C drive. You can bring it back by making C the active drive, then typing this command:

UNDELETE PROG.EXE

When you do, DOS will say that it found a file named "?ROG.EXE" and asks if the file it found is the one you want to undelete (see fig. 9.5). Press Y to answer yes, and DOS asks for the first letter of the file name. You can type any letter you want, actually, but it's obviously better to use the "P." Type the letter, and DOS tries to recover the file.

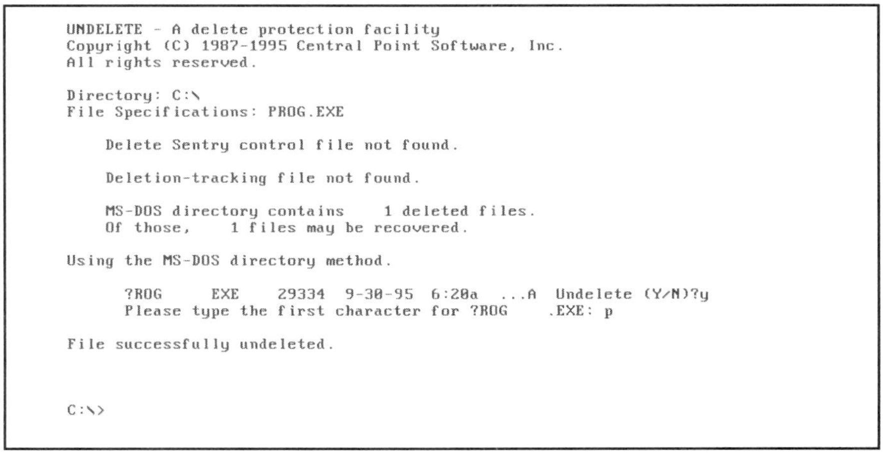

Fig. 9.5
The UNDELETE command can bring deleted files back from the great unknown.

```
UNDELETE - A delete protection facility
Copyright (C) 1987-1995 Central Point Software, Inc.
All rights reserved.

Directory: C:\
File Specifications: PROG.EXE

    Delete Sentry control file not found.

    Deletion-tracking file not found.

    MS-DOS directory contains    1 deleted files.
    Of those,   1 files may be recovered.

Using the MS-DOS directory method.

    ?ROG    EXE    29334  9-30-95  6:20a  ...A  Undelete (Y/N)?y
       Please type the first character for ?ROG    .EXE: p

File successfully undeleted.


C:\>
```

CAUTION   **The UNDELETE command works reliably only if you use it**
immediately after deleting a file. The more you use your computer before
trying to recover the file, the less likely UNDELETE will be successful. This is
because other files may get saved over the data that was contained in the
deleted file.

How to change a file's name

Often, you'll want to change the name of a file. Maybe this week's sales are
now last week's sales, or perhaps you simply don't like the name you originally gave to a file. The command REN (short for *rename*) is used to rename
files in DOS. To use this command, type **REN** followed by the file's current
name and new name. For example, to change LETTER1.TXT to
MYLETT.TXT, type this:

REN LETTER1.TXT MYLETT.TXT

This command looks similar to COPY, because you type the command word
first and then two **parameters** separated by spaces. But the result is totally
different from COPY. With REN, you still have only one copy of the file when
you're finished. It just has a different name.

Q&A   ***What if DOS tells me*** `Duplicate file name or file`
`not found`***?***

This means either that the file you want to rename doesn't exist or that
there's already a file in the active directory that has the file name you want
to use. In the first case, check your typing. In the second case, choose a new
name.

Moving files from place to place

Copying a file is like photocopying a letter. When you're done, you end up with the original plus a new copy. The COPY command is great for placing duplicates of files on another disk. When you want to just rearrange files to other directories on the same disk, MOVE is better. Your disk doesn't fill up with old forgotten copies of files because the originals are automatically deleted from their directories.

If you have DOS Version 6.0 or later, you can use the MOVE command. To move the file README.TXT from the MYSTUFF directory to your WINDOWS directory, you'd change to the MYSTUFF directory first (CD MYSTUFF), then type this:

   MOVE README.TXT \WINDOWS

Notice that this command also resembles COPY, in that it has two param-eters: a *what* and a *where*. Notice also that the WINDOWS directory has a backslash inserted just before it. This is a way of telling DOS, "Go back to the root directory (\), then turn around and go into the WINDOWS directory." Since the MYSTUFF directory is active when this command is typed, DOS can't see the WINDOWS directory at all. Inserting the backslash before a directory name is called "showing the path" to the directory. The **path** to a directory is something you type when you have to be very specific with DOS. It tells DOS exactly the route to take to get to the directory you want to use in a command.

Q&A *I have DOS Version 5. How can I move a file?*

If you have a version of DOS earlier than 6.0, you can still move a file, but you have to COPY it and then DEL the original:

   COPY README.TXT \WINDOWS

   DEL README.TXT

Going out on a limb with DOS commands

As you saw with the DIR command, DOS is pretty shortsighted when it comes to looking around on the disk. In fact, it only sees directories or files that are inside the active directory. (You couldn't get to OLDLETS without opening LETTERS first, remember?) Suppose your root directory contains several files and two directories: MYSTUFF and WINDOWS. If you change to the MYSTUFF directory and give the DIR command, DOS shows you what it sees there—lots of files, probably, but no WINDOWS directory. (That's only visible when you're in the root directory.) The DIR command can only show the directories and files immediately below the current (or open) directory.

Think of your hard disk as a tree, and all the directories it contains as branches. Your commands to DOS tell it where to climb in the tree. Let's call the trunk of the tree the root directory. When DOS is holding onto the trunk (in the root directory), it can only see two branches to start off with—WINDOWS and MYSTUFF. You can tell it to climb out onto the MYSTUFF branch with the command, **CD MYSTUFF**. Now, if you tell DOS to look around (with the DIR command), it only sees the files within MYSTUFF and any other directories that are branching off of MYSTUFF. (The other directory called WINDOWS is invisible to DOS because it's on the other side of the trunk.)

You can always tell DOS to return to the trunk of the tree (the root directory) by telling it to **CD **. The backslash is a symbol used by DOS that means the root directory. In the MOVE command, understand that the first command you typed (**CD MYSTUFF**) told DOS to climb out onto the branch of the tree containing MYSTUFF. Since the WINDOWS branch is invisible to DOS from that position, your MOVE also has to tell DOS the path to get there:

MOVE README.TXT \WINDOWS

This is like saying, "Since you're on the MYSTUFF branch already, look around for README.TXT, then move it to another directory (WINDOWS) that you'll only see if you return to the root directory (\) first." Whenever you use a leading backslash as part of the path, you are telling DOS to go back to the root directory and look around again.

Sometimes you need to work with a group of files

One daunting task that you will one day face is when you decide to copy an entire directory containing 50 files or more. Relax, you don't have to do it one file at a time. In fact, the best commands you can use will probably take *less typing* than if you try to copy only one file!

How to use a wild card

DOS allows you to use something called a **wild card** (or **wild card character**) that represents any file name. If you've ever played poker, you know that when you have a wild card in your hand, you're allowed to make that card equal to anything else in the deck. For example, if Jokers were wild and you had four aces and a Joker, you could say you had five aces. You could also say you had four aces and a three, but then you'd be a really lousy poker player.

The wild card that DOS likes to use most often is the asterisk (*). You can use it to replace parts of a file name whenever you type a command that uses a file name in its command line (COPY, DEL, MOVE, and other commands that expect a file name to appear right after the command). Suppose you wanted to copy all the files using the DOC extension from the LETTERS directory of your hard disk to a floppy disk. (Remember that COPY is a great way of making backups.) You would first change to the LETTERS directory, make sure a blank floppy disk is inserted in the A drive, then type this command:

COPY *.DOC A:

That's all there is to it! The asterisk replaces any file name that exists in the directory, but only files with the DOC extension are accepted in the command. (Of course, this command only affects the files in the open directory. There's no danger of copying all the contents of your hard disk. That's another reason why we use directories.) Still a little unclear? Suppose you now wanted to delete any file that had the first name SALES, but you didn't care what the extension was. Just type the following command:

DEL SALES.*

This could possibly delete *hundreds* of files when you consider the possible combinations of any three characters for the extension. If it starts with SALES, then it's history! (This includes SALES.XLS, SALES.OCT, SALES.1, and SALES.12—the extension doesn't matter.) The one saving feature here is that the first name must be SALES before any file can be deleted. You have to be pretty sure what you're doing before you try using wild cards with the DEL command.

Copying, moving, and deleting by the handful

You will begin truly understanding wild cards when you realize that the commands you type are still the same structure as always. You can move a file to a floppy by typing:

MOVE LETTER.DOC A:

You can just as easily move all the DOC files by typing:

MOVE *.DOC A:

If you want to get a little fancy, you can try typing something like this:

COPY L*.DOC A:

This means, "Copy all the files that start with an L and have the extension DOC." This mixing of real characters and wild cards works very well as long as the wild card comes *after the desired character*. For some reason known only to programmers, if you start the wild card expression with an asterisk (such as *L.DOC), DOS will ignore anything you type after the asterisk and will copy all the files ending in DOC instead. The fact is that there is no easy way to copy all the files that end in the letter L.

How to use a more precise wild card

The asterisk is the most commonly used wild card character because it's so powerful, but DOS has another character that you can use in special cases. The question mark (?) can be used in a DOS command to replace any single character at the position where you use it in the file name. Suppose you want to copy PILL.DOC, PAUL.DOC, and WILL.DOC to a floppy disk. Just type:

COPY ???L.DOC A:

This is like saying, "Copy any four-character file name ending with "L" to drive A:, as long as the extension is DOC." If you had a file named KNOBHILL.DOC, for instance, it wouldn't be copied by the above command since it's more than four characters long. (Remember, it's hard to copy all files ending with "L.")

Never use *.* unless you're sure!

Beware the deadly *.* when you're deleting files! Because *.* refers to every single file in a directory, you can wipe out a huge amount of information with a single blow. DOS has one tell-tale message that appears on the screen when you're about to delete everything: Are you sure? (Y/N) appears nowhere else. If you see this message at any time, stop and read the command you just typed. DOS has interpreted it as DEL *.*! Press Y if you're sure and N if you're not.

While the *.* wild card combination is very powerful and extremely useful, it can also catch you by surprise. (Remember how L* and *L are two totally different things according to DOS.) You can avoid unpleasant surprises by using the DIR command with your wild card—for example, DIR *.*— before you attempt a COPY or (heaven forbid) a DEL. The DIR will non-destructively *show* you the file names that match your wild card. Then, if you decide that these really are the files you want to erase, go ahead and type DEL followed by the same wild card.

Getting a new floppy disk ready to use

As you learned in Chapter 7, lots of disks can't be used right out of the box— you have to **format** them first. Formatting a disk is a lot like painting the white lines for parking spaces in a parking lot. Until you get those spaces marked and numbered, nobody knows where to put their car. Likewise, until you format a floppy disk, DOS can't figure out where to store your files (or how to get them back).

Make sure that the disk you want to format matches the type of floppy disk drive you have and that the disk isn't write-protected. If you're not sure, go back to Chapter 7 and read about disk types and capacities.

CAUTION **Formatting a disk also wipes out any information that was on that** disk before you started. (You can't paint the lines in a parking lot if the cars are still there!) This isn't a problem with new disks, but it can cause you a lot of heartache if you try it with just any old disk you find lying around. Always use the DIR command to see if the disk has anything important on it first (see the early sections of this chapter for more information about DIR).

Formatting a disk sounds like a highly technical task, but it's really very simple:

1 At a DOS prompt, type **FORMAT A:**. DOS asks you to insert a disk into your drive and press Enter. As DOS prepares the disk for use on your system, it displays messages showing its progress. (If you checked the disk for useful files first, using DIR, you can probably ignore the warning about erasing all the files. Type a **Y** for yes if you're sure; otherwise, type an **N** for no, so you can check again.)

2 When DOS asks for a volume label, type any name you like (up to eleven characters), or press Enter if you don't want a name. DOS shows you some technical facts about your disk, including how much information it can hold.

3 When DOS asks whether you want to format another disk, press N on your keyboard. (Or press Y if you have another disk to format and start again at step 2.)

Figure 9.6 shows the entire formatting process as it rolls across your screen. When DOS is done formatting the disk, it's ready for you to use.

Fig. 9.6
DOS tells you everything you never wanted to know about your floppy disk.

```
C:\>format a:
Insert new diskette for drive A:
and press ENTER when ready...

Checking existing disk format.
Saving UNFORMAT information.
Verifying 1.44M
Format complete.

Volume label (11 characters, ENTER for none)?

    1,457,664 bytes total disk space
    1,457,664 bytes available on disk

        512 bytes in each allocation unit.
      2,847 allocation units available on disk.

Volume Serial Number is 1239-18CD

Format another (Y/N)?n


C:\>
```

What's a volume label?

When you format a disk, DOS asks if you want to give it a **volume label**. This is simply an electronic name for the disk. You can also use the volume label to help explain what's in your files. Squeezing a meaningful description into an eight-letter file name can be hard. For example, if DIR revealed files named JANUARY.95, FEBRUARY.95, and MARCH.95, you still don't know what they *contain*. If the directory listing started with the message Volume in Drive A: is BUDGETS, however, their contents would be more obvious.

What if you want to change or add a volume label to a disk without having to reformat it? Simple. Use the command LABEL followed by the letter of the drive your disk is in (for example, LABEL A:). DOS will ask you to type in the new volume label, and you're done!

Q&A *What does it mean when I try to format a disk, but DOS keeps giving me messages about invalid media?*

The Invalid media message (and a couple of others) usually happens when you put the wrong density disk into your drive. (Check Chapter 7 for details on disk density.) Of course, it's always possible that the disk really is damaged. Try another disk from the same box to be sure. If they're both bad, then you can be sure you've got the wrong kind of disks for your drive. If the second one formats correctly, use the bad one for anything you want, *except holding data*! (They make great coasters.)

How to completely erase a disk

When you format a disk, two things happen. Any old data is erased and the magnetic "white lines" are repainted for the next set of files you plan to save there.

In the real world, parking lot attendants don't have to repaint the parking lot every night, they just have to sweep up the trash so you can see the lines. If you want to wipe everything off a disk quickly, you can do a **quick format**, which only deletes the files without bothering to reformat.

By adding the /Q switch to the FORMAT command (*Q* stands for *quick*), you tell DOS not to bother preparing the disk from scratch. Instead, DOS just erases all the data on the disk, leaving the disk blank. Just type

FORMAT A: /Q

CAUTION ***Never, ever* use the FORMAT command with your hard disk** (FORMAT C:) unless you are preparing a new one. If you format your hard disk, you will wipe out all the data stored there, leaving you with a computer that can't even start up correctly.

Uh oh—I think I just reformatted the wrong disk

Boy, are you in trouble! Well, maybe not. Any version of DOS 5 or higher includes a special command that can probably repair the damage. The UNFORMAT command can recover everything as long as you haven't placed any other files on the disk since the accidental format.

To resuscitate your files, type **UNFORMAT A:** (if A: was the disk you messed up) and read the dire warnings carefully. One or two key presses later, the lost data reappears. If you *don't* have UNFORMAT, call your computer guru for help.

Part II: Getting Comfortable with Windows 95

10

Getting Started with Windows 95

● **In this chapter:**

- **What's all the buzz about Windows 95?**

- **Mousing around in Windows**

- **Getting off to a good start with the Start menu**

- **How do I close Windows 95?**

Windows 95 is an operating system, a GUI, and a set of accessory programs and utilities all rolled into one . . . . . .

Every computer needs an operating system. (You learned about operating systems in Chapter 1.) It provides the infrastructure or platform on which the software developers can build the programs that let you do something useful with the computer.

A **GUI** (**graphical user interface**) makes the operating system easier to use. It gives the computer much of its personality by furnishing the ways for you to interact with the computer. When you use a GUI, you don't have to type obscure commands to get the computer to do something. Instead, you can give the computer and its software instructions by pointing and clicking with a mouse—much easier.

I got Windows 95 with my computer. What good is it?

These days, most new computers come with the Microsoft Windows 95 operating system preinstalled. The operating system portion of Windows 95 goes about its business largely unseen by most users. About the closest you'll come to dealing with the operating system will be to use some of the utilities included with Windows to start programs, manage files, and customize the look of your system. (You'll learn how to do these things in this and the next two chapters.)

It's the software that you run on your computer that lets you do interesting things. Because of its features and immense popularity, Windows 95 is the operating system of choice for most software developers. As a result, most of the really cool new software programs are designed to run on Windows 95.

 Q&A *I don't have Windows 95. How can I get it?*

You can buy a copy of the Windows 95 operating system software at most computer stores and use it to replace your computer's existing operating system—provided your computer is powerful enough to run Windows 95. It requires at least a 386 CPU and 4M of RAM. To run most Windows 95 programs, you'll need a 486 or Pentium CPU and 8M of RAM. Also, replacing the computer's operating system is like giving it a brain transplant—you may want to enlist the help of a computer consultant or knowledgeable friend before you attempt such a delicate procedure.

TIP **Windows 95 is a relatively new operating system. While it works** best with software designed specifically for Windows 95, it can also run most programs designed for Windows 3.1 (the previous version of Windows), and programs designed to run on plain old DOS.

For you, the end user, the major advantage of using Windows is that all the programs you use work pretty much the same. (That's the GUI part of Windows coming into play.) For instance, the way you open a file, save a file, and get help is basically the same in each Windows program. Therefore, each new program you buy is progressively easier to learn. By the time you hit your third Windows program, things start looking real familiar.

Start with an (almost) clean desktop

Since Windows 95 is the computer's operating system, it starts automatically when you turn on the computer. Although it's automatic, it's not instantaneous. Your computer and Windows 95 have to wake up and do some housekeeping chores before they're ready to start work. During that time, you may see some text messages appear on a blank screen and a Windows 95 logo screen. Just be patient for a couple of minutes and the Windows 95 desktop will appear as shown in figure 10.1.

Fig. 10.1
The default desktop starts out like this. But your screen may look a bit different, because all these elements can be moved and customized.

Shortcut icons

Desktop

Taskbar

In Windows, the working space visible on your computer screen is called the Windows **desktop**. Your office desk probably starts out with items such as a pencil holder, desk blotter, in-basket, and phone on it even before you spread out your work. The Windows desktop is the same. It starts out as an open space with a few tools placed within easy reach.

What are these little symbols?

Arranged along the left side of the Windows desktop are several small pictures, or symbols, with text labels beneath each one. These are called **icons**. They're there to give you quick access to some Windows features and programs. In Chapter 12, you'll learn how to create shortcuts of your own.

Taskbar

The bar along the bottom edge of the screen is called the **taskbar**. At the right end of the taskbar is the clock and the left end is occupied by the Start button, which you'll use to start your Windows programs. In between is space for more buttons—one for each program that is running. (Since Windows 95 supports **multitasking**, you can have more than one program running at the same time.) The taskbar buttons make it easy to switch from one program to another.

Windows and multitasking

One buzzword you hear a lot lately is multitasking, which just means running more than one program at a time. (True multitasking is a little more complicated, but this is what most people mean when they use this word.)

How does this work? Let's say you've got your Windows word processor going. Now, you'd like to use your spreadsheet program at the same time. No problem. Just start up the spreadsheet program, too.

When you run a Windows program, it appears in its own window. Because these program windows can overlap each other, there's room for any number of them on the screen. This means that you can start as many programs as your computer's memory allows.

How does Windows know which program you're using at the moment? Easy. Although you can have many programs going simultaneously, only one can be active. The active program is the one that's ready to accept your commands and is always the program in front of all the others.

The band across the top of the window (called the **title bar**) is usually a different color in the active program than it is in the programs you're not actually using. This helps you remember which window is currently active.

How do you use the mouse with Windows?

Windows is really at its best when you command it with a mouse. Using one is pretty simple: when you move the mouse on the table top, the pointer on the screen also moves. It's a simple concept, but it does take some practice to get comfortable with the exercise. So, before you go any further, look at table 10.1, which shows the things you should learn to do with your mouse.

Table 10.1   Mouse actions

Action	How to do it
Point	Place the mouse pointer over an item (such as an icon or a menu) on the screen.
Click	Press and release the left mouse button.
Right-click	Press and release the right mouse button.
Double-click	Click twice quickly.
Drag	Place the mouse pointer over an item, press and hold down the left mouse button, and move the mouse. The object you're pointing to gets dragged across the screen. Release the mouse button to drop the object.

You may have seen this information before—it's in Chapter 8. But it's important enough that we're repeating it here.

The mouse works best if you relax

For most new users, holding a mouse doesn't come naturally. Put your hand on your mouse and look at yourself. Is your elbow way up in the air with only the tips of your fingers touching the little rodent? Then you're doing it wrong and your arm will fall right off from fatigue after a few minutes.

Think of the mouse as a convenient place to rest your whole hand. Drape it across the mouse with your first two fingers placed lightly over the buttons. The mouse should touch your entire palm. Let your wrist and your whole forearm touch the table top. Now relax those tight muscles and just "droop." If it's not comfortable, you're not relaxing enough. Droop some more.

When you're ready to click a button, the way your hand drapes over the mouse should keep it from jumping around when you press with your index finger. Don't stab with your finger—just press down lightly.

It takes a bit of practice to make the mouse move where you want it. The key is to make comfortable, natural, fluid moves. You don't need to give your whole arm a workout just to move the mouse. A little wrist action is all you need to scoot the pointer across the screen. But don't try to lock your arm in one position and make all the mouse moves with cramped little wrist and finger movements either. That's a prescription for the computer user's version of writer's cramp.

Windows that stretch, shrink, and scroll

In Windows, the action takes place in rectangular sections of the screen called **windows**. That's how you can have several different programs running simultaneously. Each program runs in its own window—its own little piece of the screen. All normal application (program) windows have common features, as shown in figure 10.2. Some application windows can even contain multiple document windows to let you work on more than one document at a time.

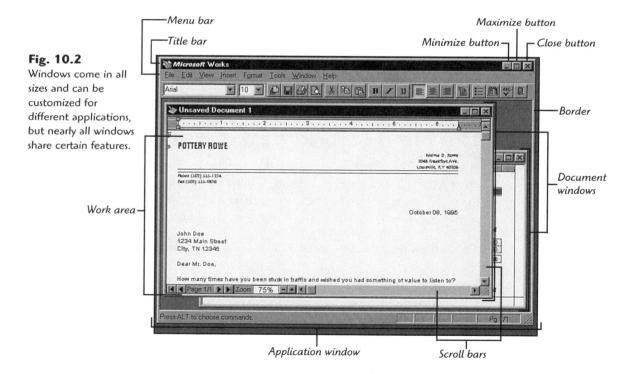

Fig. 10.2
Windows come in all sizes and can be customized for different applications, but nearly all windows share certain features.

As you become more familiar with Windows, you'll find that screen space is a precious commodity. Just like papers that sit on top of each other on a cluttered desk, each open window tends to cover up at least a portion of some icon or window on the screen. For this reason, it's important to understand how to adjust the size and placement of a window.

Double-click the My Computer icon on your desktop to open the My Computer window. You can use it to try the techniques that follow.

This window is too small

Want the biggest window possible? Use the **Maximize button**, which enlarges a window to take over the entire screen. To use the button, just click it once with your mouse. Once a window is maximized (see fig. 10.3), you don't need that button anymore, so the Maximize button changes into the **Restore button**, which returns the window to its original size when you click it. You maximize a window when you want to see all of a program clearly and you don't mind it covering up any other open windows or icons.

Fig. 10.3
A maximized window has a Restore button, which returns the window to its original size when you click it.

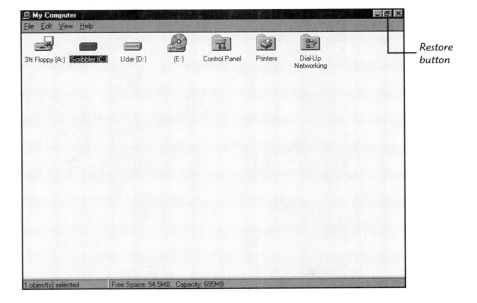

Even though a maximized window takes up the entire screen, any other programs that were running when you maximized the window are still there, unchanged. They're just temporarily hidden from view. It's like unrolling a large map or drawing on top of other papers on a cluttered desk. The rest of the stuff on the desk is still there—you just can't see it until you roll up the map or reach under the map and pull something else up to the top.

Okay, now I want this window out of my way

The **Minimize button** is a way of shrinking a window so it doesn't occupy any space on the screen. The program is still running, but it's represented on-screen by a button on the taskbar. You do this if you want to set aside a program while you do something else. Minimizing a window is like pushing your phone off to a corner of your desk until you need to make a call: it clears more desktop space for you to work.

If you click My Computer's Minimize button, you see a screen like figure 10.4. Notice that there's no My Computer window in sight, but there's still a My Computer button on the taskbar. To restore the window to its original size, simply click the My Computer button on the taskbar.

Fig. 10.4
A minimized window is hidden, but a click on its taskbar button will call it back.

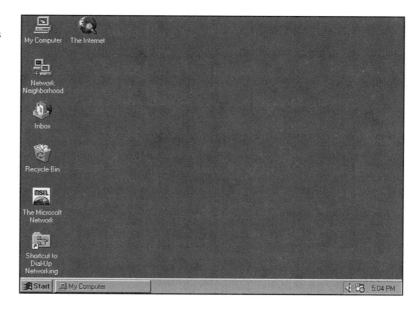

Q&A   *What happens to all the things in a window when I resize it?*

Don't worry about losing the contents of a window because you minimized it or covered it up with something else. Just because you can't see something doesn't mean it's gone for good! When you resize a window, you're just changing the appearance of it—you're not deleting things from your computer.

You can make the window almost any size with the mouse

Restore the My Computer window to its normal size. Notice that thick border around the window? If you put your mouse pointer right over this border, the pointer changes to a double-headed arrow. You can do this over any of the four sides or any of the four corners of a window. Try it and see that the arrow is sometimes straight up and down, sometimes sideways, and sometimes at an angle.

This double-arrow shape means that you can now drag the window's border to a new size. To do this, press and hold down the left mouse button while moving the mouse in one of the directions the arrow was pointing. When you do, the window's outline follows the mouse pointer. When you release the mouse button, the window shrinks or grows to fit the new outline.

TIP   **The different parts of a window's border let you change the** window in different ways. When you drag the left or right window border, you change the width of the window. When you drag the top or bottom window border, you change the height of the window. Finally, if you drag a border corner diagonally, you change the window's width and height simultaneously. Try it!

Scrolling through the world of Windows

If you drag a window's border so that it is smaller than the stuff it contains, **scroll bars** appear at the side or bottom of the window (see fig. 10.5). Scroll bars let you see information that doesn't fit in a window.

Fig. 10.5
Some windows have scroll bars, which let you control what part of a document or other information shows in the window.

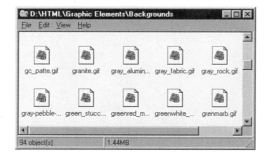

Click one of the arrow buttons at either end of the scroll bar to see more of the window contents in the direction the arrow points. To move a screenful at a time, click in the gray area on either side of the **scroll box** (the square button in the middle of the scroll bar). To quickly move anywhere in the window, drag the scroll box to a new position.

Closing a window

When you're through with a window, all you need to do is click the **Close button** (the small button with an "X" on it in the upper-right corner of the window). This will shut down the program running in the window and then close the window itself. You can use the Close button to close all sorts of windows, including program windows, document windows, and dialog boxes.

Ordering from the menu

Along the top of the My Computer window are the words File, Edit, View, and Help. Place the *tip* of your mouse pointer over the word View and click once with the left mouse button. A **menu** drops down from the word, showing you all the choices available (see fig. 10.6). The words on the drop-down menu are commands that you can give to My Computer to change the appearance of the window. Just click with your mouse on the command you want. The menu disappears and Windows does what you asked it to do. Sure beats having to remember and type in commands!

Plain English, please!

A **menu** is a list of commands that let you tell Windows or a Windows program to do something. It works like a menu in an oriental restaurant: you just point to indicate that you want "one of those." You don't have to remember how to pronounce "Mizutaki" or how to type "dir *.*/w."

Fig. 10.6
The menu bar contains drop-down menus that contain the program's commands.

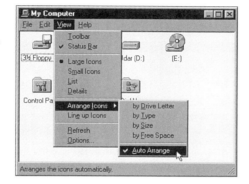

Some menu items will execute commands immediately. Some menu items have arrow heads next to them. If you let the pointer rest for a second or two on such a command (for instance, Arrange Icons on the View menu) Windows will open another menu of subsidiary commands. This is called a **cascading menu**.

 TIP If you open a menu by accident and decide that you don't want any of the options displayed there, you can close it again by clicking once more on the same command that opened it. Click once on View and the menu appears. Click again on View and it goes away. Or you can press the Esc key on your keyboard, which is the way to get out of just about anything in Windows.

Dialog boxes let you tell Windows *exactly* what you want

Maybe this sounds a little nuts, but sometimes you have to talk to Windows. Of course, Windows doesn't actually speak. Instead, it pops up a special kind of window called a **dialog box**. Dialog boxes may have important messages in them, or empty spaces for you to type in extra information that Windows needs to complete a command successfully.

TIP **When you browse through any menu in any Windows program,** notice that some of the commands are followed by an **ellipsis** (...). The ellipsis means that selecting that command will open a dialog box.

To see an example, choose the Options command from My Computer's View menu. (Click View, then Options.) The Options dialog box pops up on the screen. Just look around, then click the Cancel button to close the dialog box.

Think of a dialog box as an on-screen form that you use to give Windows (or a Windows program) detailed instructions. Paper forms often use a mixture of check-off, multiple-choice, and fill-in-the-blank questions. So do Windows dialog boxes. Figure 10.7 shows a dialog box that presents options in several ways. Once you fill in the dialog box, click the OK button to complete the command using the settings you selected. If you wish you'd never brought up the subject in the first place, click the Cancel button. The Cancel button is almost always a safe way to change your mind about a command.

Drop–down list boxes hide a pick list behind the arrow button.

Click the dialog box Help button, then click any item in the dialog box to get details on that item.

Fig. 10.7
Like paper forms, dialog boxes collect information in several ways.

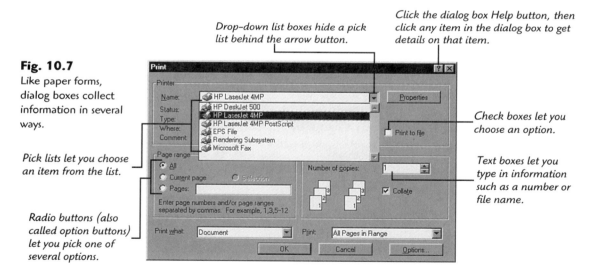

Pick lists let you choose an item from the list.

Radio buttons (also called option buttons) let you pick one of several options.

Check boxes let you choose an option.

Text boxes let you type in information such as a number or file name.

One handy feature of a Windows 95 dialog box is the dialog box Help button. If you're not sure what a dialog box option does, click the dialog box Help button (the button with a question mark on it). The pointer changes to display an arrow with a question mark. Click the dialog box option you want to know about, and a box pops up describing the option (see fig. 10.8). Click anywhere to close the Help box.

Fig. 10.8
A couple of mouse clicks is all it takes to find out what a dialog box option does.

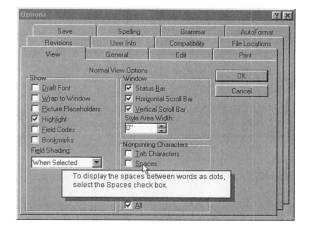

Getting more help when you need it

Dialog box help isn't the only help you can get from Windows. Nearly all Windows programs offer help in an easy-to-use, standard format. To get help on a particular program, choose Help Topics from the program's Help menu. To get help on Windows itself, click the Start button on the taskbar to open the Start menu, then click Help to open a dialog box such as the one shown in figure 10.9.

Fig. 10.9
The Contents tab of the Help Topics dialog box is probably easiest to use. The Index and Find tabs let you search for help topics by key words.

On the Contents tab of the dialog box, help topics are arranged outline style like the table of contents of a book. Double-click an item with a closed book icon next to it to see more details. Double-click an item with question mark icon to view a specific help topic in a separate window (see fig. 10.10).

Fig. 10.10
Click the Help Topics button to revisit the Help Topics dialog box to select another topic.

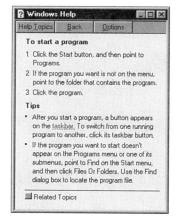

Starting programs

You probably have more than one way to get to the building where you work and to your office. You might use one route when you arrive for work in the morning, and another when you return from lunch or a meeting. Similarly, Windows 95 gives you several ways to start programs.

That's why it's called the Start menu

The first technique for starting programs is to use the Start menu. The process may seem cumbersome at first, but once you get the hang of it, you'll find that it's easy to start programs with the Start menu.

Begin by clicking the Start button on the taskbar to open the Start menu. Then point to the Programs menu item for a second or so to open the cascading menu listing groups of programs. Move the pointer over onto the cascading menu and point to one of the program groups (try Accessories). This opens another cascading menu that lists the programs in the Accessories folder (see fig. 10.11). Move the pointer over onto the final cascading menu and click the program of your choice (try Calculator). Windows starts the program immediately.

Fig. 10.11
You can click the Start
button and work your
way through the
cascading menus to
start almost any
program.

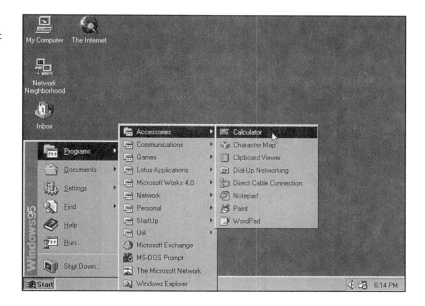

 TIP   **Normally, when you install new software, the setup program**
will add the new program to your Start menu automatically. If it doesn't,
you can add a program to the Start menu manually. See Chapter 12 for
more information.

Taking a shortcut

Want an even faster way to start a program? Try a shortcut icon. Windows 95
lets you create shortcut icons for your favorite programs. (Software installation programs often create shortcuts for you, and you'll learn how to create
your own shortcut icons in Chapter 12.) Shortcut icons can appear on your
Windows desktop, or in a folder with other tools for a project.

 Using a shortcut icon couldn't be any easier. In fact, you've already used one
to open the My Computer window. All you do is double-click a shortcut icon,
and Windows starts the associated program immediately.

Just open a document

Windows keeps track of what program creates what kind of documents. As a
result, if you tell Windows to open a document file, Windows knows what
program to run in order to work on the document.

You can use My Computer or Windows Explorer to locate a document file you want to work on. (You'll learn more about working with these tools in the next chapter.) When you open the file, usually by double-clicking the file's icon, Windows starts the appropriate program and then opens the document file in that program automatically.

When it's time to close Windows...

When you're ready to turn off your computer, you first need to follow the proper procedure to exit Windows 95. You see, Windows needs to do some housekeeping chores before you turn the lights out. There are files to save and close, accessory programs that may be running behind the scenes that need to be shut down, and general tidying up that needs to happen in an orderly fashion.

To shut down your computer, click the Start button, then click the Shut Down command on the Start menu. This opens the Shut Down Windows dialog box, as shown in figure 10.12. Select the shut down option (usually Shut Down the Computer?) and then click Yes. Windows starts its shut down routine.

Fig. 10.12
Visit this dialog box to shut down Windows before you turn off your computer.

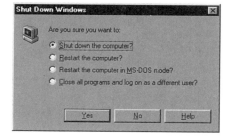

If you have any unsaved documents open, you'll be prompted to save those files before Windows shuts down. Then Windows cleans up the desktop and displays a screen advising you to wait while the computer shuts down. Finally, you'll see a message saying It's now safe to turn off your computer. You may need to wait a couple of minutes or so from the time you start the shut down until the message appears. Only then should you push the button that cuts the power to your computer.

11

Exploring Your
Files and Disks

● In this chapter:

- Getting to know your disks, folders, and files

- What's in a name?

- Exploring your folders with Windows Explorer

- Rescuing a file from the trash

A PC can hold more information than a whole room full of filing cabinets. Once you learn how the filing system works, finding the information you need is a snap! . . . . ❯

O ne of the primary functions of any personal computer is to serve as an information storage device. It stores infor- mation on disks in such a way that it can later retrieve and manipulate that information quickly and easily.

For the most part, you can leave the details of that information management to the operating system and the programs you run. However, from time to time, you'll need to work with some of that data yourself. You may need to make copies of some information, move something else to a more convenient location, or get rid of some outdated data. That's what this chapter is all about—learning how your computer and Windows 95 store information and how you can work with the documents stored in your computer.

Getting to know My Computer

The primary containers for information storage on your computer are the disks. Your computer can store information on floppy disks and the hard disk built into the computer. (It can also read information stored on CD-ROM disks—provided you have a CD-ROM drive installed.)

In Windows 95, you can get a look at those disks and what they contain by opening the My Computer window. Just double-click the My Computer icon (it's probably in the top left corner of your desktop) to open the window shown in figure 11.1.

Fig. 11.1
The My Computer window starts out showing your available disk drives.

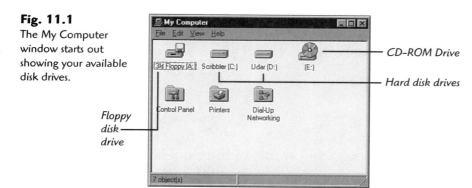

CD-ROM Drive

Hard disk drives

Floppy disk drive

Q&A *Some of my icons include a hand holding the bottom of the drive, folder, or printer. What does that mean?*

The hand means that the drive, folder, or printer is **shared**. Sharing a resource on your computer means that other network users can access that resource over the network—they can read and save files on the drive or print to the printer.

TIP **Windows 95 names your computer system "My Computer" by** default. However, like nearly everything else in Windows 95, that name (and even the icon) can be changed. The icon might be named "Silicon Giant," but it should act the same.

The My Computer window contains an icon for each disk drive in your computer (plus some other icons you don't need to worry about now). To see what's stored on a particular disk (for example, the C: drive), double-click its icon in the My Computer window. Windows opens another window, as shown in figure 11.2. This one contains icons representing the information contained in the selected drive.

Fig. 11.2
Open another window to peek inside a disk drive.

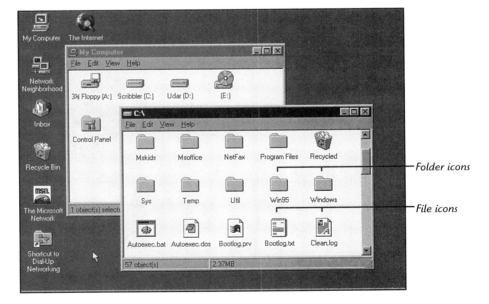

Folder icons

File icons

TIP **The operating system assigns letter-names to each of the drives** on your system so you can tell it which drive to work with. The first hard disk is always C:, the first floppy drive is always A:, and a second floppy is B:. Windows 95 lets you assign friendly names to your drives as well, but behind the scenes, it's the letter names that count.

A guided tour of your disks

Everything you store on a disk is placed in a **file**. A file is nothing more than a collection of computer information (called **data**) that's related somehow. A file can hold the words in a business letter, the information that draws a picture, the numbers that make up a spreadsheet, or the programming code that runs a program—almost anything.

Imagine an office filing cabinet. That filing cabinet has drawers that hold file folders. The file folders hold paper documents. As you can tell from figure 11.3, a computer is a lot like that filing cabinet. Instead of drawers, though, the PC uses disks. Inside the drawer of the filing cabinet, file folders organize groups of paper documents. On your PC's disk, the computer equivalent of folders (called **folders** or **directories**) organize groups of files.

Fig. 11.3
Disks are like drawers and folders (directories) are like file folders. Files are the papers that the file folders hold.

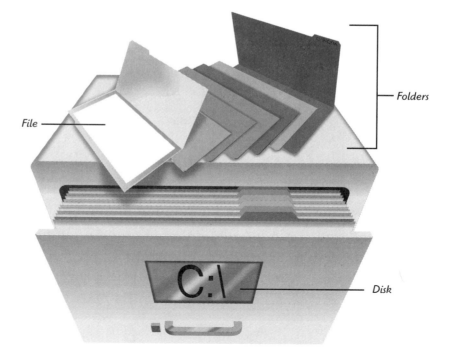

Plain English, please!
The terms **folder** and **directory** both mean the same thing. Older DOS and Windows systems used the term directory. Windows 95 uses the term folder instead.

When you get lots of files on a disk, it can be hard to find what you're looking for. To help you find information quickly, you can organize your files into folders. Just as you might keep all your tax records in one section of a file cabinet and your correspondence in another section, you might choose to store your computer graphics in one folder on your disk and your word processor documents in another folder.

A folder can contain other folders as well as files. If you have a lot of word processor document files, you might want to break them up into smaller groups to make the files more manageable. You might create within the folder for word processor documents a folder of sales reports and one for correspondence, or separate folders for specific projects. The Correspondence folder could contain separate folders for business and personal letters.

Explore your files with the Windows Explorer

Nesting folder within folder within folder helps organize files into narrower and narrower categories. However, getting to those files with My Computer can get tedious. You have to open a window for the drive, then open another window for the first folder, and another window for the next folder, and so on until you finally reach the folder containing the file you want to work on.

As an alternative to the My Computer window, Windows 95 supplies another file management utility called Windows Explorer that makes it easier to navigate through nested folders.

To try Windows Explorer, click the Start button on the taskbar, then point to Programs and click Windows Explorer on the cascading menu. This opens the Windows Explorer window, as shown in figure 11.4.

The right panel of Windows Explorer is essentially the same as the My Computer window. It contains icons for drives, folders, and files.

Fig. 11.4

Windows Explorer lets you see the structure of your folder organization.

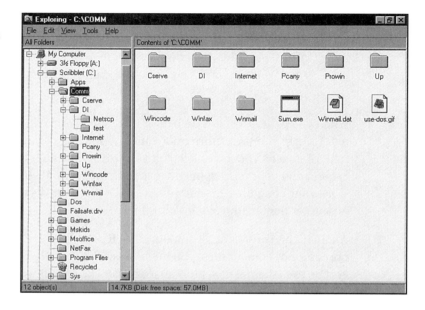

The difference is in the left panel of the Windows Explorer. It shows an outline-style, hierarchical listing of all the disk drives on your computer, including all the folders they contain. This serves as an effective map of all the folders on your system.

When you first open the Windows Explorer window, the folder list shows only one level of folders on one drive (usually your C: hard disk drive). Folders (and other drives) that contain nested folders are indicated by a small box with a plus sign in it shown beside the folder icon.

You can click the plus sign to **expand** the item and show the detail under it (the folders it contains). The nested folders are shown indented beneath the folder containing them.

When you expand a folder in the list by clicking the plus sign, the plus sign changes to a minus sign. You can click the minus sign to **collapse** that part of the display and hide the subfolders again.

The folders list lets you display folders within folders many layers deep and visualize the relationships between the folders in various levels. Once you locate a folder you're interested in, simply click the item in the folder list, and Windows Explorer displays the contents of that folder in the right panel.

TIP **Want to see more files listed in the right panel of Windows Ex-**plorer? Pull down the <u>V</u>iew menu and click <u>L</u>ist. Windows Explorer uses smaller icons, making room for more files in the window at one time. The same technique works in the My Computer window.

Every file has two names

What's in a name? It can be a lot when you're talking about file names for your computer files.

Every file must have a unique name. (At least, no other file in the same folder can have the same name.) And each file needs both a first name and a last name to identify the file and specify what kind of file it is.

The file's first name

A file's first name is usually a descriptive name that identifies the file. Program files will have names assigned by the programmers. For the files you create, you can define your own file names, such as:

1st Quarter Sales Report

The file's family name (extensions)

Following the descriptive file name is a period and a short letter/number code called an **extension**. Just as your surname identifies you as part of a certain family, a file's extension identifies what family it belongs to. The extension lets Windows identify what kind of file it is—what application created the file (or at least what program Windows should use to open the file if you want to view it). For example, the .DOC extension might identify a file as a Microsoft Word document file.

Q&A *Why do different files have different icons?*

Just as files can have different extensions, they can also have different icons. The icon helps identify the file. Typically, each program has its own icon design that will appear on the program file itself. In addition, when you save a document file, the program tacks on an icon that Windows will use when it displays that file. It's often a variation on the program's icon.

Usually, your program will add the correct extension to your files automatically when you create or save them. It's sort of like the cowboy branding his cattle. Normally, you won't have to worry about extensions in Windows 95. You just need to understand why Windows applications insist on tacking on an extension to the end of your file names.

CAUTION **File name extensions provide Windows with important information** about the file and what program it belongs to. Be careful not to confuse Windows by changing the extensions on file names, or including a period and letters or numbers in a file name that Windows might mistake for an extension.

Long file names

In Windows 95, file names can be up to 255 characters long and can include spaces and some punctuation characters. That means you can give your files truly descriptive file names such as:

> Jones Letter January 14, 1996.doc

Such a long and descriptive file name is called, appropriately enough, a **long file name**.

In contrast, DOS and older versions of Windows don't support long file names. Instead, they are restricted to an eight-character file name followed by a period and a three-character extension (sometimes called an **eight-plus-three** file name). For example, the file name for the Jones Letter above might be shortened to

> jonesltr.doc

in the eight-plus-three format.

For backward compatibility with DOS and older Windows programs, Windows 95 maintains a list of the files on your disk in the eight-plus-three format. However, you'll normally see only the long file names as you work in Windows 95.

CAUTION **Windows 95 long file names can contain spaces and some punctua-**tion marks, but you can't use any of the following characters: \ / : ? " < > | .

A file for every purpose

Now that you know files have two names and that the extension (last name) lets Windows identify what kind of file it is, it may help to know what some of those file extensions are. Just like Windows, you can use file extensions to recognize file types to help you identify the files you want to work with. File extensions can also warn you of which files you should leave alone.

Files for documents

Normally, when you work with files, they will be the document files you create with the programs you run. There are all sorts of documents created by many different programs. The following table shows the extensions for a few of the more popular document file types.

Extension	Document type
AVI	Video clip
BMP	Bitmap picture
CDR	CorelDRAW! drawing
DBF	dBASE database file
DOC	Microsoft Word document
DOC	WordPerfect document
EPS	Encapsulated PostScript drawing
GIF	Picture file
HTM	Internet World Wide Web document
JPG	Compressed picture
MDN	Microsoft Access database
PCX	Picture file
PPT	Microsoft PowerPoint presentation
PRZ	Lotus Freelance presentation
RTF	Rich Text Format—word processor document

continues

Extension	Document type
TIF	Picture file
TTF	TrueType font file
TXT	Text document
WAV	Audio clip
WB1	Quattro Pro spreadsheet file
WDB	Microsoft Works database
WK4	Lotus 1-2-3 worksheet
WKS	Microsoft Works spreadsheet
WPS	Microsoft Works word processor document
WRI	Microsoft Write document
XLC	Microsoft Excel chart
XLS	Microsoft Excel worksheet

Long file names don't work for everyone

Although Windows 95 supports long file names, DOS and older versions of Windows don't. And there are still a lot of folks using DOS and Windows 3.1. You might also run into trouble trying to use long file names on some networks.

In order to exchange files with those people who don't use Windows 95, you'll need to make sure the file names conform to the eight-plus-three format their systems require.

Windows 95 will convert long file names to the eight-plus-three format automatically, but the results may include some strange characters and be hard to use. For example, Windows 95 might shorten *Jones Letter.doc* to *Jones~1.doc* and *Jones Report.doc* to *Jones~2.doc*. To use the file in DOS, you'd have to remember whether the letter or report was number one, and you'd have to find the tilde (~) on your keyboard. (It's usually located in the upper-left corner of the keyboard to the left of the number one.)

However, if you name the files with eight-plus-three names yourself, you could choose more meaningful abbreviations such as *Jonesltr.doc* and *Jonesrpt.doc*. If you name your file using the eight-plus-three format, Windows 95 will use that name for both the long and short file names.

Files for programs

You can also recognize your programs and their support files by their extensions. Files with the extensions listed in the following table are program files. If you double-click a program file icon, Windows will start the program.

Extension	Program type
EXE	Executable program file
COM	DOS executable file
BAT	DOS batch command file

Files with extensions listed in the following table are support files for your programs. Generally, you'll want to leave these files alone. If you delete or move any of these files, your program may not operate properly.

Extension	File type
DLL	Program extension (Dynamic Link Library)
INI	Configuration information
INF	Program installation information
DAT	System data file
DRV	Device driver
REG	Registration information
VBX	Program extension
VXD	Virtual device driver
SYS	System files
HLP	Windows Help file

Working with files and folders

Now that you know something about files, you can try manipulating some of the files on your disks.

What's in this folder?

To see what files and folders are contained in a folder in Windows Explorer, click the folder icon in the left pane of the window. Windows Explorer displays the contents of the folder in the right pane of the window.

In a My Computer window (or in the right pane of the Windows Explorer), you can simply double-click the folder icon. Windows displays the contents of the folder in the same window or creates a new window to display it in.

Copying and moving files

You can make a duplicate copy of a file in a different folder or move a file to a different folder. Both processes are nearly identical.

Start by clicking a file icon in a Windows Explorer or My Computer window. Then right-drag (press and hold down the right mouse button as you move the mouse) the icon to a new location on the desktop or into a different folder in another My Computer or Windows Explorer window. When you release the mouse button to drop the file icon at its destination, a shortcut menu appears. If you want to copy the file, click Copy Here on the shortcut menu. If you want to move the file, click Move Here on the shortcut menu. As soon as you select the appropriate command, Windows completes the copy or move operation.

Changing a file's name

Assigning a new name to a file or folder is even easier than sticking a new label on a paper document or file folder. In Windows Explorer or a My Computer window, simply right-click the file (or folder) icon you want to rename, then click Rename on the shortcut menu. Windows highlights the file name in the window. To change the file or folder name, just type the new name and press Enter to record the change.

CAUTION **When you rename a file, be sure you don't change the extension.** If you do, Windows won't know what kind of file it is and won't be able to use the proper application to open and edit the renamed file.

Creating a new folder

Need to create a new folder for some of your files? That's easy. Use Windows Explorer or My Computer to open the folder or drive where you want to create the new folder. Right-click a blank space in the My Computer window or in the right panel of the Windows Explorer window. On the shortcut menu, point to Ne_w_, and then click _F_older when the cascading menu appears. Windows creates a new folder with the generic name New Folder. The folder name is already highlighted. To change it, just type in a new folder name and press Enter. Your new folder is ready for use.

Preparing your disk to drive

As you know from reading Chapter 7, every new disk must be formatted before it can be used to store files. Formatting a disk is also a way to erase all the files from an old disk and start over with a clean slate.

To format a disk, right-click the disk drive icon in My Computer or Windows Explorer, then click For_m_at on the shortcut menu. This opens the Format dialog box, as shown in figure 11.5.

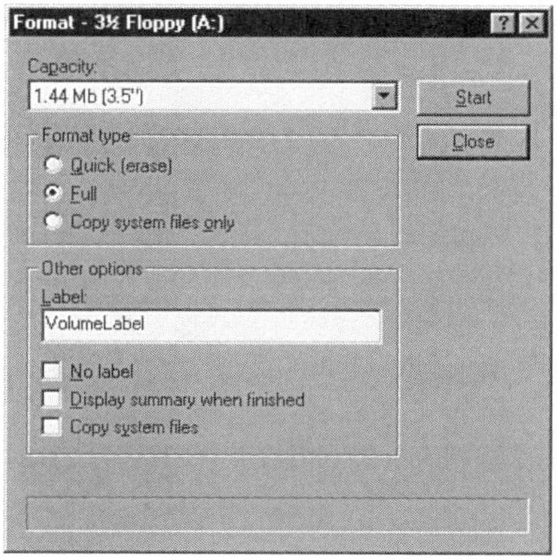

Fig. 11.5

These are the typical settings for formatting a 3¹/₂-inch floppy disk.

Adjust the dialog box settings as needed, then click the Start button. Windows begins formatting the disk. Formatting a disk takes a few minutes. The bar at the bottom of the Format dialog box shows the progress of the procedure.

When it's done, click the <u>C</u>lose button to close the dialog box. Your disk is formatted and ready to use.

If you don't need it, put it in the trash

Sooner or later, you'll need to get rid of a file. Perhaps the file is outdated or it's an unneeded duplicate copy. Whatever the reason, Windows makes it easy to delete a file. Simply drag the file icon from the Windows Explorer or My Computer window to the Recycle Bin icon on the desktop. A dialog box appears, asking you if you're sure you want to move the file to the Recycle Bin. When you click the <u>Y</u>es button, Windows deletes the file from the folder.

TIP **You can also delete a file by right-clicking the file icon and then** clicking <u>D</u>elete on the shortcut menu. The effect is the same as dropping the file in the Recycle Bin. This method comes in handy when the Recycle Bin icon is inaccessible (hidden behind another window).

Rescuing a file from the trash

But wait—you say you didn't really mean to delete that file? Don't worry, it's not really gone.

To recover a "deleted" file from the Recycle Bin, double-click the Recycle Bin icon. This opens the Recycle Bin window, which looks and acts like a My Computer window. To retrieve a file from the trash, just move it from the Recycle Bin window to another folder.

Click the file icon you want to rescue, drag it out of the Recycle Bin and drop it on the desktop, onto a folder icon, or into a My Computer or Windows Explorer window. That's all there is to it!

Don't forget to take out the trash

Windows 95's Recycle Bin makes a nice safety net to let you recover mistakenly deleted files. But it can also cause problems when you *really* want to get rid of some files. You see, the files in the Recycle Bin remain on the disk taking up space. Eventually you may need to get rid of those files for good.

 TIP **Before emptying the Recycle Bin, double-click the Recycle Bin** icon and look over the list of files in the Recycle Bin window. If there are any files you might want to recover, drag them out of the Recycle Bin before you empty it.

To finish deleting the files in the Recycle Bin, right-click the Recycle Bin icon, then click Empty Recycle <u>B</u>in on the shortcut menu. A dialog box appears, asking you to confirm the action. When you click <u>Y</u>es, Windows deletes all the files in the Recycle Bin—permanently.

12

Make Windows 95 Do It Your Way

● **In this chapter:**

- Redecorating your on-screen office

- Jump-start your favorite programs automatically

- How do I install new software?

- Building shortcuts to your favorite programs and files

Give your PC a personal touch by customizing the environment in which you work . . . .

Are you the type of person who likes to put your mark on your personal working and living spaces? Do you feel a compelling need to hang pictures in a new office, redecorate a new house, or add accessories to a new car? If so, you're gonna love Windows 95. It really lets you put the *personal* touch into your personal computer.

Windows 95 (and many Windows programs) let you change and customize lots of the details about your PC. Many of the changes, such as color preferences, are just for looks, but they can go a long way toward making your PC uniquely yours. Some changes, such as installing programs and setting up shortcut icons to start them, are more substantive and will affect what you can do with your PC.

Making Windows look the way you want

Do you yearn to repaint your drab office but you know your pin-striped boss will never go for the neon color scheme you have in mind? Or maybe you prefer pastels to blue and gray. Well, I can't help you with the rest of the office, but I can show you how to redecorate your on-screen desktop. What's more, if the boss (or your spouse) objects, you can switch back to the old color scheme faster than you can say, "It didn't look like that on the paint chip!"

Changing the screen colors

Right out of the box, Windows comes with a plain green background for your on-screen desktop, and windows appear in shades of gray with a conservative blue title bar. This standard color scheme is functional, but it's kind of boring. It's also easy to change.

To change the colors Windows uses on your system, start by right-clicking anywhere on the desktop, then click Properties on the shortcut menu that appears. When Windows opens the Display Properties dialog box, click the Appearance tab. The dialog box should look similar to figure 12.1.

Fig. 12.1

Pick one of the more than two dozen color schemes, or create one of your own.

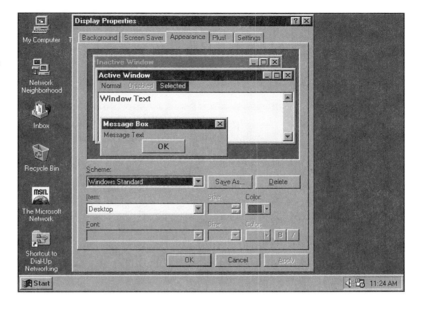

Now you can have some fun trying different color schemes. Click the arrow button at the right end of the Scheme drop-down list to open the drop-down list, then click the name of a color scheme in the list. The colors in the preview area in the top half of the dialog box will change to reflect your choice. When you find a color scheme you like, click the Apply button at the bottom of the dialog box to apply the color scheme to your entire desktop.

If you don't find a color scheme that exactly suits your taste, you can make your own. Start by selecting the standard scheme that's closest to what you want. Then move the pointer into the preview area and click the part of the scheme you want to change. For example, click the title bar of the active window. Notice that `Active Title Bar` appears in the Item box. To change its color, click the arrow button in the Color box to the right of the Item box. Instead of a drop-down list box, this opens a small color palette. Click a color, or, if you don't see a color you like, click Other to open another dialog box where you can pick from a whole rainbow of colors instead of a few standard color chips.

When you click a color, the preview area shows the effect of your choice. You can also choose a different font, size, and text color for the active title bar. Repeat the process for other screen elements until you're satisfied with your new color scheme.

Once you get a color scheme you like, you can add it to the choices in the Scheme drop-down list. Just click the Save As button, type in a name for your color scheme in the dialog box that appears, then click OK. Click OK again to close the Display Properties dialog box.

TIP **You can change back to the Windows default color scheme** quickly. Open the Display Properties dialog box and click the Appearance tab. Scroll down the Scheme drop-down list and click Windows Standard. When you click OK, your desktop is instantly returned to the default color scheme.

Wallpapering the desktop

Now that you've got a color scheme you like, let's do something about that bland, solid-color desktop background. You can apply a pattern using the existing background color and black, or you can hang some colorful **wallpaper**. Wallpaper is simply a picture file that you tell Windows to display as the background for your desktop. You can hang a large picture in the center of the screen, or you can have Windows repeat a small picture as many times as needed to fill the screen, as shown in figure 12.2.

Fig. 12.2
Tiled wallpaper repeats a small image until it fills the entire desktop background.

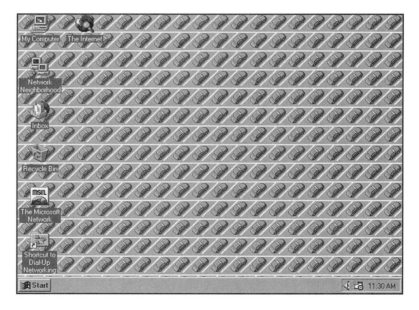

To add wallpaper to your desktop, begin by opening the Display Properties dialog box just as you did to change the color scheme, but this time click the Background tab. The dialog box that appears will look similar to figure 12.3.

Fig. 12.3
Select your wallpaper and background patterns here.

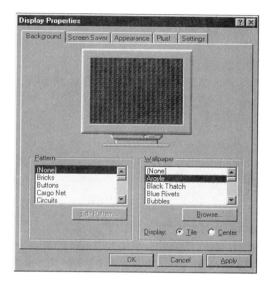

To select a wallpaper effect, click an item in the Wallpaper list, then click the Tile or Center option. The miniature monitor previews the effect. Click the Apply button to try the wallpaper on your desktop. When you're through, click the OK button to close the Display Properties dialog box.

Most of the standard wallpaper files supplied with Windows are small images that are designed to be tiled, not centered. But you're not confined to the standard choices—clicking the Browse button below the Wallpaper list box will let you select other image files as wallpaper.

If you have the Microsoft Plus add-on package for Windows 95, you have several larger, full-screen wallpaper images to choose from. In addition, you might get interesting images from clip art collections (see fig. 12.4), user groups, and on-line services. You can draw your own wallpaper with the Paint program (it's in the Accessories program folder on the Start menu), and even scan in family photos if you have access to a scanner. Basically, any image file saved in the BMP file format can be displayed as wallpaper.

Fig. 12.4
You can use photos and drawings as personal wallpaper.

TIP **Instead of wallpaper, you might want to try a Pattern. The proce-dure** for picking a pattern is the same as selecting wallpaper. Remember that in Windows, wallpaper covers patterns. So to see your pattern, be sure to choose None from the Wallpaper list.

Adding a screen saver

Screen savers were developed to address a problem with computer moni-tors being damaged when a static image remained on the screen too long. The image could become permanently "burned" into the screen.

The screen saver software works by monitoring keyboard and mouse activ-ity. After a specified period of inactivity, the screen saver replaces whatever was showing on-screen with a randomly changing pattern (or just a blank screen). Then, when you move the mouse or press any key on the keyboard, the screen saver returns your screen to normal operation.

Newer computer monitors are much less susceptible to damage than older models, but screen savers are more popular than ever. Many people found that the screen savers enhance computer privacy by hiding the document you're working on from prying eyes if you leave your desk for a few minutes. Also, some of the patterns and effects the screen savers display are just plain fun.

Windows 95 includes a built-in screen saver. To activate it or change the settings, open the Display Properties dialog box (as described earlier) and click the Screen Saver tab (see fig. 12.5).

Fig. 12.5
You can select screen saver effects ranging from plain to hypnotic.

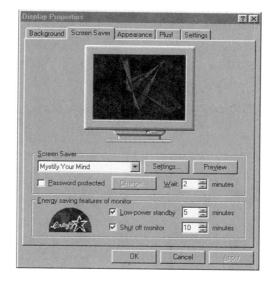

The Screen Saver box is a drop-down list box. Click the arrow button to open the list and pick a screen saver by clicking an item in the list. The miniature monitor graphic previews the screen saver effect. To see the effect full-screen, click the Preview button. Then just move the mouse to restore the dialog box to the screen.

The next thing you need to do is type a number of minutes in the Wait box. After that amount of time without any keyboard or mouse activity, Windows will automatically activate the screen saver.

If you have an energy-saving monitor, you can also adjust the time delay before the monitor reduces power to save energy. Finally, click OK to apply the settings and close the dialog box.

Other stuff you can play with in Control Panel

There are still more ways to customize Windows 95.

The Windows **Control Panel** is a special folder that contains icons for **applets**, mini-applications that let you adjust various Windows settings and options. You probably shouldn't mess with most of the Control Panel applets without help from someone who's knowledgeable about such things. However, there are some applets you can experiment with.

To open Control Panel, click the Start button on the taskbar, then point to Settings, and click Control Panel when the cascading menu appears.

Sounds

The Sounds applet lets you associate sounds with certain Windows events such as minimizing a window. (You need a sound card to get the full effect.) Double-click the Sounds icon to open the Sounds Properties dialog box, as shown in figure 12.6.

Fig. 12.6
You can instruct Windows to play a sound effect every time you maximize a window or select a menu command.

To assign a sound to an event, click an event in the Events list box, then pick a sound from the Name drop-down list box. To hear the sound you chose, click the arrow button that's just to the right of the Preview box. Once you assemble a set of sounds you like, you can save it as a **sound scheme**—just like saving a color scheme. When you're through adjusting sound settings, click OK to close the dialog box and apply the settings.

Mouse

Are you left-handed? If so, you can swap the functions of the left and right mouse buttons to make the mouse easier to use in your left hand. Double-click the Mouse icon in Control Panel to open the Mouse Properties dialog box shown in figure 12.7.

Fig. 12.7

Use the options in this dialog box to train your mouse.

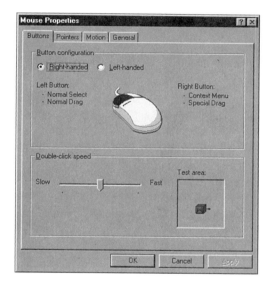

Besides switching mouse buttons for left-handed use, you can select alternate pointer shapes, adjust how fast or slow the pointer moves when you move the mouse, and more. After making your adjustments, click OK to close the dialog box and use the new settings.

Themes

If you have Microsoft Plus for Windows 95 installed, you can choose from several different **desktop themes**—sets of colors, wallpaper, sounds, pointers, and even custom icons for things like My Computer and the Recycle Bin. Double-click the Desktop Themes icon in Control Panel to open the Desktop Themes dialog box (see fig. 12.8).

Fig. 12.8
Desktop Themes are available only if you have the optional Microsoft Plus package installed.

Pick a theme from the Theme drop-down list box and check out the effect in the large preview box. The Screen Saver and Pointers, Sounds, etc. buttons let you preview those aspects of the chosen theme. The column of check boxes on the right give you the option of applying all or part of the chosen theme to your Windows environment. Click OK to apply the settings, then close the dialog box.

TIP **Microsoft Plus Companion for Windows 95 requires at least a 486** CPU and 8M of RAM. It also includes some other features besides the Desktop Themes.

Date/Time

If you ever need to reset your computer's clock, you can do it with the Date/Time Properties dialog box, shown in figure 12.9. To open the dialog box, simply double-click the Date/Time icon in Control Panel.

Setting the correct date is fairly straightforward. There are drop-down list boxes for the month and year. To set the day, just click the date in the calendar. You set the time in the time box below the clock. To change the hour, click the hour part of the time and then adjust the value by typing a new number, or by clicking the up- or down-arrow button at the right end of the box. Repeat the process to adjust the minutes, seconds, and AM/PM setting. The Time Zone tab lets you specify what time zone you're in and instruct Windows to automatically adjust the clock for daylight savings time.

Fig. 12.9
Here's where you set
your computer's clock
and calendar.

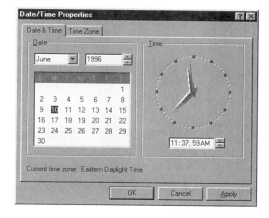

Installing that new program you just bought

Windows 95 includes a mini program called a **wizard** to help you install new oftware. To use the Install Wizard, open Control Panel as described earlier and double-click the Add/Remove Programs icon. In the Add/Remove Programs Properties dialog box (see fig. 12.10), make sure the Install/Uninstall tab is selected, then click the Install button to launch the wizard.

Fig. 12.10
Start here when
you need to add or
remove software in
Windows 95.

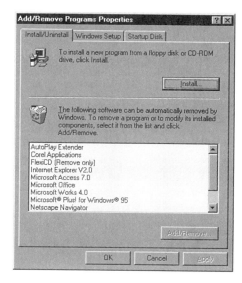

When you run the Install Wizard, you'll see a series of dialog boxes giving you instructions and prompting you for information. Just follow the instructions in each dialog box and then click the Next button to go to the next step.

The first dialog box instructs you to insert the new program's first installation disk. When you click the Next button, the wizard searches for a setup utility program on a floppy disk or CD-ROM and displays the result in the next dialog box. Just click the Finish button to run the setup program.

 Q&A *What should I do if the Install Wizard can't find the new software's setup program?*

Try clicking the Browse button, which lets you tell the wizard where the setup program is. You'll need to do this if the setup program has an unusual name that the wizard doesn't recognize, or if the setup program is tucked away in a folder on the disk.

If all else fails, click Cancel to close the dialog boxes and read the instructions that came with your new software. Follow the manufacturer's instructions for installing the program manually.

The setup program will install your new software on your PC. You simply follow the instructions that appear on-screen. The setup program may ask questions and offer options. Be prepared to insert other disks when instructed to do so.

The setup program will probably create one or more folders on your hard disk and copy files into the folders. Then it'll add the new program to your Start menu and operate behind the scenes to introduce itself to Windows 95.

Add programs to the Start menu

Normally, a program's installation utility adds a new program to your Start menu automatically. However, some small accessory programs don't have installation programs. You may need to add those programs to the Start menu manually. It's easier to do than you might think.

Start by right-clicking the taskbar, then click Properties on the shortcut menu that appears. (Make sure you click the background of the taskbar and not a button for a program.) This opens the Taskbar Properties dialog box. Click the Start Menu Programs tab, as shown in figure 12.11.

Fig. 12.11
This dialog box lets you customize your Start menu.

Now click the Add button. This opens the Create Shortcut dialog box, which contains a text box intimidatingly labeled Command Line. It needs the drive, folder, and file name of the program you want to add to the Start menu. But don't worry. You don't have to type it in from memory.

Click the Browse button to open the Browse dialog box, as shown in figure 12.12. Now you can browse through your folders and files until you find the program you're looking for.

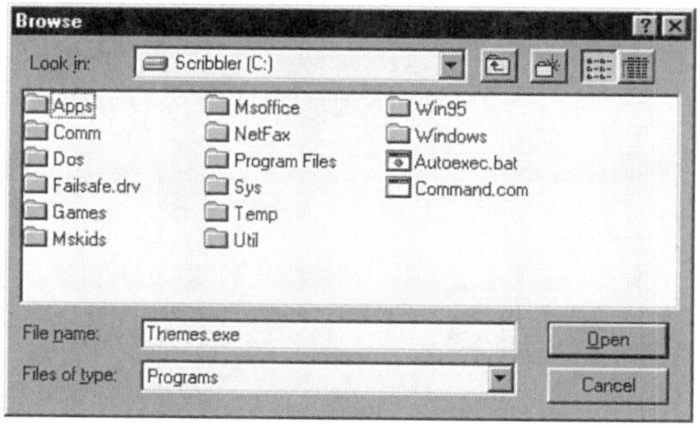

Fig. 12.12
This is the same kind of dialog box you see to open files in most Windows programs.

Double-click a folder icon to open the folder and display its contents in the Browse dialog box. If you need to look on another drive or in a higher level folder, you can choose it from the Look In drop-down list box. When you find the correct folder, click the program's executable file, then click the Open button. Windows closes the dialog box and adds the correct path to that file to the box in the Create Shortcut dialog box.

Click the Next button to continue to the Select Program Folder dialog box, as shown in figure 12.13. This is where you pick the folder where you want to place the new program shortcut. The indented folders in the list correspond to the cascading menus of the Start menu. Click the Next button.

Fig. 12.13
The cascading menus of the Start menu are really just folders within folders.

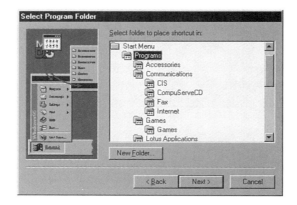

In the next dialog box (shown in fig. 12.14), type a title for the new shortcut as you want it to appear in the Start menu. Click the Finish button to complete the process, then click OK to close the Taskbar Properties dialog box. You'll find the new program available the next time you open the Start menu.

Fig. 12.14
Now you get to name your program. You can name your word processor Fred if you like.

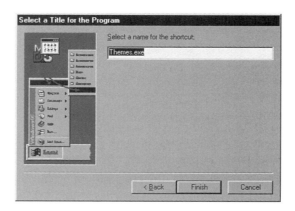

TIP **You can add a few of your favorite programs to the top of the first** layer of the Start menu so you don't have to work through the cascading menus to get to them. Use Windows Explorer or My Computer to open the folder containing the program's executable file. Then drag the program file's icon from the folder to the Start button on the taskbar. That's all there is to it. The program will appear on the Start menu.

Create shortcuts for your most-used programs and files

You can have icons on your Windows desktop to give you instant access to your most-used programs and document files. **Shortcuts** are handy tools. They can make any program or file as accessible as the My Computer icon on your desktop.

A shortcut isn't a copy of a program or file—it's just a way to access a program or file. It's like having more than one extension telephone on the same line. You can answer or place calls from any extension, but there's still only one phone line into the house. Similarly, you can have multiple shortcuts to the same program or file. The shortcuts can be anywhere—in a folder, or on your desktop.

Shortcuts are easy to create; and they're easy to get rid of when you don't need them anymore. As a result, you can create a shortcut to a file you're working on so you can access it directly from the desktop—you don't have to dig through several folders to get to the file. Then, when you finish working on the file, you can get rid of the shortcut to keep it from cluttering your desktop. The file itself remains intact.

To create a shortcut, use Windows Explorer or My Computer to open the folder containing the file for the document or program. Right-drag the file icon from the folder to the desktop (or into another folder). When you release the mouse button, Windows opens a shortcut menu. Click Create Shortcut(s) Here to have Windows create the shortcut icon. Notice the small arrow in the lower-left corner of the icon. The arrow indicates that the icon is a shortcut and not the document or program file.

To use the shortcut, simply double-click it. The effect is the same as double-clicking the file icon in its home folder. It opens the file or starts the program associated with the shortcut. When you don't need a shortcut anymore, just drag it into the Recycle Bin. The shortcut icon will be deleted without affecting the file to which it refers.

Part III: You Need Software!

13 Word Processing Makes Your Written Work Look Good

● **In this chapter:**

- Other than letters and memos, what can I produce with a word processor?

- How is word processing different from typing on a typewriter?

- Hot new features of today's word processors

- Take a look at some of the best word processors

A word processor's job is to make your writing efforts look good, whether this means a grant proposal, a term paper, or the most stunning grocery list you've ever seen . . . .

It's safe to assume that 99.9 percent of all home computers have a word processor of some kind installed on them. In fact, it's very likely that your operating system has a built-in word processor with limited capabilities, but to get all the features you want in a word processor, you might feel the need to also buy a commercial one.

 TIP **A word processing program is generally just called a word processor** in the computer industry (and in this chapter). The term word processor also applies to a piece of hardware much like an electronic typewriter, but that equipment isn't discussed in this book.

What can I do with a word processor?

Basically, you can use a word processor to do anything you used to do with a typewriter—and more. Because word processors are flexible and smart, the things you can do with your documents are practically limitless. You can move things around, fix problems, and change the whole shape of a document with remarkable ease.

You'll find that many of the limitations on what you can produce will come from your printer rather than your word processor. With the right paper or forms, here's a partial list of things you can create using your word processor:

- File folder labels
- Disk labels
- Business cards
- Greeting cards and invitations
- Menus
- Letterhead
- Newsletters
- Brochures and flyers
- Banners
- Bumper stickers

Most programs throw in extras, too

Remember when power steering, power brakes, and an automatic transmission were options on most cars? Well, these days, all of those are standard features on nearly every car. The new generation of options includes things like sunroofs, anti-lock brakes, and separate temperature control for each seat. Word processors have likewise evolved—some features that once made a splash on the PC software scene for being brand new and different are taken for granted now because almost every word processor on the market includes them. Among these well-established features are:

- Adding headers and footers

- Inserting footnotes

- Using different character fonts in a variety of sizes

- Changing text to **bold**, *italic*, <u>underlined</u>, <u>double underlined</u>, ~~strikethrough~~, and more

- Checking for spelling errors (and in some programs, checking for grammatical errors)

Some word processor features remind me of car airbags (that is, many modern word processors have them, but some don't, even though they ought to). These include:

- Adding lines or boxes in a variety of widths and styles

- Inserting digitized photos and artwork

- Making charts and tables with newly entered data or by linking to data that already exists in a database

- Drag-and-drop editing (you really gotta have a mouse for this sleight-of-hand stuff!)

- Creating a table of contents or index automatically

- Executing complex macros

Plain English, please!

A **macro** is a bunch of commands that do a specific job, which you save as a unit. Macros are handy for automating repetitive tasks. For example, you might create a macro that swaps transposed letters in a word (such as "center" for "centre"). **,,**

Building a masterpiece

You'll probably end up using your word processor to type everything—not just documents that need to look great (like quarterly reports and monthly newsletters) but rough transcripts of phone conversations or even notes to your significant other.

The first thing you do with a word processor is create a new document, which you'll eventually save in a file on disk. This task is a lot like sticking a new piece of paper in a typewriter. Some word processors have a new document ready to go as soon as you start them. Others make you choose a command (such as <u>N</u>ew on the <u>F</u>ile menu) before they'll give you a clean window in which to type your document (see fig. 13.1).

Do I have to spend a fortune to get a decent word processor?

Many new PCs come with a variety of software packages, including a word processor. If yours didn't, however, you're probably interested in knowing how much a good word processor costs.

Word processors can be expensive, with street prices of $300 or more. However, there are ways to avoid spending such big bucks. One way is to purchase a **competitive upgrade** package. You can only do this, however, if you already own another word processor and are "trading up" to the new one. Another way is to purchase **software suites**. See Chapter 16 for details.

How to jazz up those boring documents

*This newsletter page uses a **three-column layout**. Note the **vertical and horizontal lines** that are used to separate the columns and other elements on the page.*

*You can add a variety of **graphics** to most word processing documents. This scanned photograph straddles two columns and adds visual interest and balance to the page.*

THE LAKES

Contained within the National Park are three very famous, and pulchritudinous, lakes. The first you come to by jaunting car is the Lower Lake, also called Lough Leane. The second, or Middle Lake, is also called Muckross Lake. The third is simply known as the Upper Lake. In addition, don't miss Torc Mountain and its stupendous waterfall. Water from the Devil's Punch Bowl rushes over Torc's 60' waterfall, gushing and glorious, it is a sight you will not want to miss.

THE PEOPLE

Of course, as we have said before, the people of Ireland are its main tourist attraction. Their warm, friendly smiles await your visit. Their music greets you; their song welcomes you. Men resting along the side of the road from working in the peat bogs. Their worn, shiny suits a symbol of days gone by. The women, with their rosy red cheeks, shopping for fresh bread and potatoes; chatting with their

beauty and solitude of the landscape, and the love of life from the people. It is a memory to cherish your whole life through.

MUCKROSS ESTATE

Also located near Killarney, County Kerry, is a tremendous National Park called Muckross Estate. Over 10,000 acres of mountains, lakes, and green, green flora preserved by the Republic for your enjoyment. Cars are not allowed on the estate; there are, however, alternatives. You may rent or bring your own bicycle. Or take a jaunting car. Jaunting cars line the entrance to the park (as well as line the streets of Killarney), ready to transport you to this scene of serenity and beauty. The horse-drawn carriages are driven by gents who spin tales and weave stories of old Ireland, Killarney, Muckross, and the fairies.

Your first stop on the Estate is Muckross Abbey. A Franciscan Abbey built in the 15th century,

it is one of the best kept and restored abbeys in all of Kerry. Your next stop is Muckross House. A monumental 19th century home donated, along with the land, to the people of Ireland by its former owners. The house is filled with intricately hand-carved furniture, home-made crafts, tapestries, and original art works. The basement contains a stable, and fully stocked print shop, pub, blacksmith shop, kitchen, and weavers shop; all have presenters working as you tour, answering any and all questions.

*A variety of **fonts** and **font sizes** creates different types of emphasis in certain parts of the page.*

TRAVEL AIRLINES

presenting our
Spring Specials

| Round Trip to Shannon | $695 |
| Round Trip to Dublin | $795 |

Restrictions and limits apply
Call for information and prices

CALL TOLL FREE
1-800-009-9900

*Centered text provides emphasis and enhances readability. Note the use of **white space** to make information easy to read.*

Graphics lines such as this create a page border and add visual interest.

Clip art can add drama or even humor to your documents. With most word processors, you can move clip art or inserted pictures, and the program adjusts the text to flow around the new location.

Fig. 13.1
All word processors
have a command for
starting a new docu-
ment that leads to a
blank page like this.

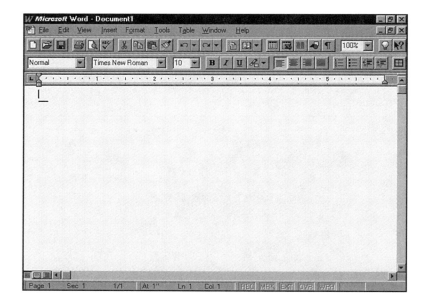

Just start typing

Once you have a new document started, type everything you want on the
page, just as you would with a typewriter. The big difference is that mistakes
you make with your word processor aren't permanent—you just press the
Backspace key to get rid of the troublesome characters and then retype the
word.

Another difference is that you don't press the Enter key at the end of each
sentence like you use the carriage return with a typewriter. Today's word
processors all perform **word wrap**, so you only press Enter when you've
finished a paragraph.

 Plain English, please!

> **Word wrap** means that your cursor (often called the insertion point) goes
> down to the left edge of the following line when the word you're typing
> won't fit within the margin. **99**

Q&A ***Why can't I use the space bar to line up columns of figures?***

Unlike most typewriters, word processors typically use proportional fonts, which means that some letters are wider and some are narrower. That makes it nearly impossible to line things up by counting spaces. Use tabs instead. Most word processors have rulers that make it easy to set and adjust tabs.

Edit the heck out of it

In the old typewriter days, producing a second draft of a document was as much physical labor as it was mental; you had to retype the whole thing.

A word processor makes editing a document as easy as rearranging magnets on a refrigerator. Decide which parts of the document need to be lifted, moved, or added. The rest of your writing stays put on the screen as you use commands like Copy, Cut, Paste, and Replace to move the parts around, so you never have to retype anything that was done properly the first time.

Fancy it up

You can spruce up your document as you write, or add the pretty stuff when you're done typing—fancy borders, different fonts, tables, and so on. The latter approach lets you focus on the content and worry about adjusting the presentation later, but plan ahead to get a rough idea of how you want the final document to appear.

Your letters, memos, and reports make a statement about you. Should a memo to your boss have the same look as an invitation to a surprise birthday party? Of course not. Your new business plan needs a nice, conservative, dressed-for-success look, while a flyer for next week's big sale demands a bold, attention-getting look.

Every major word processor comes with a huge wardrobe of accessories to help you dress your documents appropriately—for success, to get attention, or just for fun.

Get it out on paper

When you have a dazzling document, you're ready to print. Printing a document is probably the most complicated task you'll have to do with a word processor (outside of figuring out when to use "who" and "whom"). This is because you have to make sure that the printer and word processor can work together.

If you use a Windows-based word processor, Windows handles most of the printing details for you, making sure that what comes out on the page looks the same as what's on the screen. If you're using a DOS-based word processor, though, you may need to refer to your word processor's manual to be sure that you have both the word processor and the printer set up correctly.

Save it for posterity

Another great thing about word processors is that once you create a document, you can save it onto a hard disk or floppy disk. Then, anytime you like, you can open the document (that is, display it on the screen) and print a few extra copies, or do additional editing.

The latest and greatest word processors

Each word processor has its own strengths and weaknesses. It's crucial that you decide which tasks matter most to you and choose a word processor that excels at those tasks.

 TIP **Windows 95 comes with its own word processor, WordPad. Before** you spend a lot of money on a word processor, try WordPad to see whether it'll do enough things to satisfy your word processing needs. WordPad isn't as powerful as the major word processors, but it may be good enough for many home computer users.

Microsoft Word for Windows

The Windows version of Microsoft Word (called Word for Windows or just WinWord for short) has long been a consumer favorite. This is thanks to its ease of use, its full supply of state-of-the-art word processing features, and its extra goodies. Incorporating tables and graphs into your documents is a snap with WinWord (see fig. 13.2).

Fig. 13.2
Microsoft Word for
Windows is one of the
leading word processors
because of its solid
selection of standard
features and healthy
dose of extras.

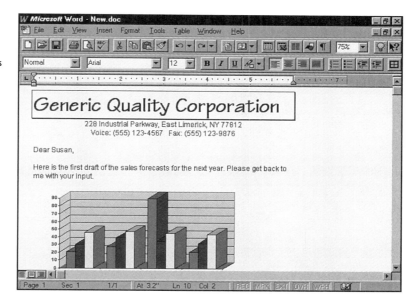

Word, like all major word processors, features a spelling checker and grammar checker, along with customizable toolbars and menus. Word has automated many activities, including checking spelling (it can catch errors as you
type) and adding numbers to numbered lists (it can pop up each subsequent
number for you). Word also handles special chores like adding borders,
graphics, and tables to a document.

66 *Plain English, please!*

A **toolbar** is a row of on-screen buttons, with each button representing a
command that you can give to the program. To issue the command, you just
click the button with your mouse. 99

Word includes numerous **wizards**, plus supplemental programs (called
applets) to create graphs, edit scientific equations, manage a gallery of clip
art, and create fancy text treatments. Word also includes templates for
getting documents started quickly, and for prewritten business letters.

Figure 13.3 shows an invoice template.

Fig. 13.3
This invoice template is one of a dozen templates that Word provides to help you create business documents quickly.

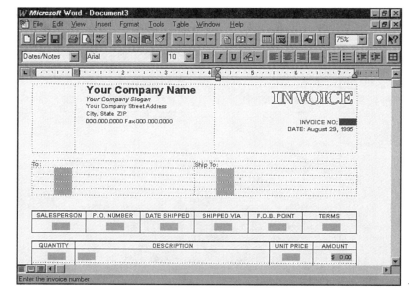

66 *Plain English, please!*

A **template** is a document that has been created and laid out for you. To use a template, all you do is open it with your word processor and fill in the blanks with your own text. Think of templates as electronic versions of those preprinted forms you can buy at a stationery store. 99

Wizards

To make creating documents easier, Word includes **wizards**, which are automated helpers that lead you, step by step, through the creation of a certain type of document. Working with a document type you've never dealt with before is as easy as following the instructions on your screen. Word includes wizards for fax cover sheets, letters, memos, and resumes, to name a few.

WordPerfect for Windows

The Windows version of Novell's WordPerfect (see fig. 13.4) includes toolbars, templates, a spelling checker, drawing, charting, and more. As I write this, the latest version (6.1) of WordPerfect for Windows is designed to run under Windows 3.1, but a new version designed for Windows 95 is in the works and due out soon. With WordPerfect 6.1 for Windows, you can:

- Assemble a variety of charts (for example, pie and bar charts)
- Fax documents from within WordPerfect for Windows
- Copy formats from one section of text to another
- Create mini-spreadsheets
- Assign special effects to text, such as color, shapes, or shadowing
- Create and edit graphics images with WP Draw, a scaled-down version of WordPerfect Presentations

The DOS version of WordPerfect is probably the most popular word processor of all time. Although it lost ground when Windows exploded in popularity, the DOS version of WordPerfect 6.0 is still a very impressive program. In fact, it looks and acts deceptively like a Windows program.

Fig. 13.4
WordPerfect for Windows is the successor to the world's most popular word processor, WordPerfect for DOS.

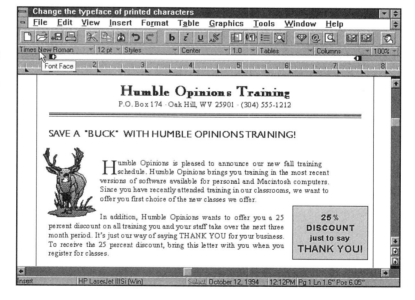

Word Pro

Although Lotus Development Corporation's Word Pro (formerly called Ami Pro) is not as popular as Word for Windows or WordPerfect for Windows, it boasts some significant strengths—especially its ease of use for complex things like page layout. Word Pro makes it simple to create newsletters and documentation, for example, thanks to its graphics capabilities and ready-to-use templates (see fig. 13.5).

Fig. 13.5
With its superior graphics handling and outstanding templates, Word Pro deserves to play in the majors.

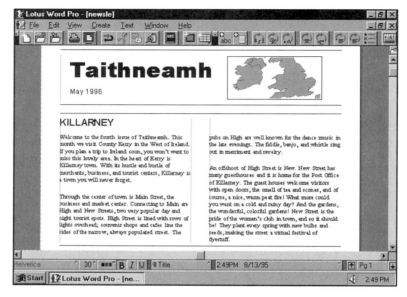

 Plain English, please!

Page layout is the process of determining how a page will look. This process includes setting margins, positioning headlines, creating headers and footers, and choosing styles for paragraphs.

In addition, Word Pro's workgroup editing helps set it apart from its competitors. Like most modern word processors, Word Pro's screen includes a toolbar at the top and a status line at the bottom, from which you can quickly select character types and styles.

In addition to the usual spelling and grammar checkers, Word Pro sports handy tools for making the program work the way you want it to. For example, you can create a new icon, place it on the toolbar, and assign a macro to the icon. Presto! You've got your own custom command button.

14

Crunch Numbers with Spreadsheets

● **In this chapter:**

- **What's a spreadsheet, and why do I need one?**

- **Parts of a spreadsheet**

- **Text, numbers, and formulas**

- **The "Big Three" Windows spreadsheets**

- **Spreadsheets that work with DOS**

You've seen a sort of spreadsheet if you've ever seen a baseball scoreboard . . . . **>**

Aspreadsheet is pretty much like a scoreboard or a book-
keeper's ledger sheet, with rows and columns. But you don't
need a scorekeeper; you can change and update information instantly,
correct mistakes without erasing, and even whip up a chart or graph showing
statistics at a moment's notice. You can use a spreadsheet program for all
kinds of instant calculations, such as finding the amount of interest you'll pay
on a loan.

What's a spreadsheet program good for?

Numbers, of course, are the heart of the spreadsheet. Very few people use
a spreadsheet program to write letters or memos, although you can do that
with recent versions. Most of the time, you use a spreadsheet program to
handle anything where you want columns and rows of numbers, you need
financial calculations, or you want to show statistics in a graph or chart:

- How much money did your business make last year?

- What was the average grade earned by your students on the last test?

- Which meetings are being held in which ballrooms or suites, and at
  what time?

- How much did your advertising expenditures increase over the last five
  fiscal years?

Figure 14.1 shows a typical spreadsheet. In this example, the owner of a
small restaurant calculates costs and profits. Notice the bar graph that shows
at-a-glance which product line is most profitable.

An important spreadsheet feature is its ability to recalculate constantly. As
you insert new information, the spreadsheet can recalculate totals instantly,
so your information is always up to date.

Another useful part of current spreadsheet programs is their ability to do
"what-if" thinking. This lets you try to come up with the "best plan" in the
easiest manner. Suppose you increased your production output for the
second half of the year. What kind of profit could you expect to make?
Would it offset the additional production costs, such as overtime?

Fig. 14.1
A typical spreadsheet program, with rows and columns.

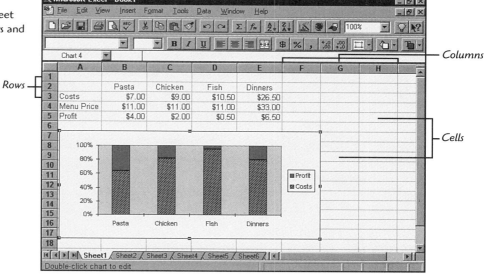

How is a spreadsheet different from an accounting package?

A spreadsheet isn't a substitute for a business accounting software program. Rather, a spreadsheet is a versatile tool that you can use to analyze a lease or get the big picture by charting total sales for a month. An accounting software program is a specialized product for recording the details that make up those sales.

Parts of a typical spreadsheet

Spreadsheets are composed of columns and rows, and the intersection of a column and row is called a **cell** (refer to fig. 14.1). Spreadsheets have millions of cells. You simply scroll the screen horizontally or vertically to see the ones outside the current view.

Just like houses on a street, the cells are given unique addresses. Most spreadsheets use letters to name the columns of cells. Numbers are used to name each row. The upper-left cell in a spreadsheet is A1. The cell below that is A2. The cell one place to the right of A1 is B1, and so on. A rectangular bunch of cells—either a single column or row or multiple columns or rows—is called a **range** or a **block**, depending on the program you use (see fig. 14.2).

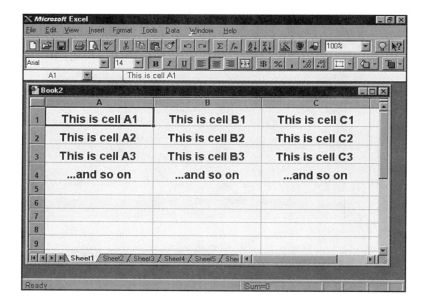

Spreadsheet cells can be filled with numbers, text, or formulas.

Numbers and text in cells

Text in a spreadsheet is often used to describe a row or column, such as GROSS SALES or JANUARY PROFIT. You can also write paragraphs that explain the information in the spreadsheet, annotate graphs, and so on.

Recent spreadsheet programs allow extensive formatting of numbers and text. In many cases, the programs include special features that automatically format the spreadsheet. You can choose from quite a variety of formats that include shadow boxes, drop shadows, color bars, and various type sizes and typefaces.

Formulas perform calculations

The true power of the spreadsheet is the **formula**. Formulas command the spreadsheet to do a calculation. A spreadsheet may have formulas that tally the interest on an outstanding loan, or simply total a range of values.

For example, you could add up 12 monthly sales numbers, one for each month of the year, which appear in column A. The formula might look like this:

A1+A2+A3+A4+A5+A6+A7+A8+A9+A10+A11+A12

If you change any of the numbers being added, the total changes automatically. For example, if you have a revised sales figure for June (in cell A6), just pop that new number in the cell. As fast as you can press Enter, your spreadsheet changes the total at the bottom of the column.

 TIP

These days, you don't even have to type most of a formula.
Modern spreadsheet programs let you click the cells you want to add, subtract, or whatever. You can even drag the mouse over a bunch of cells at a time to select a column or row.

Formulas also let you multiply, divide, and subtract, as well as perform other math operations.

Functions are even more powerful than formulas

If you don't want to keep typing the addresses of individual cells to make a formula, or even clicking the ones you want ("A1 *plus* A2 *plus* A3…" gets pretty boring), try a **function**. Functions are just built-in formulas. The manufacturers of spreadsheet programs pretty much know the kinds of things you need to do, and have already thought up formulas for most situations.

For example, virtually all spreadsheet programs have a function that adds a column or row of numbers, because everybody who uses a spreadsheet needs this formula at some point. Remember the example from a few paragraphs ago?

This formula says that you want to add the contents of cell A1, A2, A3, and so on through cell A12. Here's how the equivalent function might look, depending on what spreadsheet product you use:

=SUM(A1:A12)

@SUM(A1..A12)

These two formulas say exactly the same thing as the earlier formula: you want to add up all the numbers in cells A1 through A12. And the result will be identical, too.

 TIP The @SUM in the second example is pronounced "at sum."

Keep in mind that the program doesn't care whether you use a formula or a function, but the function saves on typing for you. Some spreadsheets even have buttons on a toolbar that you can click to enter the function you want—talk about convenience!

What-if calculations

Remember, cells with formulas recalculate results if you change any of the numbers used for the formula. This automatic "ripple effect" allows you to create a financial plan, and then plug in different assumptions. The automatic recalculation immediately shows you the impact of the new numbers.

Spreadsheets are even smarter than you think!

One of the coolest (and most labor-saving!) features in a spreadsheet is its ability to copy your formulas from one cell to another. This doesn't sound like any big deal, because you can copy and paste in almost any program.

The big difference in a spreadsheet program is that when you copy a formula, the program is smart enough to guess what you're trying to do, and helps you fix the formula so it works somewhere else!

For example, look at figure 14.3. Notice the amount 15,507.00 in cell C12? You can't see it in this picture, which shows the results rather than the formula, but that's a calculation for the amounts in the cells above—all in column C. If you copy that formula and paste it into cell B12, though, the program assumes that you want to calculate with the amounts in column B, not column C, and fixes all the addresses in the formula. You don't have to do a thing!

Fig. 14.3

This may become your favorite part of using a spreadsheet. If you have lots of columns or rows to calculate, let the program figure out what you need.

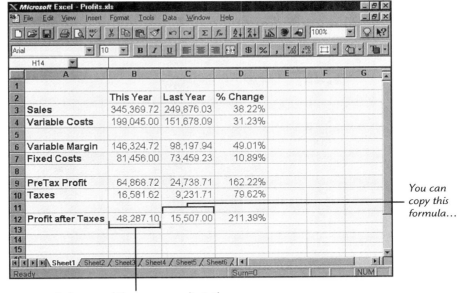

You can copy this formula...

...to here, and the program adjusts the addresses automatically.

Color and pictures, too

Spreadsheets are well known for their ability to turn a slew of numbers into an insightful (and even pretty) pie or bar chart. There are also 3D charts, line charts, histogram charts, and many, many more kinds! These charts can often be displayed in the corner of the spreadsheet, and the size of the bars or pie slices automatically changes as you change your numbers (see fig. 14.4).

To improve reading, you can color your worksheet. You can paint an entire worksheet, color specific ranges, add tinted drop shadows and cell borders, or set off a chart by adding special shading.

Fig. 14.4

A typical column chart—one of several chart types available in spreadsheets.

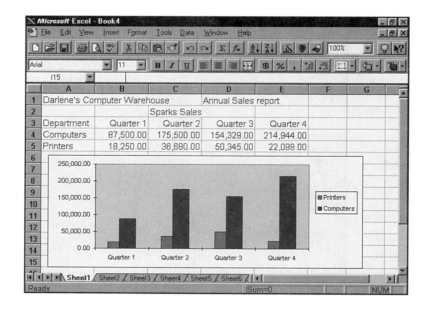

The "Big Three" Windows spreadsheets

Like car manufacturers, spreadsheet software has evolved into the Big Three: Lotus 1-2-3, Excel, and Quattro Pro. All share many common features, while each has specific strengths. For example, all use the tabbed-notebook approach to three-dimensional spreadsheets.

Q&A *What's a 3D spreadsheet?*

A regular spreadsheet is like an accountant's ledger sheet with columns and rows of numbers. A 3D spreadsheet adds another dimension—multiple sheets. It's like a whole stack of ledger sheets. The advantage is that formulas on one sheet can refer to values from other sheets. It's great for consolidating monthly results and such. All the leading spreadsheet programs today are 3D spreadsheets.

Another novelty being adopted is the editing of cell contents in the cell. You used to edit the cell contents in a narrow box at the top of the screen. Now, your eyes no longer have to bounce between the cell and the box. Both Lotus 1-2-3 for Windows and Excel offer this **in-cell editing**.

Lotus 1-2-3 for Windows

Think of Lotus and most people think of the world's number-one spreadsheet program, 1-2-3. Figure 14.5 shows Release 5 of 1-2-3 running in Windows 3.1. A new version of the program, designed for Windows 95, should be available by the time you read this.

Fig. 14.5

Lotus 1-2-3 is available in DOS and Windows versions. Here's Release 5 for Windows.

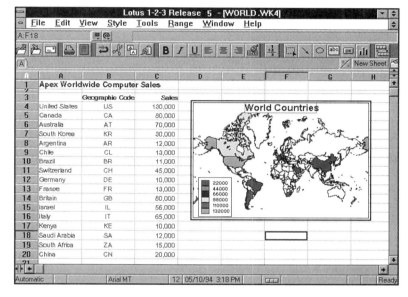

One interesting feature of Release 5 is that it allows you to view your data geographically—by state, region, or country, for example. You'll find maps of the United States, Canada, Mexico, Japan, and Europe, as well as 1,500 cities worldwide. You can even map your data by ZIP code.

Another handy feature is SmartMasters, a collection of ready-made templates for common spreadsheet tasks. A template is the framework for a particular task, such as an income statement or personal budget. The template contains all the formulas for the task, so that all you have to do is insert your specific numbers.

Microsoft Excel

Microsoft Corporation's Excel is full of significant features, such as true 3D worksheets, and "IntelliSense," the ability of the spreadsheet to sense what you want to do next. For example, Excel will automatically enter a closing parenthesis to your formula so you don't have to.

One of Excel's strengths lies in how well it works with other Microsoft programs, such as Word for Windows. Excel 5.0, for Windows 3.1, also provides useful what-if capabilities and includes Visual Basic for Applications, which is a programming language you can use to automate tasks and even build your own programs. Excel 7.0, the new Windows 95 version, adds even more formatting power and lets you get help by asking questions in plain English. The figures earlier in this chapter show Microsoft Excel in action.

Quattro Pro for Windows

Quattro Pro (a program that is now owned by networking giant Novell through its WordPerfect Corporation subsidiary) offers a little something for everyone, from the beginner to the power user. Toolbars make a wide variety of commands available with the click of a mouse.

Like 1-2-3's templates, Quattro Pro has **experts** that automate creating budgets, what-if analyses, and bullet charts. The Formula Composer shows complex spreadsheet macros as a tree structure. With this feature, you can easily handle the most difficult spreadsheet macros. Figure 14.6 shows Quattro Pro 6.0 running in Windows 3.1. If you use Windows 95, look for a newer version designed for your environment.

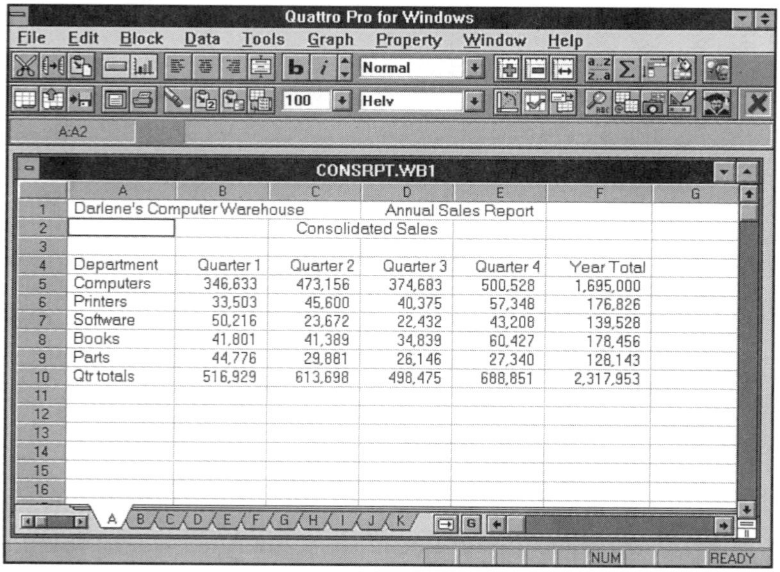

Fig. 14.6
Quattro Pro is one of the easiest spreadsheets for beginners to use.

Spreadsheets that work with DOS

Using a DOS spreadsheet could be like going down a dead-end street. As the world further embraces Microsoft Windows, there is likely to be little improvement to existing DOS products. Still, a DOS spreadsheet program can operate on older, slower computers in the office.

Lotus 1–2–3 for DOS

Lotus 1-2-3 Release 4.0 for DOS (see fig. 14.7) adds a souped-up interface and 3D spreadsheets to the old standard. It includes a spelling checker, and lets you assign names to ranges of cells. A status bar at the bottom of the screen shows at a glance the current cell's number format, named style, and font. You can then change those settings with a few clicks of the mouse.

Fig. 14.7
Lotus 1–2–3 for DOS has undergone its last face–lift.

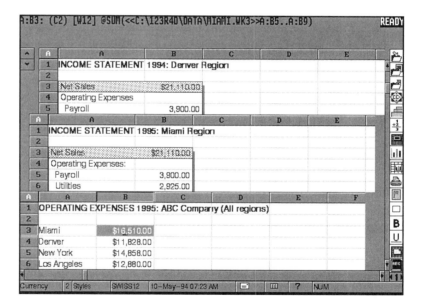

Release 4.0 for DOS is best for people who have a fast computer, 1.5M of memory, and the need for a 3D spreadsheet. If you lack any of these, you may be wise to stay with the older version of 1-2-3.

Quattro Pro for DOS

Quattro Pro for DOS 5.0 is an excellent value for a DOS spreadsheet. It includes a "slide-show" facility for showing charts one after another. It can also directly use database files from Paradox 4.0. Figure 14.8 shows Quattro Pro 5 for DOS.

Fig. 14.8
Quattro Pro offers multiple-window capability, even in the DOS version.

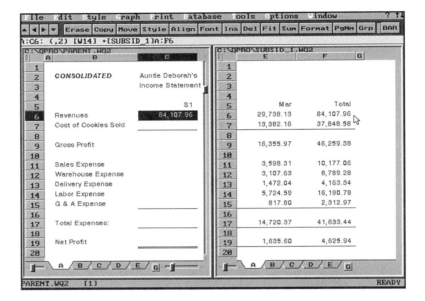

While Lotus 1-2-3 for DOS uses extended memory to handle large worksheets, Quattro Pro for DOS uses your hard disk for extra memory. As a result, the program runs okay with as little as 512K of memory and on the oldest PCs. However, the drawback for this backward compatibility is that calculations may take longer. Also, the size of your spreadsheets is limited. (However, most spreadsheets aren't very large, anyway.)

15

Databases Can Help Manage Your Lists

● In this chapter:

- A database is like an index card file

- What can I use a database for?

- Some of the more popular programs

If you've ever used an address book, you're already an expert at using databases . . . . ▶

Ask any computer guru what a database is, and you may hear that a database is "a collection of data structured and organized in a disciplined fashion so that quick access is possible to the information of most interest at the present time." Your response, of course, is "Could you translate that into English, please?" For the simplified version, read on!

You already know what a database is

You might not realize it, but you've no doubt used a database before. Very simply put, a **database** is a collection of information. For example, an address book is a database. Think of a database like this:

- You collect similar types of information from different sources (your friends' addresses and phone numbers).

- You store them all in one place (in an address book).

- You can look up a single **record** ("What's Uncle Bob's address in North Carolina?").

- You can **query** to find out various things that are similar about each record ("Make a list of friends who are in the sailing club.").

- You can perform **calculations** on the data ("What's the average age of the members of the sailing club?").

- You can prepare **reports** based on the data or calculations ("Print address labels for all my friends who have birthdays this month.").

What's so great about a computerized database?

There are several fantastic elements involved with computerized databases:

- *Maintenance.* Like life itself, a database is always changing. Just look at the scribbles in your own address book. If you keep your database on a computer, updating—or **maintenance**—is a snap!

- *Space.* A computerized database stores a lot of information in a small amount of space. You would need hundreds of address books to store the amount of information you can store in just one computer database. Also, the database doesn't take up any extra room on your desk.

- *Speed.* Think about how long it takes to flip pages and find an address. A computer database can find your addresses in a mere fraction of the time.

- *Efficiency.* If you have all your addresses stored in a database, you can print them on envelopes or mailing labels. You no longer have to type or hand-write each address on each envelope.

What can you store in a database?

Just about anything! You might keep financial data in a database and make decisions about how to manage and invest your money based on that data. Catalog all your favorite recipes, baseball cards, or CDs, tapes, and videos.

A business can keep virtually all the information it needs in a database. This information may include data about its customers, employees, salaries, and its product line.

Anatomy of a database

To make the database's job easier, it stores information in groups known as **records**. A single record might be all the information you have about your friend Jim: his wife's name, their anniversary, the names and birthdays of all their kids, where he works, and so on.

One record usually contains several types of information. Thus, records are divided into separate **fields**. Here are some typical field types:

- **Character fields** are typically used for names, addresses, and other alphabetic information.

- **Date fields** store information such as a birthday, anniversary, or purchase date.

- **Time fields**, such as 12:01 p.m., can be used to show exact times, such as what time a customer's order was delivered.

- **Logical fields** are for yes or no answers, such as "Anniversary card sent?" or "Shipped?".

- **Number fields** track numbers and money. For example, how many children each person in your address book has, or the total amount due on a customer's order.

- **Memo fields** might hold directions on how to get to a friend's house, special shipping instructions, or other extraneous information.

By breaking down all this information, the database can work more efficiently and answer your questions a lot faster. If you want to find the names of all your friends in California, the database only needs to search character fields that you have probably labeled "State." It doesn't have to read every single field in every single record to find the answers.

Relational versus flat-file databases

An address book is a good example of a **flat-file database**. All the information about a particular subject is stored in a single place.

A more sophisticated type of database is a **relational database**, which lets you store related information in several places and link the information together. Why do this? Because relational databases eliminate redundant information.

Imagine you have a database of patients in a doctor's office. This database may have fields for their names, addresses, and so on. You must also track each patient's visit. In a flat-file database, you would have to add several fields for each doctor visit—Visit 1, Visit 2, Visit 3, and so on. As the years go on, adding these new fields for subsequent visits would make the database ugly and unwieldy. Some patients would have only a few Visit fields, but the hypochondriacs would have scores of them.

In a relational database system, you create the following individual databases that contain only a few fields:

- Database 1 contains all the patients' names, addresses, and insurance information.

- Database 2 contains information about each office visit, such as the patient's name, the date, and the fee.

- Database 3 contains information about the doctor's diagnoses, such as the patient's name, symptoms, treatment, and prescriptions written.

If you link the patient database (Database 1) to the visit database (Database 2) through a common thread called a **key field** (in this case, the patient's name), you create an efficient relational database.

Once linked, all the related information is retrieved quickly and without much effort from you. For example, you could look up a patient's last visit in Database 2, then, using the key field to cross reference to information in Databases 1 and 2, you could prepare a bill for the insurance company that includes the diagnoses. (This actually takes longer to describe than to do.)

A relational database is very powerful, but it can be a lot harder for beginners to create.

What to look for in a database program

A variety of database programs are available. Here are some features to look for:

- The **search** feature helps you find the information you want without having to know fancy programming code. The best search is called **query-by-form** or **query-by-example**. This means you just enter in the field what you are looking for. For instance, if you wanted to search for your friends and relatives who live in New York, you would enter **NY** (the "example" of what you want to find) in the State field of a form very similar to the one you used to enter the data into the database.

- **Sorting** organizes information in the order you want. You should be able to sort in either **ascending order** (1 to 10, A to Z) or **descending order** (10 to 1, Z to A). Sorting by last name, state, birthday, and so on should be simple.

- **Data entry validation** and **default values** ensure that the data entered is correct. If your database knows what city is assigned to every ZIP code, you might have your database look at the ZIP code to make sure the city and state were typed correctly. If most of your customers are in the local area, you can enter the city, state, and telephone area code as default values to save typing those values when you enter data.

- **Importing data** and **exporting data** should be a snap. Lotus Approach, for example, can use files that are in Paradox, dBASE, or FoxPro format. If the information is easily exported, you can use it in other programs. For example, you could export an address list to your word processing program to use in creating a mass mailing.

- **Programming features** are found in some high-end, complicated databases. Others include **macro** capabilities that record your keystrokes for later playback to perform certain tasks. For example, if you routinely sort and print your address list by birthday, you can record the process once and then assign it to a particular keystroke to use in the future.

- Designing **forms** and **reports** should be easy. Most databases support various report formats.

The following sections describe some popular Windows-based databases so you can see some of the features of these packages.

Windows databases offer a good balance between ease of use and power. Windows-based databases provide a friendlier face to your data entry. Instead of typing Yes or No in a field, you can click a button. For multiple-choice fields, you can just click a choice from the list.

 TIP Many other databases than those described here are available. In addition to Access, for example, Microsoft offers FoxPro, a higher–end database for those with programming experience. Be sure to consult with your software dealer for details before choosing a database package.

Approach

Approach for Windows (see fig. 15.1) was one of the first easy-to-learn and easy-to-use relational database products available for Windows. Approach is perfect for business persons, consultants, and even developers who don't want to pull their hair out over a complicated programming language.

Fig. 15.1
This particular database form uses graphics and list boxes to make entering the data easier and faster.

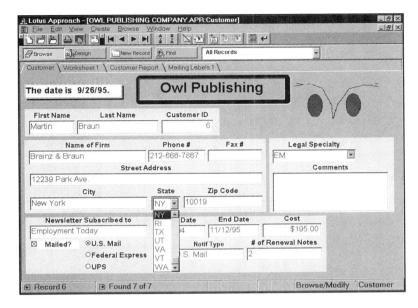

The icing on the cake is the addition of special reports for analyzing your data in a different light and a charting feature for viewing colorful graphs of your data. Even a spell checker is included. Approach is included in the Lotus SmartSuite suite of programs.

Access

Microsoft Access (see fig. 15.2) has burst onto the database scene within the last couple of years as a middle-of-the-road package. While Access qualifies as easy to use (especially for a relational database), it's still suitable for the database developer. In fact, Access includes a programming language—Microsoft's Visual Basic for Applications.

Access includes plenty of features that make it easy to use, such as wizards, cue cards, and other learning aids. By using **wizards**, you can automate many database tasks. For example, if you also have Word for Windows, the Report Wizard can run a mail-merge to generate instant form letters. Access is included in the Microsoft Office Professional software suite.

Fig. 15.2
One nice feature of Access is its capacity to create forms like this—easy to read and use.

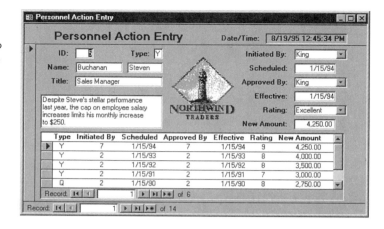

Paradox for Windows

Paradox for Windows from Borland International (see fig. 15.3) has always been a bruiser of a database. In the hands of an experienced developer, the program really packs a wallop. Recent versions of Paradox for Windows have become an all-around better product: more compact, more powerful, and easier to use.

Fig. 15.3
This view shows a table, a form, and a report—all containing related information.

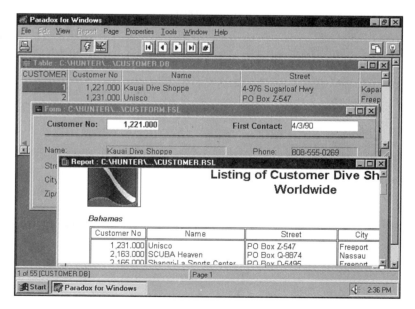

Like Access and Approach, Paradox includes interactive on-line helpers (Borland calls them **experts**). Experts contain more forms and reports than wizards, and they show you a preview of sample output so you'll have less backpedaling to do if you choose the wrong layout. Paradox for Windows is included in the Novell PerfectOffice Professional software suite.

dBASE

Visual dBASE for Windows from Borland International (see fig. 15.4) is intended for use by hard-core dBASE programmers. For years, dBASE has been one of the leading database development tools for DOS-based developers. Visual dBASE for Windows lets many of those programmers move easily to the Windows version.

Fig. 15.4

Keep in mind that dBASE for Windows is intended for people who know some programming. This figure shows the design view of a custom database form.

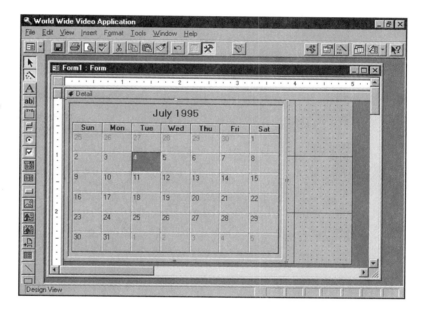

The prompt (a single dot) found in the DOS version is replaced in dBASE for Windows with the **Command window**, allowing commands to be executed on-the-fly. Although dBASE for Windows provides a complete set of tools for creating forms, queries, and menus, you can also work visually or directly with code.

TIP **dBASE III and dBASE IV were so popular that their file format**
(.DBF) is still used for sharing data between programs. If you keep your own
database but send it out to a service that does your mass mailings for you,
they'll probably want your files sent to them in DBF format—regardless of
what program you use.

FoxPro for Windows

Like dBASE, FoxPro is another major player from the days when DOS-based
databases were king. Now owned by the giant Microsoft, FoxPro has made
the transition to the Windows platform as well (see fig. 15.5). FoxPro is the
realm of serious programmers, but you may run into it if you use a database
application created and maintained by professional developers.

Fig. 15.5
FoxPro is a serious
programmer's tool with
versions for both DOS
and Windows.

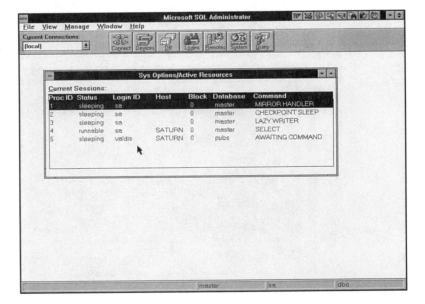

16

Integrated Packages and Suites

● In this chapter:

- What's a software suite?

- Suites aren't the same as integrated packages

- Which is better for me?

- Meet the top-selling software suites

Software suites started as a marketing gimmick. Microsoft put several programs into a single box, labeled it Microsoft Office, and sold it cheap . . . . ●▶

Imagine you're writing your quarterly budget report using your favorite word processor and need some figures from a spreadsheet file. No problem. You just click a button to jump over to the spreadsheet, grab the figures, and pop them into the word processor. Even better, you bring the numbers in as a linked table. That way, not only does the table look great, but when you update the numbers in the spreadsheet next week, your report will be updated automatically.

This typical scenario embodies the heart and soul of **software suites**, the bundles of vendors' top word processing, spreadsheet, and database programs sold for one rock-bottom price.

How "suite" it is

What's in a typical suite? A software suite will often include at least these programs:

- Word processing
- Spreadsheet
- Database
- Presentation graphics
- Personal information manager

You've already learned about word processors, spreadsheets, and databases in the preceding chapters. A brief overview of presentation graphics and personal information managers is included in the following sections.

How does a suite work?

The programs in suites transfer and share information because of a thing called **OLE** (pronounce it like a cheer at a bullfight). OLE is short for **object linking and embedding**. Basically, OLE lets you pull chunks of information or a whole file from one Windows program into another.

As nice as OLE sounds, not all Windows programs have it. Although Windows provides the tools to make OLE possible, it's up to each software company to make its software use OLE. Some do, some don't.

Most suite packages offer two options: a standard suite and a professional version. Typically, the professional version adds the database program and perhaps some other software to the standard set of programs, but costs more money. Your software dealer can help you decide which options you need.

Presentation graphics

Originally, "slide" shows were literally that—photographs were developed in a slide format, and flipped through one by one on a big screen. An alternative method was an overhead projector with images hand-drawn or transferred onto transparent film.

Now, the computer has replaced the camera and the graphics artist for creating slides and overheads—especially for business presentations. Presentation graphics programs let you use a computer to create **slides** (sometimes called **pages**) with text, graphs, or clip art images such as a company logo.

Using the computer to create presentation materials has two major advantages:

- It automates creating text and charting data, so that anyone can build attractive slides quickly and easily. Figure 16.1 shows an example of one presentation program, PowerPoint 7.0.

- It lets you view the slides in a variety of formats—printed out, on-screen, and more—so that you can use the slides for a variety of business purposes.

What can I do with a presentation graphics program?

Of course, you can use presentation graphics to create a traditional business presentation—a series of slides that you display to an audience with a slide projector—explaining the data on each slide as you go along. Fortunately, you're not limited to just that traditional format. Here are more ideas:

- Create printed reports, handouts, or notes to use while you're speaking.

- Traveling with a laptop computer? Use the laptop to display your sales presentation.

- Create self-running slide shows that can play on any computer—regardless of whether the presentation graphics program is installed on that computer.

- Explore multimedia by adding sound to a slide show.

 TIP   **Multimedia presentations generally require that your computer** have a sound card, CD–ROM drive, and speakers.

- Send your slide show to a company specializing in presentation graphics program output, and get 35mm slides or color transparencies made.

Fig. 16.1
Presentation graphics programs like PowerPoint 7.0 let you create slides with text, charts, and graphics.

This slide has a large heading to explain what it's about.

You can even add graphics to make your slide show more interesting!

The software did most of the work involved in charting this data.

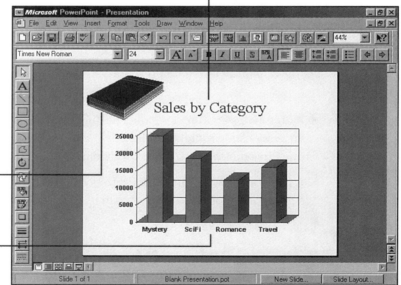

How to start your own slide show

When you start a slide show file in a presentation graphics program, you pick a "look" for all the slides by choosing a **design template** (or **master**) for the slide show. The design template sets the default colors, margins, and so on for all the slides you create. This saves you from having to set the colors and other settings each time you create a slide. Most presentation programs come with dozens of different design templates (see fig. 16.2), to ensure that no matter what you're showing on the various slides in your show, all the slides look consistent. You look like a pro without even trying!

Fig. 16.2
Most programs offer many "looks." Here, PowerPoint lets you preview a design template before picking it.

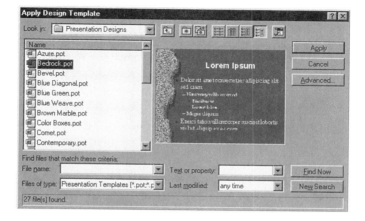

I'm not an artist; how do I design a slide?

A slide can hold text, data, and graphics in different combinations. Each combination of elements is called a **slide layout**. Along with design templates, each presentation graphics program comes with several preformatted slide layouts. You simply choose the one you want, and the program displays your new slide, complete with **placeholders** for various elements, as you can see in figure 16.3.

Fig. 16.3
Placeholders let you add text and data easily. Here, the slide has predefined areas for a title, bulleted list, and clip art.

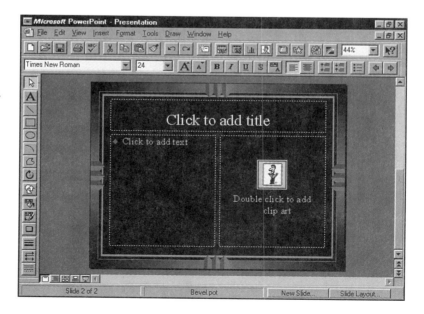

Q&A   *What if I want to do something totally unique? Am I stuck with one of the prefab layouts?*

No. Preformatted slides are only there to serve as shortcuts when you're doing routine stuff. You can create a slide from scratch by making areas for text, graphs, and clip art wherever you want them.

Once you pick a layout, you can add your own text, charts, and clip art to your slide. With presentation graphics programs, you don't have to do anything by hand. Creating a graph, for instance, takes about three steps in most programs:

1 Activate (or create) the placeholder for your graph.

2 Choose the type of graph you want (see fig. 16.4).

3 Fill in the data you want in a form that resembles a mini-spreadsheet, and then return to the slide. The presentation graphics program will generate the chart for you.

Fig. 16.4
You can choose a new look for your chart at any time—while you're creating it, or any time later.

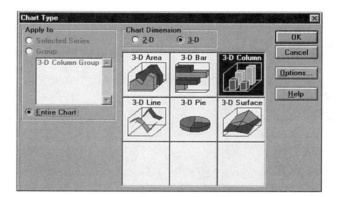

Creating slides that contain tables, organization charts, and clip art is just as simple as creating charts.

Now view the whole slide show

Most presentation graphics programs let you choose from several different working views:

- **Slide Editor view** lets you see one full slide at a time. Figure 16.1 earlier in this chapter illustrates this view. This is the view you'll use for editing details and formatting the slides.

- **Outline view** lets you view your slide show as an outline of the slide text (see fig. 16.5).

Fig. 16.5
Outlining a slide show is just like working in Outline view for a word processor. This is PowerPoint's Outline view.

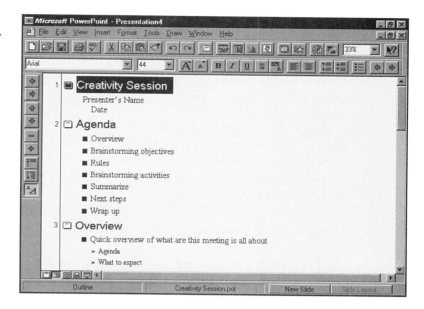

- Most presentation programs offer a view of the slide show with a **thumbnail** picture of each slide (see fig. 16.6). This view lets you reorder slides (often just by dragging one to a new location).

Fig. 16.6
Use this view to drag slides to a new position in the slide show.

Thumbnails show different slide layouts. Click the one you want, then click OK.

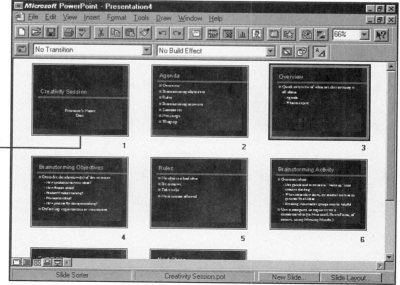

Print, make slides, and create screen shows

Most programs let you print the show slide-by-slide with each slide at full-page size. In addition, you can print each slide with a list of speaker notes or print reduced-size slides for use as audience handouts. If you need traditional 35mm slides or overheads, you can send your presentation file to a **service bureau** that will use specialized equipment to "print" your slides to that format.

More and more, business presentations are viewed directly on computer screens instead of being projected from slides or overheads. Most of the popular presentation graphics programs support this option—and even let you add sound and video clips to your presentation to create a multimedia production. All the major presentation graphics programs also include small viewer programs that let you view, but not edit or create, your slide show.

A look at the choices in presentation graphics

Microsoft Office, Lotus SmartSuite, and Novell PerfectOffice suites each include a major presentation graphics program (PowerPoint, Freelance, and Presentations, respectively). If you're using a suite of Windows programs, you should probably stick with the presentation graphics program that's part of that suite. However, all three of the programs are also available separately and deserve consideration on their own merits.

You might also want to consider these other presentation graphics programs:

- *Harvard Graphics.* Harvard Graphics, from Software Publishing, was the number one DOS-based presentation graphics program. The Windows version doesn't enjoy similar prominence, largely because it's not part of a major software suite. However, it's a very competent program and you should consider it—especially if you or your company used the DOS version and have a large collection of Harvard Graphics presentation files that you may want to reuse.

- *Adobe Persuasion.* This is another very competent presentation graphics program. It tends to be favored by graphics professionals familiar with PageMaker, PhotoShop, and other graphics programs from Adobe.

The same program is also available for Macintosh computer users, which is an advantage for companies that use both computer platforms.

- *Corel PRESENTS.* This is a new entry for Windows 95 from Corel Corporation. Its strength lies in its integration with the graphics programs of the CorelDRAW! suite of graphics programs (covered at the end of this chapter), instead of integration with the word processor and spreadsheet of an office suite. You get tons of fonts and clip art, plus the power of CorelDRAW! for editing your graphics.

Personal information managers

Being organized can't guarantee you a promotion, but getting your act together certainly can't hurt you in your climb toward the big bucks. Better organizing and prioritizing of your work improve your personal productivity and let you get more done in less time. What a concept—more work in less time! If your organizational skills and memory could use a boost, you can benefit from using a **personal information manager**, or **PIM**.

PIMs are programs that act much like your very own personal assistant. Personal information managers are intended to prevent you from overlooking important tasks, meetings, commitments, and golf outings. They help you keep track of appointments, to-do lists, and information on your contacts.

Using an information manager can help organize much more than just tasks and meetings. For example, information managers can:

- List all the phone calls you need to complete today.

- Check coworkers' schedules for conflicts and automatically set up meetings that everyone can attend.

- Prioritize your daily tasks so that the most important work gets done first.

- Track completed work, so you can tell someone exactly when you finished a certain report.

- Let you check your workload for the day, week, or month at a glance.

The major software suites all include a personal information manager. Most of those PIMs also support some **groupware** features as well, meaning that your PIM can communicate with the PIMs of coworkers on the same network in order to coordinate scheduling meetings and facilitate other communications and group activities.

Picking a PIM

Ideally, you'd choose a PIM based on which program meets your own needs and matches your own working style. If you work independently, that's exactly what you should do. If you use a software suite, start your search with the PIM that's included with the suite. But be sure to consider other programs as well.

Here's a list of some of the more popular personal information managers:

- *Schedule+*. Included with Windows for Workgroups and the Microsoft Office suite (version 7.0).

- *Lotus Organizer*. This one is in the Lotus SmartSuite, and it's also sold separately.

- *GroupWise*. The resident PIM in Novell PerfectOffice.

- *Act!*. A very popular PIM optimized for managing sales contacts. It's available for DOS, Windows, and Macintosh.

- *On Time*. This popular PIM is also available in both DOS and Windows versions.

- *Ascend*. This PIM is a computerized version of the Franklin Day Planner.

 TIP **If you are part of a networked workgroup and want to take** advantage of the group scheduling features offered by a PIM, you won't have much choice of which PIM you use. Generally, everyone has to use the same PIM for the groupware features to work.

Get organized with Organizer

Suppose you have a meeting with your boss every Thursday at 10 a.m. You're such a busy and dedicated worker (naturally) that you occasionally forget the time and arrive at your boss's office late—or worse, not at all. If these meetings were entered in a PIM such as Lotus Organizer, your computer would beep and flash a message on your screen telling you when it's time to leave—thus preventing CLMs (career-limiting maneuvers) like skipping meetings.

Organizer is great for scheduling meetings (you can schedule a recurring meeting once and Organizer takes care of filling in all the future dates!), maintaining to-do lists, and keeping a name and address list. By far, Organizer's greatest strength is that it's easy to understand and use. It looks and acts just like organizer notebooks you're used to seeing (see fig. 16.7).

Fig. 16.7
Organizer looks just like a normal organizer notebook—and you'll never forget your pen.

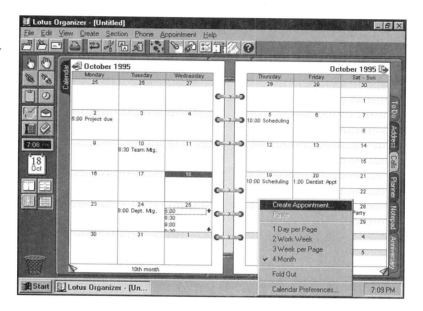

Schedule a meeting with Schedule+

You can turn a bunch of independent PIMs into a program that can manage the resources of dozens, maybe even hundreds, of people and projects. The first step is to get everybody connected somehow. That requires the business to install a network and get everyone hooked up to that network.

Then, suppose you want to schedule a meeting with several coworkers. Normally, you'd pick up the phone and start calling everyone, trying to find a mutually agreeable time to meet. In many cases, you spend more time setting up a meeting like this with multiple participants than you spend at the meeting itself.

With a product like Microsoft Schedule+ (shown in fig. 16.8), everyone's schedules are available on the network for the computer to check. Instead of calling everyone, you tell the software the names of the people with whom you want to meet, and it tells you the earliest available time when everyone is free to attend. If that time is okay with you, the program automatically puts your meeting on everyone else's schedule.

Fig. 16.8
The Meeting Wizard in Schedule+ handles the details of scheduling a meeting with several attendees.

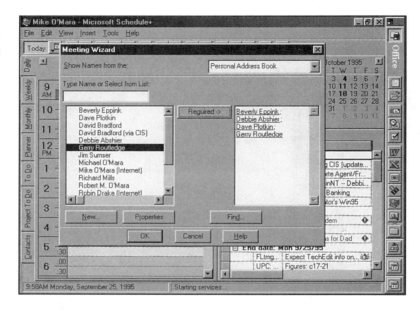

A PIM for keeping in touch: ACT!

ACT! is a great PIM for people who need to keep in touch with a large number of people. ACT! isn't part of a software suite, but its many built-in features make it especially useful for people in sales, public relations, or market research:

- ACT! can store an unlimited number of contacts (there is a practical limit, however, because your computer doesn't have endless resources) and lets you track up to 70 different items per person or company. Figure 16.9 shows a typical contact record.

- ACT! can schedule and prioritize as many calls, to-do items, and meetings as you care to enter.

- ACT!'s word processor is perfect for short business letters. The word processor works with the database, so mass mailings are a breeze.

- A report generator lets you create any kind of report you like—from a "what I did this week" report for your boss, to a "whose birthdays are coming up this month" list for yourself!

Fig. 16.9
Act! lets you keep track of everything you need to know about each contact.

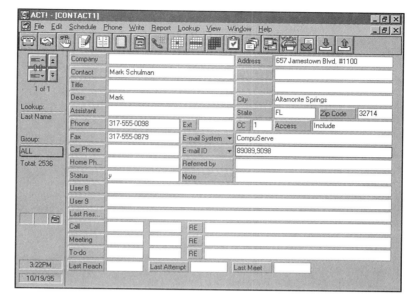

Integrated packages

Integrated packages and software suites are kind of the same idea, but the products are quite different.

A software suite is a collection of top-of-the-line application programs from the same vendor. An **integrated package**, on the other hand, is a single program with modules to do things such as word processing, spreadsheets, graphics, database management, and/or communications (see fig. 16.10).

Integrated packages usually don't have as many features as their suite cousins. On the other hand, the integrated package can be a lot cheaper than the suite. Think of it as the difference between buying a Honda Civic and an Acura Legend. Both are reliable transportation, but the Acura version (like a suite) offers more power and more bells and whistles. If those features are important to you, you pay more to get them.

TIP Software suites are huge compared to integrated software packages, which typically require only about 5M of disk space. For a suite, be prepared to sacrifice up to 80M of hard disk space.

Fig. 16.10
If you don't need all the power of the applications in a major software suite, an integrated package such as Microsoft Works offers a simpler and less expensive alternative.

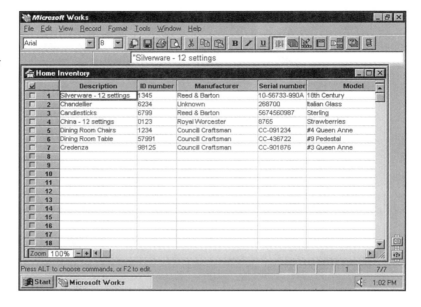

Should I buy a suite or an integrated package?

Integrated software and suites are both excellent bargains. In fact, suites may turn out to be the software deal of the century. For the price of a stand-alone package, you can own a collection of three or more powerhouse programs, all conveniently supported by the same vendor. Entire suites can often be bought for under $300 through special "competitive upgrade" programs.

Some vendors, such as Lotus, even offer "mini-suites." Instead of combining all five of their top-selling programs, you can buy Lotus 1-2-3 and Approach bundled together for less than $150.

The following sections give you some pros and cons on buying suites versus integrated packages. Both versions have advantages and disadvantages.

 TIP **Many computer dealers offer an integrated package or a suite as** part of the deal for the equipment. Don't let the offer make the decision for you, or you may regret it! If all you need is to write a few letters and memos, do a couple of spreadsheets, and maybe draw something once in a while with a graphics package, an integrated package should suit you nicely. If you want to share files with clients, do multicolumn statistical analysis with graphs, or produce presentations and newsletters, a suite is your best bet.

A suite is a good bargain

With a suite, you own a group of programs that have been designed to work together in the same way. The common design makes you feel at home among multiple, complex programs. You can work smarter and more efficiently. Better yet, all the software you'll be using is sold by the same vendor, so you're able to direct all your product questions to one company.

If you opt for the security of a suite such as Lotus SmartSuite or Microsoft Office, though, this convenience comes at a price. If you buy a software program outside the suite, you do so at an additional cost. Not only do you pay for the extra software, but you're generally on your own when it comes to getting all the programs to work well together.

There are some notable exceptions to this last point, however. Microsoft Office has spawned an aftermarket in add-on software specifically designed to extend the capabilities of the Office suite. Several programs, such as Visio (a popular drawing program), are available in "Office-compatible" versions. The Lotus SmartSuite is designed to connect with the famous electronic mail program cc:Mail and powerful groupware product Lotus Notes.

 TIP **If you buy a suite, you may also have to invest in more memory.** Most suites require at least 8M of memory—since more than one component may have to be open simultaneously. Many businesses and homes still use computers with only 4M.

An integrated package may be a better choice for you

If your needs are modest, you could buy an integrated software program, such as Microsoft Works for Windows 4.0. This inexpensive (less than $100) program provides word processing, database, spreadsheet, and communications software in one package. It doesn't offer all the features of high-end suites, but Works' components share a common home screen, making it easy to move data among the applications. One-step printing of envelopes and labels is included. For some home users and small-business owners who will be using a computer occasionally, it is an ideal package.

Popular integrated packages include the following:

- Microsoft Works

- GeoWorks Pro

- ClarisWorks

What suites are available?

Three major companies offer general office software suites: Microsoft, Lotus Development, and Novell. All of these suites include word processors, databases, spreadsheets, presentation graphics, and personal information managers. But the concept of bundling several software applications together for one price is catching on. For instance, Corel offers a suite of graphics programs.

Microsoft Office

Microsoft started the suite boom with its popular Office suite (see fig. 16.11). Since then, Microsoft has stepped up its intensity by incorporating Word, Access, PowerPoint, Excel, and Schedule+ into a competitively priced Microsoft Office suite of programs.

Microsoft Office includes the following programs:

- Word for Windows (word processor)

- Excel (spreadsheet)

- PowerPoint (presentation graphics)

- Schedule+ (personal information manager)

- Office Binder (document management utility)

- Access (database)—in the "professional" version

One nice feature of this suite is Microsoft's "IntelliSense" technology, which recognizes what you want to accomplish next and adapts to the way you work. Toolbars, menus, dialog boxes, and screen layouts are consistent in all the programs. Most of the menus are identical among Excel, Word, and PowerPoint. Because of this common look, common tasks are faster and easier to complete.

The Microsoft Office application menus and toolbars
are consistent among the different programs.
Note the toolbar on the right side of the screen.

Fig. 16.11
The great thing about
suites is that you can
work in one program
and use the info from
another. Here, the user
has stuck an Excel
spreadsheet into a
Word document.

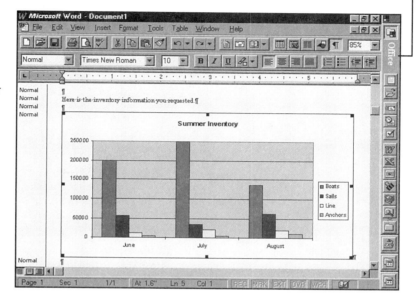

Lotus SmartSuite

The Lotus SmartSuite has evolved from a collection of dissimilar programs
to a truly integrated suite. With Lotus 1-2-3, Word Pro, and Approach as core
programs, SmartSuite is poised to compete with big-boy Microsoft Office.
SmartSuite's strength is that it's great in a client/server environment.

 Plain English, please!

> **Client/server** refers to a computing system that splits the workload
> between PCs and one or more larger computers on a network. It's like a
> restaurant where the waiter (server) takes your order for a hamburger, goes
> to the kitchen, and comes back with some raw meat and a bun. You (the
> client) get to cook the burger at your table and add your favorite condi-
> ments. Although it sounds like more work, the service is faster and the food
> (data) is cooked to your liking. Also, the giant, expensive stove (the main-
> frame computer) in the kitchen can be replaced by lots of inexpensive little
> grills (desktop PCs). Computer specialists refer to this as **distributed
> processing**. 99

The major improvement in the latest version of SmartSuite is its common design (see fig. 16.12). It's now more consistent with 1-2-3 and Approach, with a convenient SmartCenter icon box for switching among the three. You can just click the icon for the program you want to go to.

Lotus SmartSuite includes the following programs:

- Word Pro (word processor)

- 1-2-3 for Windows (spreadsheet)

- Freelance (presentation graphics)

- Organizer (personal information manager)

- ScreenCam (screen and sound capture utility)

- Approach (database)—in the "professional" version

Online Help Cards help you figure out how to do stuff with more than one of the SmartSuite programs. Bubble help, which debuted in Organizer, now appears in all the SmartSuite applications. Place the pointer on a toolbar icon, and a balloon tells you what the icon does. Sure beats clicking it and maybe sending yourself into limbo!

Fig. 16.12
This figure shows some of the powerful features available with SmartSuite.

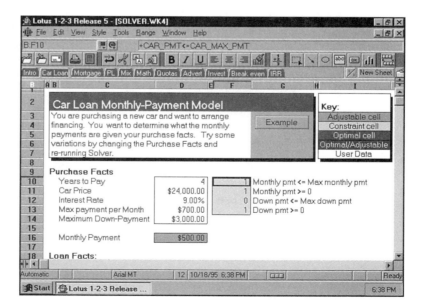

Novell PerfectOffice

Novell has come up with the perfect name for its office suite. The PerfectOffice bundle differs significantly from its predecessor Borland Office, which included WordPerfect, Quattro Pro, and Paradox.

PerfectOffice includes the following programs:

- WordPerfect (word processor)
- Quattro Pro (spreadsheet)
- Presentations (presentation graphics)
- GroupWise (e-mail, calendaring, and scheduling client)
- Envoy (electronic publisher and viewer)
- InfoCentral (personal information manager)
- Paradox (database)—in the "professional" version
- Visual AppBuilder (visual application development program)— in the "professional" version

All the programs in PerfectOffice look pretty much alike, have the same tools, and use a customizable toolbar for starting and switching among programs. Part of the strength of the Novell PerfectOffice suite is its integration with Novell's networking products.

One very useful part of this suite is PerfectSense Technology, a feature similar to Microsoft's AutoCorrect. PerfectSense understands the meaning and context of words, and can therefore correct your grammar and spelling errors.

Also, QuickTasks automate many simple and complex tasks for you from the desktop. You don't even have to know which programs you need to open.

CorelDRAW!: a different kind of suite

Corel in Canada has long been a leader in the graphics field. Their CorelDRAW! program has evolved from being the leading drawing program for Windows users to being a suite of tools geared towards making your PC a fully featured graphics studio. The latest version of the CorelDRAW! suite (see fig. 16.13) includes the following features and programs:

- CorelDRAW! (a powerful and full-featured drawing program)

- Corel PHOTO-PAINT (a program for retouching, editing, and manipulating photographs and scanned images)

- Corel PRESENTS (presentation graphics program)

- CorelDREAM 3D (three-dimensional rendering software)

- A huge selection of clip art and fonts

- Utilities for multimedia file management, screen capture, a utility to convert scanned images into graphic drawings or text, and more

Corel takes the unusual approach of continuing to sell and support older versions of its software. Instead of each new version superseding the previous version, the new version takes over as the top-of-the-line package with all the latest features for the most demanding users. But older versions continue to be sold at a somewhat reduced price for users who don't need all the bells and whistles.

Fig. 16.13
CorelDRAW! is the namesake program of a suite of graphics software that also includes an extensive clip art and font collection.

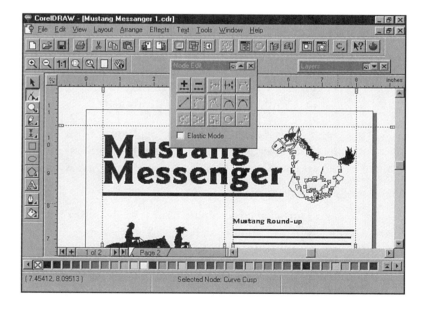

The result is that you can pick how much power you need—and how much you want to pay. As this book goes to press, CorelDRAW! 3.0 is still available and sells for less than $150. It includes the basic drawing program, a simpler version of the PHOTO-PAINT program, rudimentary charting and screen show programs, some utilities, and a nice assortment of clip art and fonts. Versions 4 and 5 are also available at increasing prices for progressively more features, more clip art, and better quality fonts. The latest version—6.0—is designed for Windows 95 and adds more new features to the drawing and paint programs, 3D rendering and animation, and the new presentation graphics program.

17

Games and Family Software

● **In this chapter:**

- **Who's playing games with these CDs?**

- **Take time to relax with computer games**

- **Learning can be fun with Edutainment software**

- **A world of data on a disk**

- **Let your computer help you pay the bills!**

Enough of the serious stuff—in this chapter, you'll see how computers can also be fun! . . . . ⟩

Word processing, spreadsheets, databases, software suites—
these software categories cover the routine uses most
people have for their PC. But there are other software categories that may
have more impact on you and your family. You can also use your computer to
have fun, learn new things, and even manage the family finances.

For the greatest selection, you need a CD-ROM

This chapter is about family software. However, by extension, it's also about
software on CD-ROM (pronounce it *seedy-rahm*). Why? Because, increas-
ingly, the most popular family software (especially games and reference
materials) comes on CD-ROM instead of floppy disks.

The **CD-ROM drive** provides a way to distribute hundreds of megabytes
(about 600M) of information on a small silver disc. That's about equal to
240,000 pages of text. With such storage capabilities, owning a CD-ROM drive
in the 1990s will soon be as necessary as owning a hard drive was in the
1980s.

 Plain English, please!

> If you want to impress friends, remember that CD-ROM stands for **com-
> pact disc, read-only memory**. By the way, the word disk becomes *disc*
> when referring to CD-ROMs. Floppy disks and hard disks also contain discs—
> round platters made of some kind of material that can store data.

Although CD-ROMs look remarkably like audio CDs, you can't just hook your
audio CD player to your computer. However, you can play your audio CDs on
your computer. (Strange, huh? Just don't try to listen to your Microsoft Office
CD-ROM in your stereo—unless you enjoy listening to spreadsheets singing!)

The read-only portion of the CD-ROM name means that you can load information from the CD, but you can't save information to the disc. See Chapter 20
for information about selecting and using a CD-ROM drive and the sound
card that comes with it when you make your PC "multimedia compatible."

TIP **Although a CD-ROM is a self-contained disc, its installation** program may still place some files on your hard disk. Why? Your hard disk is much faster than a CD-ROM drive. The program would run very slowly if you ran it from your CD-ROM drive.

Simpler software installation

Installing large programs from a CD-ROM is easy. A single disc provides enough room for an entire software program. You can slip in a CD-ROM and make installation a breeze instead of inserting disk after floppy disk.

Perhaps CD-ROMs will even save some trees. Lotus 1-2-3 is provided on CD-ROM. No paper documentation or disks are included. The program and documentation, except for a tiny startup booklet, are all on a single CD-ROM. The printed documentation is available for an additional $59.

More and more information at your fingertips

Software makers often use the leftover room on a CD-ROM to add tutorials for the new software program, complete with animation, sound effects, and graphics. A CD-ROM edition of Microsoft Publisher 2.0, for example, provides additional desktop publishing templates, artwork, and a tutorial.

Having fun with your PC

Your PC can be a super game machine. All you need is the right software. There's a tremendous selection of games available.

A few very simple games come with Windows: Solitaire, Minesweeper, and Hearts. They can provide a brief diversion from more serious pursuits, but they don't begin to demonstrate the diversity of the games available for your PC. Here's a short list of popular games:

- Microsoft Golf
- Dynamix's Stellar 7
- LucasArts' Loom
- ChessMaster 3000
- King's Quest VI

- Microsoft Flight Simulator

- Sim City 2000

- Falcon

Games, which require both excellent graphics and sounds, are best suited for CD-ROM. Game makers can add more and more detail, sound, and musical scores with little regard to space. Games such as Broderbund Software's Myst, with its hauntingly beautiful graphic images and multi-level strategies, are provided only on CD-ROM.

Two of the most popular games on CD-ROM are DOOM and DOOM II: Hell on Earth. The DOOM games are perhaps the most realistic, addicting, and frightening games ever. They've been so popular that an entire industry of DOOM add-ins has sprung up. For example, you can add your own levels to the game. While DOOM is virtually a free game—about $7 in the store (but you'll pay an additional $40 for two more levels)—DOOM II: Hell on Earth is a package for which you'll have to pay the full price (see fig. 17.1).

Fig. 17.1
DOOM, one of the more popular games available on CD-ROM, provides an eerie set of corridors and enemies that you must escape from.

 TIP **You can purchase CD-ROMs with sneak peeks of games for as** little as $5. Companies such as Electronic Arts, Microsoft, and Software Toolworks have sold hundreds of thousands of CD-ROM "samplers"— inexpensive demos of games that let you "test drive" a game before plunking down $49.95 or more for the full version.

Your PC as an electronic tutor

In addition to playing games on your PC, you can also use it for something productive—like sharpening your skills and furthering your education. If you're looking for serious educational software, you can find plenty of it. There are computer-based tutorials on all kinds of subjects. You can learn about other computer software, practice taking college entrance exams such as the SAT, or study for professional certification.

But learning doesn't have to be dull. In fact, software developers have combined educational qualities with entertainment value to create a new software category called **Edutainment**. As a result, learning can be fun!

Here's a brief sampling of some popular edutainment titles:

- *Math Blaster.* Practice math while shooting down aliens.

- *The Magic School Bus Explores the Human Body.* A fanciful cartoon adventure that teaches anatomy.

- *Reader Rabbit.* A vocabulary-building game for beginning readers.

- *Creative Writer and Fine Artist.* Kid-friendly cartoons encourage creativity (see fig. 17.2).

- *Where in the World is Carmen Sandiego?* Is it a game show, a spy adventure, or a geography lesson? Who cares; it's fun! Play along with your kids.

A library on a disc

A single CD-ROM can easily hold the contents of an entire encyclopedia set. For a comprehensive encyclopedia, consider the *New Grolier Multimedia Encyclopedia*. This CD-ROM is based on the 21-volume *Academic American Encyclopedia* and includes 10 million words, 4,000 photos and illustrations, 53 video clips, and 300 maps.

An electronic encyclopedia can make information come to life in a way that traditional printed books can't. For instance, you might look up Martin Luther King, and in addition to the usual facts and background information, be able to hear a recording of his famous "I have a dream" speech.

While an entire encyclopedia of hardback books costs over $1,500, you can purchase electronic versions for less than $150. For that price, you can afford to update your encyclopedia every year. Figure 17.3 shows another of the popular CD-ROM encyclopedias.

Fig. 17.2
Cartoon characters in Microsoft Creative Writer and Fine Artist encourage kids to use their creativity to write stories and draw pictures.

Fig. 17.3
Another popular encyclopedia is the Software Toolworks Multimedia Encyclopedia. Here you see a photograph from the Civil War entries.

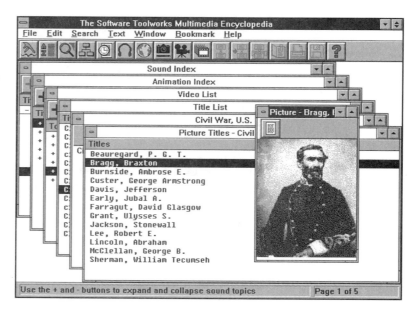

TIP **You might have seen the popular Microsoft Encarta Multimedia** Encyclopedia CD-ROM in your local software stores. Although it's not quite as complete as Grolier's, Encarta offers much more multimedia dazzle. It's a good choice if your PC is equipped to let you fully appreciate the multimedia effects.

Another popular CD-ROM reference work is Microsoft Bookshelf. This multimedia reference includes:

- Dictionary
- Book of quotations
- Thesaurus
- Chronology of world events
- Encyclopedia
- World atlas
- Almanac

Bookshelf is updated yearly by Microsoft, so you are assured of using the most current references available. Bookshelf's QuickShelf feature puts volumes of data at your fingertips. When you're creating a document in a Windows word processor and you need to flesh out an idea, highlight the word you're stuck on and click the QuickShelf tool on the toolbar. From there, you can access any work in the library for more information about the highlighted word. And since all seven volumes are linked, you can search all of them for citations—any of which may have accompanying photos, sound, or video clips. For all that, Microsoft Bookshelf requires just 2M of hard disk space—slightly more than a single floppy disk contains!

What Microsoft Bookshelf is to the consummate writer, the *Allegro Reference Series Business Library, Vol. 1*, is to entrepreneurs. This collection of 12 books provides answers to questions such as: What are the principles of a successful telemarketing campaign? What's the tax benefit of real-estate trusts? This collection includes superb books on marketing, finance, real estate, international business, selling your product, and promoting your own career.

Need a handy reference on public relations? The *Public Relations Handbook* from Compton's NewMedia is filled with general advice, along with specific examples that can be adapted easily to your own PR events. The Windows interface makes it simple to get all you need to hold down the fort until the spin doctor arrives.

Another type of CD-ROM package that you might find useful in the office for marketing is one of the many phone directory applications. Pro CD's ProPhone line is such a tool, providing you with company names, phone numbers, mailing addresses, sizes, and numbers of employees—great for putting together mailing lists. Its $299 SelectPhone is a four-CD-ROM set providing over one million U.S. residential and business listings, along with 2,700 SIC code headings.

There are other, more specialized CD-ROM references available and more coming out every day. For instance, if you need to stay current on the computer industry, you can subscribe to Computer Select, a service from computer magazine publisher Ziff-Davis. You get full text or abstracts of articles in 170 publications, all indexed for instant searches.

Graphics and photos on CD-ROM

You can liven up your presentations and newsletters with digitized photos and artwork on CD-ROM. Using a Kodak Photo CD-compatible drive (most CD-ROM drives are), you can place images in any document.

There are two types of photography you can use: **stock photography** and **clip images**. Stock photography requires you to pay fees for using each image. Clip images, on the other hand, are the perfect alternative. Unlike stock photos, which you can only use once, clip images are yours to use however and as often as you'd like. Both types of photography can be found through the same sources—retail software stores or mail-order catalogs.

Clip image libraries, such as Corel's Professional Photos CD-ROM ($49.95 each) and Digital Stock Professional's images ($249 each), are relatively inexpensive sources of high-quality images. Often, you can find them at even lower prices as part of a special offer, or even get some free as a bonus or incentive for buying other products.

You can even get your family photos recorded on CD-ROM. You shoot your photos normally on 35mm film, then take the film to a specially equipped lab for processing. You get back your normal prints or slides and also a CD-ROM containing your snapshots converted to digital files—ready to add to the family newsletter you're publishing on your PC.

Personal finance software

Quit punching numbers on a pocket calculator, trying to balance your family checkbook. Let your computer do the dreaded task for you. All you need is some inexpensive (about $50) software to put the power of your computer to work straightening out your family finances.

Programs such as market leader Quicken from Intuit (see fig. 17.4) make the job easy. You don't have to get involved in complicated bookkeeping procedures or obscure accounting lingo. Instead, you work with on-screen versions of your familiar checks and check register. You can enter information with a few keystrokes and have the program print checks for you.

Fig. 17.4

No confusing debits and credits here. If you can use your paper checkbook, you can use personal finance software.

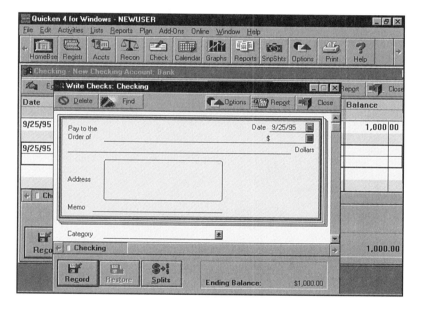

Entering your information into a personal finance manager takes some time. But once the data is entered, you can quickly and easily use that information to develop an instant picture of your family's financial health. Reconciling a bank statement is a breeze. Plus, you can develop a budget, predict cash flow, analyze investments, compare loans, and develop a retirement plan.

Soon, personal finance software such as Quicken and Microsoft Money will go beyond recording the checks you write to replace the teller and ATM card as your primary mode of interacting with your bank. On-line banking is moving out of the experimental stage and into the mainstream. When it becomes fully operational, you'll be able to check your balance, transfer funds, pay bills, apply for loans, and more—all from your computer keyboard.

18

Communications Packages

● **In this chapter:**

- **Do I really need a communications package?**

- **What communications software can do for you**

- **I need a communications software relevant to what I do**

- **What's an on-line session like?**

Without communications software, about all you can do with your modem is dial; you can't send messages or download or do anything to promote world peace . . . . ▶

One of the cool things you can do with your computer is to connect to the outside world through normal telephone lines. A device called a **modem** (more on modems in Chapter 21) serves as your passport to the world of on-line communication, but the passport isn't the trip, is it? You see, your modem only connects you to other computers—it doesn't help you do anything once you get connected.

To do anything on-line, you need special **communications software**. Communications software gives the directions that your modem needs to properly connect to other computers.

 TIP **With the right software, you can use your modem to send faxes** to and receive faxes from other computers and fax machines.

Communications software controls your modem

Communications software issues strings of commands to your modem. These commands instruct your modem to do various things at various times. Basic communications programs do at least these things:

- Pick up the phone line and get a dial tone
- Dial the number
- Connect when it hears a tone from the other computer
- Display a screen of information from the other computer
- Relay signals and instructions from your computer to the other computer
- Download files from the other computer to your computer
- Send and retrieve messages and e-mail between the two computers

Plain English, please!
When you copy a file from another computer to your personal computer, that's called **downloading** the file to your PC. When you send a file, on the other hand, it's called **uploading**.

More advanced communications software allows you to save electronic **address books** with frequently dialed phone numbers. With some software, you can even automatically log on to other computers through **scripts** that contain the necessary commands.

 CAUTION   **When you download program files (that is, files with EXE or COM** extensions) from other computers, you run the risk of infecting your computer with a computer virus.

How to choose the right communications software

There are a variety of communications programs on the market. They all do pretty much what you need them to do—some just pay more attention to certain types of tasks. To make things simple, let's just take a look at three core programs.

 TIP   **Many of the major on-line services, such as America Online and** Microsoft Network, require you to use specialized software to access their services. General-purpose communications software such as that described in this chapter won't work.

Simple (and free): HyperTerminal

HyperTerminal (see fig. 18.1) is the communications package included with Microsoft Windows 95. It's a fairly easy program to use, in part because it doesn't have a lot of advanced features.

If you don't do a lot of on-line communicating, you can probably get by with HyperTerminal. HyperTerminal isn't a very robust package, but the price is right! If you plan to participate in on-line cruising more than once a week, however, you probably want to invest in a more fully-featured program.

Fig. 18.1
Simple communications software you already own—Windows HyperTerminal.

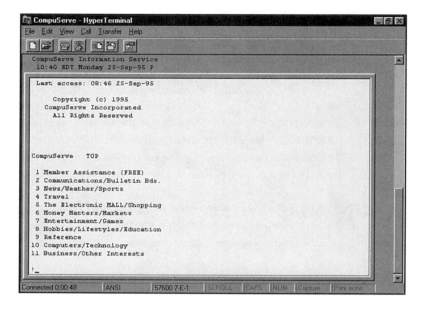

An all-around performer: ProComm Plus for Windows

ProComm Plus is a program that's been around a long, long time. Consequently, the program has evolved into what may be the best all-around communications program available. Here's what you get with ProComm Plus:

- Basic on-line communications

- Automated logon scripts

- Multiple dialing directories (address books)

- Basic fax operation

ProComm Plus is a good program to use for most basic on-line communications (see fig. 18.2). It's easy to use, yet powerful when you need advanced features.

Fig. 18.2
Good software for
computer communica-
tions—ProComm Plus
for Windows.

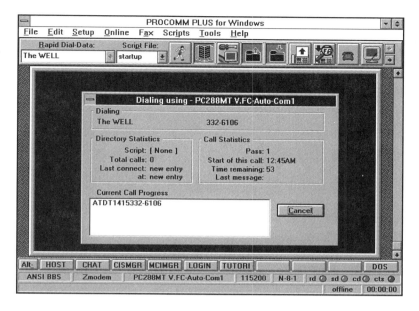

When you need the fax:
WinFax Pro for Windows and the
Delrina Communications Suite

WinFax Pro is a program specifically designed for sending and receiving
faxes with your personal computer (sure, ProComm Plus does faxing and
Microsoft Fax is free with Windows 95, but WinFax Pro does it better).
WinFax Pro includes numerous predesigned fax cover sheets and can
automatically receive faxes when you're away from your computer. You can
also program it to "broadcast" a single fax to hundreds of different recipients.

But what if you need to do faxing *and* normal PC communications? Then
turn to a combination of products called the Delrina Communications Suite.
This product includes WinFax Pro and its sister product, WinComm Pro (see
fig. 18.3). WinComm Pro does most of what ProComm Plus does, but has the
added benefit of working alongside WinFax Pro.

Fig. 18.3
The best software for faxing from your PC—WinFax Pro for Windows.

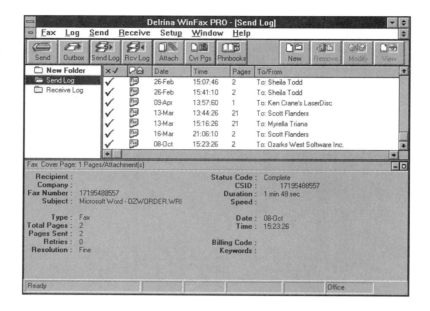

Which software is right for me?

Perhaps the best thing to do at this point is to list some common communications needs and then match them up with the right programs. And to help speed you through this process, table 18.1 provides a brief roadmap to help you choose the right software for your needs.

 TIP How frequently you use bulletin board systems will have an impact on what kind of software you need. See Chapter 23 for more details on BBSs.

Table 18.1 Finding the right communications software

Your needs	The right software
Occasional BBS use, occasional or no faxing	HyperTerminal
Occasional or regular faxing, no BBS use	WinFax Pro
Regular BBS use, occasional or no faxing	ProComm Plus
Regular faxing, occasional or regular BBS use	Delrina Communications Suite (WinFax Pro and WinComm Pro)

If you use Windows 95, be sure that you get the latest, TAPI-compliant version of the communications software you choose. You don't need to be concerned with what TAPI stands for or how it works, just that it will allow your communications software to share your modem with Windows 95 and other Windows applications.

I have a modem and software. How do I get on-line?

An on-line session is really quite simple. And the process is pretty much the same no matter what service you're connecting to.

The following steps walk you through a typical on-line session:

1 Start your communications software.

2 Tell your software where you want to connect to (what phone number). If you work in an office that requires you to dial 9 first for outside calls, you may need to add a 9 and a comma (so it looks like **9,**) to the beginning of the number. The comma is a special character that tells the modem to wait a bit for a dial tone before dialing the rest of the number.

Q&A *I keep getting disconnected when I'm on-line. What's happening?*

You might have "call waiting" service on your phone line and you're getting a second call while you're on-line. To turn off call waiting, change your calling setup to include ***70,** before the number you're calling. When you hang up the phone, call waiting will automatically be reset.

TIP **Most software lets you keep frequently dialed numbers in an** electronic address book (you know, that speed-dial concept). Otherwise, you have to enter the phone number manually.

3 Tell your software to start the connection process. Most software will display some strange-looking commands on-screen (see fig. 18.4). These commands tell your modem to get ready. Make sure you have a dial tone on your phone line, and then dial the number you entered.

Fig. 18.4
These weird command lines indicate the commands your software is sending to your modem.

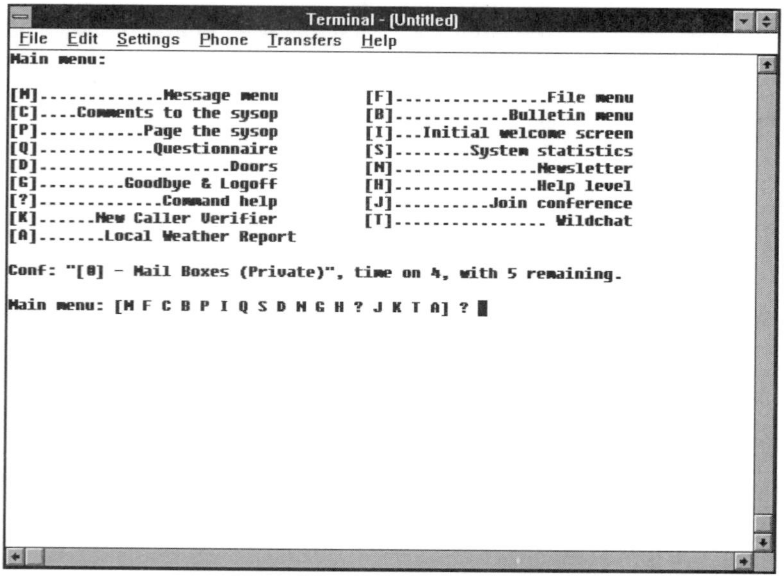

This line resets and configures your modem.   This line confirms the reset.   This line dials the number.

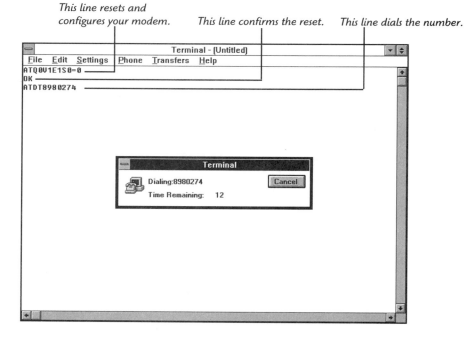

Fig. 18.5
Your modem dialed and your communications software kicked in, and next thing you know—you're on-line!

It's really that easy—when you type at the keyboard, the information appears on your screen and goes to the other computer. It's as if your keyboard and screen were attached directly to the other computer. The communications software takes care of all the details automatically.

Q&A *Why won't my communications program dial?*

If your software won't dial, there are several things to check. Is your modem properly installed and configured? Is your modem connected to your phone line? Is your communications software properly configured for your modem? Any of these things could cause the problem. You can also try shutting everything down and starting over. That often clears up modem problems.

Part IV: Other Equipment to Buy for Your PC

19

Printers and Scanners

In this chapter:

- **What types of printers are available?**

- **What's a font?**

- **Features to look for in a printer**

- **What's PostScript?**

- **I really want to print in color**

- **Do I need a scanner?**

"Experts" may predict the paperless office, but most offices find that PCs add to the paper blizzard. We can now spew reams of paper at up to 20 pages per minute . . . . ➤

Although the information in a computer is electronic, you often need to print that information on paper (thus creating a **printout** or **hard copy**). On the other hand, sometimes you need to get stuff *into* your computer that has already been printed—such as a company logo or the text of a product sheet. This process is called **scanning**. This chapter covers both.

What kinds of printers are available?

PC printers come in several designs. One may print envelopes, while another excels at carbonless forms. One may offer high quality, the other is amazingly fast. There are three basic types of printers:

- **Dot-matrix printers** use a combination of small pins that strike an inked ribbon, like a typewriter.

- **Laser printers** work much like a copier. With these printers, an ink substance called **toner** is "melted" onto the page to leave a permanent, high-quality image.

 TIP   **Some printers are mistakenly called laser printers but don't** actually use lasers. Okidata's OkiLaser 400E and 410E, for example, use shutters of light–emitting diodes (LEDs) to create the image. Despite the operating difference, the quality is the same as laser printers.

- **Inkjet printers** are like a "poor man's" laser printer. They use small nozzles that spray fast-drying ink onto the page. The quality is high, but the speed is low.

What are fonts, and why should I care?

A **font** is the style of letters (both shape and size) that your printer puts on the paper. Most printers come with a bunch of fonts built-in. These fonts are known as **internal** or **resident fonts**. All you have to do to use these fonts is tell your software what printer you have. Your software tells the printer to print the following text using this font, then switch to a different font to print the next batch of text on the page, and so on.

Some printers also support **font cartridges**, stored in little boxes that look like an 8-track tape or Nintendo game. They plug directly into the printer and then act like internal fonts.

 Plain English, please!

The term **support** gets thrown around a lot in the computer industry. If a printer (or program, or whatever) *supports* cartridges (or features, or whatever), that just means it allows them to be used. In the example above, some printers can use font cartridges, so they're said to *support* font cartridges.

Besides built-in fonts, most laser printers support **downloadable** fonts, sometimes known as **soft fonts**. (Some dot-matrix and most inkjet printers can also use downloadable fonts.) These fonts are contained in files on your hard drive and are transferred (downloaded) to the printer as they are needed. To use these fonts, you have to tell your software what kind of printer you have and what soft fonts you have.

In Windows you can use the printer's resident fonts or downloadable fonts. Windows will try to approximate on-screen the appearance of the fonts you choose. Most of the time, however, you'll probably use Windows' own **TrueType** fonts. TrueType fonts are **scalable fonts**, meaning that Windows can enlarge or reduce (**scale**) the font as needed to get the size you want. Windows can also use the same TrueType font file to create a downloadable font for the printer and screen font for your display, so the on-screen preview matches the printed output as closely as possible.

What kind of fonts are best?

There are distinct advantages and disadvantages to each font type. Internal fonts print faster and generally look better. Soft fonts come in endless varieties, from standard Times Roman to "PostCrypt," where the letters look like ghouls and goblins.

When buying a printer, look for one that comes with several internal fonts and that supports soft fonts. When buying fonts, make sure they are scalable—that is, they can be printed in many sizes. (Many printers have scalable internal fonts.)

If you use Windows, your best bet is to get a printer that works well with Windows and with Windows' TrueType fonts. Then buy your fonts in TrueType format. This advice holds true unless you have a particular need for a PostScript printer. (You'll know if this applies to you.) In that case, you should standardize on PostScript fonts.

 TIP **If you have Windows and at least one popular word processor, you** probably have more fonts than you can handle. Windows, and most of the word processors, come with a bunch of TrueType fonts. Before investing in more fonts, check out what fonts are already listed in your word processor's font menu.

How to choose a printer

Picking the right printer is like picking the right vehicle. How many miles will you be driving? How fast do you want to go? Will you be hauling anything heavy? Some questions you should consider:

- What quality of printing do you require? Do you need to impress or just show the facts?

- How fast do you need your printing? Can you afford to wait a little for the pages to print, and thus buy a less expensive printer?

- What type of paper do you have to print on? Do you need a wide printer for 11×17-inch ledger sheets or mailing labels? Do you need to print carbon or carbonless forms? What about envelopes?

- How much printing do you intend to do? Are you just printing occasionally or do you need to print massive numbers of pages?

- How expensive are the **consumables**—that is, the inked ribbons, toner, ink cartridges, or special paper the printer uses?

- Does your software support your printer? Some non-Windows programs may work with only a handful of printers. In Windows, things are easier. Once you set up your printer to work with Windows, all Windows applications can use it. But you'll need to make sure the printer comes with software—called a **driver**—to let it work properly with Windows.

When to choose a dot-matrix printer

Dot-matrix printers are the cheapest printers available (see fig. 19.1). Compatibility with your software is rarely a problem because most software can print easily to an Epson printer or IBM Pro Printer, and most other brands of dot-matrix printers can act like the Epson or IBM.

Fig. 19.1
A dot-matrix printer is cheap to own and operate.

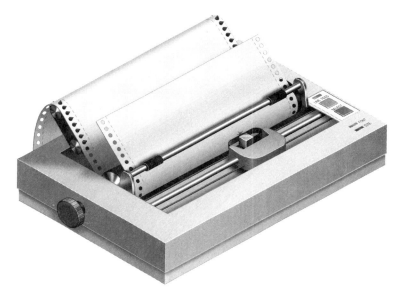

These printers form text and images by hammering away with several small pins against an inked ribbon. The more pins used, the better the image (and the noisier the printer because more pins are striking the ribbon). Dot-matrix printers typically come in two choices of quality: **9-pin** and **24-pin**. Nine-pin printers are used for inexpensive but fast printing. At best, these printers provide **near-letter-quality** (**NLQ**) printing. That is, they do the job, but you wouldn't want to print your resume on them.

The term **letter-quality** (**LQ**) used to be common to describe the final product of good printers; that is, good enough to use for your important letters. Near-letter-quality is considered pretty close to that letter-quality standard. But don't be fooled by a salesperson. Near-letter-quality is just that—close, but no cigar.

A good 24-pin dot-matrix printer can provide real letter-quality printing. Although typically slower than a 9-pin printer, these printers can be used for important correspondence. They can also be scaled back to **draft mode** so that you can print quickly—the printer just uses a handful of the 24 pins to produce a result that is just legible, not attractive.

 Plain English, please!

The term **mode** or **print mode** describes which way you're printing: draft, near-letter-quality, or letter-quality. Often you can specify in your software program how you want something to print. If you just need a quick copy you can show to somebody for corrections or for a meeting, use draft mode. When the document is ready to be finalized, then you want letter-quality, or near-letter-quality if it's not very important.

How fast is a fast printer?

The speed of dot-matrix printers is measured in **characters per second**, or **cps**. The speed in a printer ad may be given in draft, near-letter-quality, or letter-quality modes. Advertisers typically print only the draft speed because that's the fastest speed of the printer.

Dot-matrix printers are sometimes very slow compared to laser printers, which are measured in **pages per minute**, or **ppm**, instead of characters per second.

If you'll be printing hundreds of mailing labels or long reports, get a printer with a high cps rating. Also, you may want to get a printer that has a **noise-reduction** feature, so it doesn't interrupt nearby conversations.

Don't forget the paper issue

Dot-matrix printers use various types of paper: **continuous-feed** or **fanfold paper** (the paper with those pinholes on the sides and perforated edges), mailing labels, forms that create duplicate copies, and even single sheets. Printers that can print on single sheets are often known as **sheet-fed printers**. Some include a gadget called a **sheet feeder** to put the paper into the printer page by page, so you don't have to do it. Some printers can use either kind of paper.

Dot-matrix printers are the only printers covered here that can print on two-, three-, or four-part carbon or carbonless forms. Why? These printers hit the page and can make duplicate copies. Almost every business needs such a printer for printing invoices, service orders, and so on.

Some dot-matrix printers come in two **styles**: **narrow carriage** and **wide carriage**. Narrow printers can handle letter-size sheets ($8\frac{1}{2}$ inches wide). (These are also called **80-column printers**.) Wider printers can handle 11×17-inch ledger sheets and mailing labels on sheets wide enough to hold three or four labels. (These are also called **136-column printers**.) If you need to print only letter-size sheets, you can save about $100 by choosing a narrow printer.

 Q&A *I need to be able to switch between continuous-feed paper and letterhead. What kind of printer is best for me?*

Get a dot-matrix printer with a paper-parking feature, which pulls the continuous-feed paper out of the way so you can print on single sheets without having to unload the continuous paper.

Pros and cons of dot-matrix printers

The pluses of dot-matrix printers:

- Prints reports and mailing labels cheaply since the inked ribbons are cheap

- Can print on carbon and carbonless forms

- Relatively inexpensive

The downside of dot-matrix printers:

- Often slower than other printers

- Generally noisy

- Paper jams may occur if unattended

Maintaining a dot-matrix printer

Simple maintenance can prolong the life of a dot-matrix printer.

- Clean and lubricate the track on which the print head moves. Wipe it periodically with a soft cloth and use a light oil, such as sewing machine oil. Don't use motor oil or synthetic oils, though, because they can ruin the printing mechanisms!

- Use manufacturer-recommended ribbons. A ribbon not only provides ink for printed characters, but contains lubricant to keep the small pins in the print head moving freely (see fig. 19.2). Cheap or re-inked ribbons may skimp on the lubricant.

Fig. 19.2
The correct ribbon lubricates the dot-matrix pins.

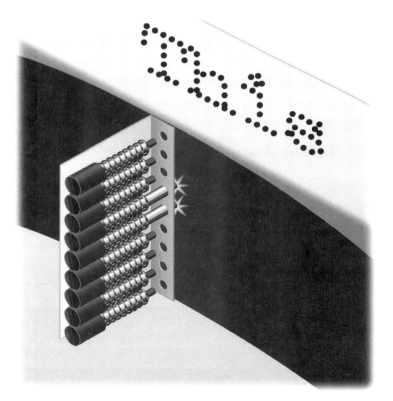

- Clean the print head occasionally. A build-up of ink may cause one or more of your printer's pins to stick. A sign of this build-up is a continuous white horizontal line through your type or graphics. Use isopropyl alcohol with a foam (not cotton) swab.

- Position the print head according to the thickness of your paper. If you set the print head too close to the surface of the paper, you shorten the life of your print head. Some printers, such as those from Okidata, intelligently sense the thickness of your paper and set the print head accordingly. Check your printer's manual for the correct setting for the paper you use.

- Use the correct paper path. Your printer may be able to accept paper from the front, rear, bottom, and top. Select the best path for the paper being used. Mailing labels, for example, are best used through the front or bottom paper path—not the rear, where they are more likely to jam.

When do I need a laser printer?

For about $500 and up, you can get a high-quality laser printer (see fig. 19.3). These printers use laser beams to burn special toner onto the page for a permanent impression.

The most popular laser printer is the **Hewlett-Packard LaserJet** (it has various models, often just referred to as **HPs**). Most laser printers imitate the LaserJet and many are less expensive alternatives. One HP-compatible printer is the OkiLaser 400E from Okidata.

Fig. 19.3
The laser printer is quiet and fast but more expensive than dot–matrix printers.

Laser printers use a **toner cartridge**, a plastic box that contains enough toner to print about 3,000 pages before being replaced. Toner cartridges are not cheap, costing from $25 to $95 each.

Whereas a dot-matrix printer uses a number of pins to determine its print quality, laser printers use **dots per inch** (**dpi**). Most print at 300 dpi. This is fine for most work, such as correspondence and simple newsletters. A 300-dpi laser printer prints at essentially the same resolution as the best 24-pin dot-matrix printers, but since there is usually some slight smudging of the dot-matrix output, the laser output usually looks better.

High-resolution laser printers, such as the HP LaserJet 4 and OkiLaser 410E, print at 600 dpi. High-resolution printers are best for creating in-house ads, material that needs to be "camera-ready," or other documents that need the finest resolution.

The need for speed

Laser printers are fast. Most come in speeds ranging from 4 to 20 pages per minute (ppm). If you print only a few pages per day, you can save money by buying a slower 4-ppm printer. A small office might be better served by a mid-speed model rated at 8 ppm. Businesses that love to crank out paper should choose the 12-ppm (or more) printers—especially if several people will be sharing the printer.

 TIP **Don't be too impressed by page-per-minute speeds. These rated** speeds are the top speeds at which the printers can print. The complexity of the pages you print will determine how fast you'll see some output. If you use lots of fonts and have several pictures, for example, you can expect the printer to slow significantly.

The speed of the printer's processor is often more important than the page-per-minute speed. Some printers, such as the LaserJet 4 Plus, use a special processor that helps the printer print close to its top speed even with complex documents.

Space and paper requirements make a difference

As a rule, 4-ppm printers tend to be smaller, requiring little desk space. (The amount of desk space used is called a **footprint**, so you might hear these small printers called **small-footprint** machines.) Some printers, such as the Panasonic KX-P4401 SideWriter, stand vertically and require very little desk space.

If you'll be printing several pages quickly, your printer will need to hold several sheets of paper. Some only hold 50 sheets of paper, requiring frequent reloading. Others may hold 200 to 250 letter-size sheets. Most printers can also print envelopes, one at a time. An optional envelope feeder allows you to print up to 50 before reloading. If you often switch between blank paper and special letterhead, you may want an optional sheet feeder that allows you to specify which paper bin the paper should feed from.

And then there's PostScript

Laser printers must use a common language for describing how text and graphics should be placed on a page during printing. This **page description language**, or **PDL**, determines which fonts work with your printer.

Most laser printers understand one of two page description languages that have become standards. The most prevalent is the **Printer Control Language** (**PCL**), developed by Hewlett-Packard for its LaserJet printers. The newer HP LaserJet III and LaserJet 4 use a version called **PCL5**. The other PDL standard, **PostScript**, was developed by Adobe Systems.

Both have their advantages and drawbacks. Most PostScript printers cost more than PCL printers and print more slowly. However, PostScript printers usually have better fonts, produce better gray scales, and are better supported by high-end graphics and design packages. The newer PCL printers have better resolution and incorporate support for special effects (like adding a drop-shadow).

Almost every laser printer imitates the Hewlett-Packard LaserJet. (This imitation is called an **emulation**.) Other printers may use the PostScript standard. The important point is that your software must be capable of working with whichever standard your printer uses and vice versa. Not all software programs can work with a PostScript printer; on the other hand, some programs require PostScript printing. Some more expensive printers support both printing standards.

Pros and cons of laser printers

The pluses of laser printers:

- Fast printing

- High quality

- Quiet operation

The downside of laser printers:

- Can't print carbon or carbonless forms

- Per-page cost of printing is expensive

- Can be expensive to buy and to maintain

A couple of other little things may not bother you at all. A laser printer cannot print to the edge of the page. At least one-quarter of an inch around the entire page is unprintable. And you can only print 60 lines of text per sheet of paper, rather than the usual 66 (assuming six lines per inch, like a typewriter).

Laser printers print an entire page at once, not one line or character at a time. To prepare a page for printing, laser printers require some memory. Most include at least 1M of memory, which is adequate for a page of simple text. However, if you intend to print several fonts or lots of graphics, your printer may need more memory installed. Otherwise, you may see partially printed pages.

Maintaining a laser printer

Because of their price, laser printers are worth caring for. If you own a laser printer, follow these tips:

- Clean your printer. Most printer manuals tell you how to clean the printer, and most recommend that you clean the corona wire and fuser. (The **corona wire** creates the electric charge that attracts the toner to the paper.) If the corona wire gets dirty, it won't be able to apply the proper charge to the paper. If this happens, you'll get light or even blank streaks on your page. The **fuser** is the part that melts the toner onto the page. If it's dirty, the toner may not stick. Clean these parts with a soft cloth and cotton swabs or the built-in cleaning brush. Avoid solvents and liquid cleaners.

- Protect the **printer drum**. Don't touch it or expose it to light for long periods. The laser's drum may be part of the machine or built into the replaceable toner cartridge (such as in the HP LaserJets).

- Keep toner cartridges level. Never tilt or store your toner cartridges on one end. This shifts the toner to one side, causing uneven printing.

- Use top-quality toner cartridges—either new or recycled. Recycled toner cartridges can save you some money (and reduce waste going to landfills) but be sure you get a quality product. If the recycler is careless or uses substandard materials, the cartridge may leak and not last as long.

TIP **If your laser printer says that the toner is low, remove the** cartridge and rock it gently from side to side to redistribute the toner powder within the cartridge. Reinsert it into the printer. The low-toner light may go out and you'll be able to squeeze a few more pages from the cartridge.

- Keep the **print density** (how heavily the toner is placed on the page) as low as possible. Some laser printers have dials for adjusting the print density. For drafts, keep this setting low, conserving toner. For final copies, set the dial to its normal level.

What about inkjet printers?

An **inkjet printer** provides print quality that rivals laser printers for a portion of the price. An inkjet printer, such as the Hewlett-Packard DeskJet 600, can produce sharp-looking letters and reports for an initial investment comparable to a decent dot-matrix printer.

Inkjet printers spray a fine quick-drying ink onto the page from several small nozzles. Despite earlier problems with ink smudging and fading, the latest printers are inexpensive and quiet…but not fast. Also, the output isn't quite as crisp as the output of a laser printer. One other strike against inkjet printers is that their ink cartridges are expensive and do not last long. Despite their drawbacks, inkjet printers can provide high-quality output for a very attractive price. For that reason, they've become very popular for home use and as low-volume, personal printers in offices.

How the printer forms and aims ink drops is only part of the print-quality factor. If you use a porous paper, the drops will tend to bloom as they soak into the paper, leading to a fuzzy appearance.

One niche inkjet printers serve is as portable printers for laptop computers. An inkjet printer such as the Canon BJ-230 is the size of a notebook computer and sells for under $400.

TIP   **Thermal printers are also used by laptop computers. These printers** use heat to print on a special wax-like paper. They're declining in popularity because the paper is flimsy and the type fades.

Pros and cons of inkjet printers

The pluses of inkjet printers:

- High-quality output
- Quiet operation
- Low initial cost

The downside of inkjet printers:

- Slow printing speed
- Ink cartridges are relatively expensive
- Paper selection impacts print quality

Color printing—ready for prime time

Not long ago, color printers were priced at a minimum of $3,000. The first color inkjet printers could print a limited range of colors on paper but produced washed-out colors on transparencies, and they couldn't print plain black-and-white text at all.

Color is still far from the norm in business, mostly because of cost—the up-front costs for the printer, and the continuing costs for expensive color printer supplies. But that's changing. New inkjets offer both text printing at reasonable speeds and impressive color at reasonable costs. The Hewlett-Packard DeskJet 660C provides respectable color quality on plain copier paper for under $500. Move a notch higher and you can get the HP DeskJet 1200C for about $1350. This inkjet printer can use either copier paper or transparencies.

You could try thermal wax transfer or dye-sublimation (what?)

For serious color, consider thermal wax transfer technology. Usually priced at $3,000 to $5,000, thermal wax transfer printers produce rich, full colors on transparencies as well as on specially coated papers. Fargo Electronics offers the Primera, a low-volume thermal wax transfer printer that sells for just $995.

The next step up—with prices near $10,000 despite declines over the past year—is dye-sublimation technology. (Recently, Kodak set a low price point for dye-sublimation printers by pricing its ColorEase PS under $8,000.)

Dye-sublimation printers, sometimes called **thermal dye transfer printers**, are known for producing photographic-like colors. These printers vaporize and merge color dyes, rather than ink or wax.

Color printing prices vary with how you print. Dye-sublimation pages cost about $2 to $5 per page. Thermal wax transfer printers cost about 50 cents to $1.50 per page. Pages from a color inkjet printer cost about 15 cents.

Scanning printouts *into* your PC

Whereas printers get information *out* of your computer, **scanners** put the information from paper documents and images *into* your PC. Like a photocopier, a scanner takes a "photograph" of a paper document. Instead of getting a duplicate sheet of paper, though, you get an image stored on your computer (see fig. 19.4).

A scanner can be used two ways:

- To save an artwork image—such as a company logo or a photograph—as a graphics file you can use in a newsletter or on letterhead

- To turn text on the paper document into typed text for your word processing program

Scanner types for different purposes

A **hand scanner** (or **handheld scanner**) allows you to scan small areas of text and graphics, typically about four inches wide (see fig. 19.4). You roll the scanner across the page you want to scan. Don't worry if your page is wider than the scanner; many scanner software programs allow you to "stitch" together multiple scans.

Fig. 19.4
The less expensive handheld scanner allows you to scan portions of a page and is ideal for occasional use.

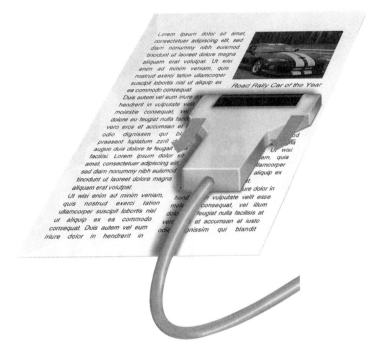

Handheld scanners require a steady hand and a flat surface so that the scanned image is smooth. You can often preview an image and repeat the scan until you get it right.

Flatbed scanners are ideal for scanning entire pages quickly (see fig. 19.5). Like a photocopier, you place the entire page on the glass surface. To speed scanning, optional document feeders can automatically feed subsequent pages into the scanner so you don't have to.

Fig. 19.5
The flatbed scanner is like a photocopier, with a glass surface on which you place the page to be scanned.

Page scanners are a recent addition to the list of scanning alternatives. They're bigger than hand scanners but much smaller than flatbed scanners. A page scanner accepts a full-width page, fed into a slot. Rollers pull the paper through the scanner in a manner similar to a small fax machine.

Page scanners provide a convenient way to scan pages for faxing and OCR. They frequently come bundled with OCR software (see the next section for details on OCR).

Whichever scanner size you pick, you'll have to add a special card inside your computer. You can't hook a scanner to your PC's printer port.

Scanners come in gray scale (capable of detecting only shades of gray) and color. More expensive color scanners can record more subtle shades of color and higher resolution, but they are typically used only by professional graphic artists and others with demanding needs.

And what about OCR?

While scanning artwork sounds cool, it is most often used by desktop publishers and artists. The truly handy use of scanners is for **optical character recognition**, or **OCR**. With OCR, you can scan and have words on a piece of paper appear quickly and almost error-free in your document. OCR is like having a 200-word-per-minute typist. Software programs such as Caere OmniPage Professional and Calera's WordScan Plus are leaders in the OCR software marketplace.

TIP **Packages such as OmniPage Professional and WordScan Plus can** take fax transmissions and turn them into text files. The fax/communications program WinFax Pro can also turn fax transmissions into text through OCR, but not with the same accuracy.

OCR isn't perfect. If you're lucky, OCR accuracy rate can reach about 98 percent, or one mistake for every 49 characters scanned, so you'll still need to proofread your final document. Most errors come from similar-looking characters, such as "0" and "O" or "c" and "e." This confusion is multiplied if your original page is of bad quality, such as a fax transmission or a copy of a copy. In the worst cases, an average typist can retype the text faster than they can correct the mistakes made by the OCR program.

20

Multimedia Mayhem: CD-ROMs and Sound Cards

● **In this chapter:**

- **Why all the excitement about multimedia?**

- **Equipment you'll need**

- **How to select the right CD-ROM drive (at the right price)**

- **What makes a sound card sound good?**

- **What features to look for in a multimedia computer**

You haven't heard of multimedia? Well, it's happening all around you and growing fast! . . . . ●>

The term multimedia is being used almost as often today as the word Internet. Everybody wants to use it, but few people know what it is. In a nutshell, it means using sound, images, and data on a computer all at the same time. This is kind of like using Tchaikovsky's "1812 Overture" to help present the end-of-year fiscal data you have assembled.

 Plain English, please!

Multimedia is the blending of video, graphics, text, and sound. It was invented when somebody decided that CD-quality sound would go well with high-resolution computer monitors.

Although multimedia can be very useful in business, most of the multimedia programs sold today are designed for education, entertainment, or reference. And because of the sheer size of multimedia files, most of these programs are delivered on compact disc. A CD-ROM can hold as much as 600M (more than 400 floppy disks!), so you can stuff volumes of information on a single disc (see fig. 20.1). By the way, that wasn't a typo. A CD is a disc (with a "c") and a floppy is a disk (with a "k"). Go figure.

Fig. 20.1
The CD-ROM delivers over 200,000 pages of information on a single disc.

Is multimedia all play and no work?

Sound cards and multimedia aren't just for kids anymore. Business users and educators also have a lot to gain from multimedia. For example, you can:

- *Add sound effects to business presentations.* Businesses are discovering that multimedia presentations that combine graphics, animation, and sound are more impressive, and often less expensive, than those tired old slide shows. See Chapter 16 for more info on presentation software.

What can multimedia do for me?

The multimedia encyclopedia is a perfect mainstream example of what multimedia can do for you. You might begin a search for information about the Watergate scandal. By clicking the entry for Richard M. Nixon, you can jump to the former president's biography. Click the movie camera icon and the encyclopedia plays a video of Nixon's farewell address, complete with sound.

When the speech is over, you can look up cross-references to H.R. Haldeman, impeachment, Khruschev, and more. You might start out at Watergate and end up at the Berlin Wall! The endless avenues you can explore using a multimedia encyclopedia keep your interest, so you learn better.

You can search an encyclopedia on CD-ROM and listen to history.

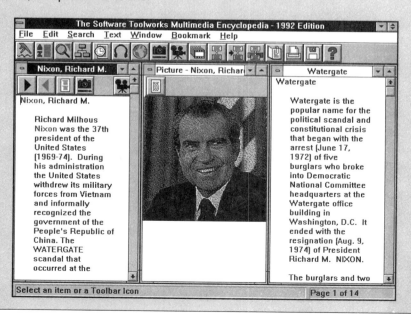

- *Install new software with ease.* Many software manufacturers give you the choice of buying your programs on CD-ROM or disks. Running the installation program on one CD is much faster and easier than swapping floppy disks over and over for a half hour or more.

- *Enhance training programs.* The CD-ROM versions of many software products often include goodies not found on the disks. You may find animated on-line Help, complete with music, extra documentation, or complete tutorial programs that show you how to use the new software.

- *Add voice notes to Windows files.* A business executive could pick up a microphone and place a spoken message into a contract to give her assistant explicit instructions, like in the spreadsheet in figure 20.2. This message is called a **voice annotation**—but think of it as a verbal Post-It note.

Fig. 20.2
This message might say, "Joan, remember this figure is based on third-quarter sales only."

	B	C	D	E	F	G	H	I
22	Net Profit and Break-even Point							
23	Units Mailed						5,013	
24	Response Rate						12.00%	
25	Unit Sales						602	
26	Gross Margin						$6,304	
27	Mailing Costs						$1,780	
28	Fixed Costs							
29	Creative Development						$200	
30	Allocations, Other							
31	Total Fixed Costs						$200	
32								
33	Total Net Profit						$4,325	
34								
35	Break-even Unit Sales						27	
36	Break-even Unit Mailing						222	

Click here to play back the message.

- *Give your PC voice commands.* Some computers are capable of voice recognition. This technology is still growing, but imagine giving your PC voice commands from within Windows 95: "File open. Page down! Left. Enter."

- *Make your computer talk back.* Text-to-speech utilities can read back a list of numbers or text to you. (Kind of like a proofreader you don't have to pay.) Hearing a letter read aloud may reveal forgotten words or awkward phrases. Accountants can double-check spreadsheet numbers, and busy executives can have their e-mail read to them while they are doing paperwork.

What kind of equipment do I need?

A group called the **Multimedia PC Marketing Council** has set the Multimedia PC Level 2 standards (known as MPC 2.0), for what a multimedia PC should have. These specifications should be considered a bare minimum and are probably too low for most people. The MPC 2.0 specification says you must have at least:

- A 25MHz 486SX processor

- 4M of RAM

- 160M hard disk space

- 3.5" high-density (1.44M) floppy drive

- 16-bit stereo digital sound card

- A pair of speakers or headphones

- 300-Kbps (or **double-speed**) CD-ROM drive

- SuperVGA (SVGA) monitor and display adapter

- Windows 3.1

The last requirement in the list is why all the other items should be considered a bare minimum. Windows 95 is much more powerful than Windows 3.1. That means it needs more RAM, disk space, and processing power to obtain satisfactory results. Maybe the Multimedia Council will decree a new specification (3.0?) in the future.

 Q&A *My computer meets the specs here, but my multimedia programs run really slow and clunky. What's wrong?*

Sometimes the MPC 2.0 standards are too small for even Windows 3.1. If your computer is on the low end, you can use multimedia, but you can't use it very well. If you think you'll want to use multimedia a lot, get a computer with more power, like a 486DX or a Pentium with 16M of RAM. This is more realistic for either flavor of Windows.

Why do I need a CD–ROM drive?

Today's hottest games and reference materials come either optionally on CD-ROM or exclusively on CD-ROM. The sheer capacity of a CD-ROM allows you to get massive libraries of data on a single disc, as well as vast collections of stereo sound clips, high-color graphics, and full-motion video. Trust me. All those high-resolution images, colors and sounds take *lots* of storage space! (One minute of stereo sound can fill over 10M of your hard disk.) This makes the CD-ROM ideal for providing

- Encyclopedias

- Technical reference information

- Databases of phone numbers and marketing leads

- Games and educational software

Remember that a CD-ROM is *read-only memory*. That means you can't save anything on it yourself. Practically any information that doesn't change much and takes up a lot of space is a perfect candidate for CD-ROM.

Why do I need a sound card?

Folks who have used computers for years usually don't see the big deal with **sound cards**—until they get one. But that's understandable. If you've always driven a car that doesn't have a radio, and then you get one that does, it doesn't take long for you to wonder how you ever remained sane without it.

A sound card is a small piece of hardware (like the one shown in fig. 20.3) that goes inside your computer and lets you record and play sounds. You can hook up microphones and speakers to sound cards, giving you all kinds of new toys to play with.

A sound card doesn't work like a tape recorder, though. Instead of going onto a tape, the sound is **digitized** and stored in a disk file just like any other data.

Here are just a few of the things you can do with a sound card:

- *Add stereo sound to computer games.* Today's multimedia games often include movie-quality musical scores, recorded human voices, or video clips. Without the sound card, all you hear are crude beeps from your PC's speaker.

- *Create your own original music, or edit music "entered" from a synthesizer.* **MIDI**, pronounced *MID-ee* and short for **Musical Instrument Digital Interface**, is essentially a musical programming language that lets your computer record and play back music. It's much fancier than a tape recorder, though. By connecting a keyboard (the musical kind with 88 black-and-white keys) to a MIDI sound card, you can compose and edit music, learn about music theory, or turn your PC into a music mixing studio.

- *Make your Windows programs talk to you.* You can use a sound card to jazz up your everyday computing experience. For example, you might want Windows to play a loud "Ta-da" when it starts or say "Adios, amigo!" when you exit a program.

- *Play your favorite music CDs on your computer.* A good multimedia computer can play Billy Joel in the background while you type away in Word for Windows, without missing a beat.

- Record your own sounds (called **WAV files**), or get them from other places. Prepackaged sounds are available from lots of different sources.

Fig. 20.3
The connections on the back of a sound card are for the speakers, a micro-phone, and a joystick game controller.

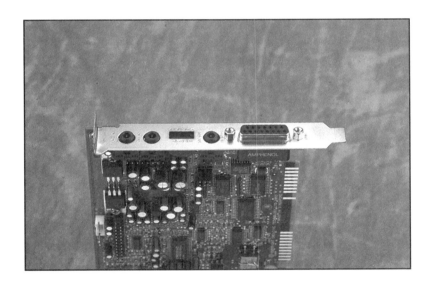

What do I look for in a multimedia system?

Most multimedia PCs being sold today easily exceed the outdated MPC 2.0 standards discussed earlier. Let's take a look at some realistic features that match the way you probably work.

How to choose a CD-ROM drive

The CD-ROM drive is the heart of your MPC system. To ensure that your computer is compatible with current and upcoming CD-ROM software, keep these things in mind (and ask the salesperson for more information) as you shop for a CD-ROM drive:

- *How fast can this CD-ROM access data?* You will want a CD-ROM drive with an average seek time of about 300ms or less. The faster your CD-ROM drive's access speed, the quicker you'll be able to get certain tasks done, especially those that frequently search the CD-ROM drive, such as a CD-ROM encyclopedia or magazine index.

 Plain English, please!

Access speed, usually referred to as **seek time**, is measured in **milliseconds (ms)**, or thousandths of a second. This is the time it takes the drive to find the information. The data transfer rate is measured in **kilobytes transferred per second (Kbps)**. This is how fast the data is transferred to the computer once it is found.

- *How fast can this CD-ROM transfer data?* After you find the data, you'll need to use it. The old specs state that a drive should be able to transfer data at 150Kb per second *and* 300Kb per second. This is called **double-speed** or simply 2X. Why have both rates? NEC Technologies, for example, uses its **MultiSpin** technology on its CD-ROM drives, which doubles the speed of the drive when reading certain kinds of information off the disc. See the following sidebar, "What's the CD-ROM speed limit?".

- *What basic controls do I need?* A CD-ROM drive should have a few controls. Look for an accessible **eject button**. A smooth, motorized load/eject tray is best. External controls for audio CDs, ranging from a thumb wheel for controlling volume (see fig. 20.4) to a full set of play, pause, next-track, and previous-track buttons, is handy. This way, you can load, play, stop, eject, and even change CD tracks without having to use software utilities.

Fig. 20.4
Most CD-ROM drives include the basics, such as a volume control and a headphone jack.

What's the CD-ROM speed limit?

When it comes to CD-ROM drives, the choices of speed and cost can be very confusing. As you flip through magazines, you'll see ads for single-speed drives (yuck!), double-speed drives, and then a bunch that just use Xs to denote their limitations: 3X, 4X, and 6X. Picking the right one means striking a fine balance between what you use it for and the thickness of your wallet.

Today's double-speed drives are cheap and work fairly well for reference work in encyclopedias, dictionaries, and other text-based media. They begin to show their limitations when accessing a full-fledged multimedia presentation. Animation and full-motion video will appear jerky and sometimes will be forced to "skip a frame." (What you see is more like an old Keystone Kops movie.) The presentation degrades even more when sound is added. Sound and video are stored in different

tracks on a CD and the drive has to jump back and forth, then mix them together before sending them to the computer.

Faster drives definitely produce better video and sound presentations, but beware the drives labeled **triple-speed**, or 3X. Nobody ever wrote any software for these drives, so most computers just run them as double-speeds (but at a triple-speed price)!

Quad-speed drives are a good trade-off for price and performance today, but as multimedia programmers become more sophisticated in their work, a 6X drive might be the ideal a year or two down the road. Buying a good drive now might mean not having to upgrade in the future. Isn't it funny how the words *powerful, sophisticated,* and *user-friendly* always mean you have to buy a better computer?

- *How much should I spend?* What you spend on a CD-ROM drive depends on what you want. Some low-end, single-speed drives are currently being sold for under $100. But beware! These drives are very slow and limited in capabilities. Double-speed drives (around $200) are better. The current speed demons (4X and 6X, or *six times* as fast) can be found for between $350 and $450. Shop around for the lowest price.

Best features for sound cards

Selecting a sound card is like buying a car. They're all basically the same, but oh, the difference a few features can make! Be sure to ask your hardware dealer these questions and get as many of these features as you can afford:

- *Is my game supported?* There are no official sound card standards, but the Sound Blaster from Creative Labs is the closest thing yet. Although nearly all sound cards claim to be Sound Blaster-compatible, you can only be sure of two: Creative Labs themselves and IBM, which has licensed the technology from Creative Labs. (They use it in their Aptiva machines.) If you stick to either of these two cards, you can be sure that almost any game will work. At least look for a card that says it is 100-percent Sound-Blaster-compatible.

- *MPC ready?* Most sound cards meet or exceed the Multimedia PC (MPC) Level 2 specifications (unlike the other multimedia hardware).

- *Can I add a CD-ROM?* Most stereo sound cards not only provide great sound, but also provide a connection for certain types of CD-ROM drives at the same time. It's a plus when the sound card can tell the CD-ROM what to do.

 *CAUTION* **Make sure your CD-ROM drive and sound card are compatible, or** as a second choice, that your CD-ROM drive comes with its own controller card. For maximum compatibility, buy a multimedia kit that contains both in one package.

- *DSP included?* One new addition to many sound cards is the **digital signal processor**, or **DSP**. DSPs add intelligence to your sound card, freeing your computer from some tasks, such as filtering noise from recordings or compressing your recorded sounds.

- *Can I add a Wave Table card?* If you plan on doing your own composing and playback using MIDI (discussed earlier in this chapter), you might want the highest fidelity sound around. **Wave Table cards** connect to the sound card and add their own quality and realism to your music. Some sound cards come with Wave Table features built in.

 TIP **If you're seeking to add both a sound card and a CD-ROM drive,** consider a **multimedia upgrade kit**. These kits bundle a sound card, CD-ROM drive, CD-ROM titles, software, and cables in an attractively priced package. Just like buying a stereo, you'll probably find superior components sold separately, but it's hard to beat the price of the prepackaged systems. Plus you'll have peace of mind knowing that the components will work together.

Don't forget speakers!

Quality sound depends on quality speakers. This applies to all audio systems, from your home theater setup to the radio in your car. Computers are no exception! An expensive sound card may provide better sound, but if the speakers can't play it, you wasted your money. Even a cheap sound card sounds better from a good speaker. Never skimp on the speakers!

Speakers come in several styles and price ranges. A growing number are designed specifically for multimedia and sound cards (see fig. 20.5). Some systems offer individual satellite speakers that can be placed anywhere; others come preinstalled in a cabinet that matches the case of your PC, fitting between it and your monitor. True audiophiles will be very impressed with how far PC sound has come in recent years.

Here are some tips to remember about the audio end of your multimedia setup:

- Take speaker specifications with a grain of salt. On paper, one product may seem superior to another. You can't listen to paper, so tell the salesman you want to audition the sound card or speakers before you buy.

- You'll get even better results if you plug your sound card into powered speakers; that is, speakers with built-in amplifiers. These speakers have on/off switches, bass and treble controls, and power cords. (Another alternative is to patch your sound card into your stereo system for greatly amplified sound.)

- Although most computer speakers are magnetically shielded (make sure that the ones you buy are!), do not leave recorded tapes, watches, personal credit cards, or floppy disks near the speakers.

- If you are short on cash, consider buying a pair of headphones. The sound can be just as good as a pair of speakers and they provide privacy.

Fig. 20.5
They might look small, but don't be fooled. These little guys can blow you away!

And none of it works without software!

Okay, you've purchased all the hardware and hooked it up. What can you do with it? Nothing! At least, not until you get some software that gives it the commands to unleash the awesome spectacle. Remember the MPC 2.0 specs that we discussed at the beginning of this chapter? Windows was a very important part of it, because you need an operating system that can talk to all this hardware.

Windows 3.1 was a good start because basic multimedia capabilities were built into it from the beginning. Its one problem was that every company that ever made a compact disc drive or a sound card also had to write a computer program (called a **driver**) to tell Windows how to use the new hardware. Asking a hardware company to write software is like asking all the car builders to refine gasoline. Everybody makes their own special brands that don't mix together well. (And sometimes there's an explosion.)

Windows 95 is a major step forward because it already knows how to use most of the multimedia equipment you can buy. Better yet, it keeps an eye on your system for you and detects when you've added something new. (At Microsoft, they call this **Plug-and-Play**.) Want proof? Place an audio CD into the drive of any Windows 95 system. The CD will be scanned and will start playing all by itself. This will also work with software programs that come on CD. After you use the program once, Windows 95 will always recognize it. The next time you insert the same CD, the program will be loaded for you automatically. (They have a name for this one too: it's called **Spin 'n Grin**!)

21

Modems:
A Phone for Your PC

● In this chapter:

- **Who needs a modem anyway?**

- **I already own a phone. Why should I get a modem?**

- **How to choose the right modem**

- **What do I need to make a modem work?**

The information superhighway is a giant computer network connected through telephone lines, and your modem is the entrance ramp . . . . ●>

If you've never heard the phrase information superhighway, then you've probably been living in a cave for the past three years. Hardly a day goes by where the media doesn't mention it in some (usually hokey) way. *Stranded on the shoulder of the information highway?* If you are, don't worry—we get you into the fast lane in Part V of this book. Don't jump ahead (pull out to pass?) just yet though, because you'll need to find out how to hook your PC up to your phone line first. Then you can merge onto the information superhighway and the multitude of information that flows along it. And I promise that's the last annoying analogy I'll use.

Since your PC speaks bits and bytes and your phone line speaks in sounds, you need something to translate between them. That's where a modem comes in.

Your modem: the phone inside your PC

A **modem** is really just a special telephone that's designed to work with a PC. That means it doesn't have a handset. Then again, your computer doesn't have an ear or a mouth. It does have a basic dialing apparatus, though, and it can send or receive calls depending on the commands that come from your PC.

The commands that make a modem work are usually generated by a com-munications software program that you run. You just tell the program the number you want to phone and it controls the modem from there. How does it work? Well, pretty much the same way you do when you want to use the phone: it picks up your telephone line and gets a dial tone, then dials the number and waits for the call to connect. If the modem receives a busy signal, it hangs up, and might try again in a few seconds (or a few minutes, depending on how you've told it to behave).

When a modem on the other end of the line answers, it issues a brief spurt of noise, a "hello, I'm a modem" signal. Your modem recognizes this noise and begins to **handshake** (negotiate the fine points of how the two will talk to one another). Once the two modems are connected, they begin "talking" to each other. That is, they start sending bits and bytes of data back and forth; this data can be commands, or output from your keyboard, or even a com-puter file. Whatever it is, it's sent from one modem to another modem over your phone line (see fig. 21.1).

Fig. 21.1
At its most basic form, this is how the information superhighway works. Your PC sends a signal to your modem, which sends a signal over normal phone lines to another modem, which talks to that PC.

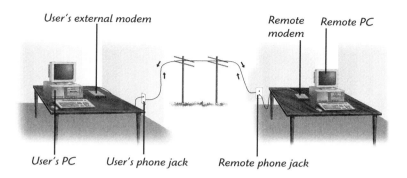

User's external modem

Remote modem   Remote PC

User's PC   User's phone jack   Remote phone jack

Q&A *I only have one phone line. Can I still hook up a modem to my PC?*

You bet! All modems allow a regular telephone signal to "pass through" without interruption when the modem isn't in use. Although a second, modem-only phone line is nice, it certainly isn't necessary.

What can you do with a modem?

Now that you know how a modem works, you might be asking, "Yeah, but what can it do for me?" That's a fair question, and here are some answers:

- It can dial up other computers to let you transfer (**download**) information.

- It can let you exchange electronic mail with other computer users all over the world.

- It may be able to send and receive faxes, depending on the type of modem you have.

- It can search giant electronic libraries of information, retrieving the data that best fits your needs.

- It can connect to national on-line services, such as CompuServe and America Online (see Chapter 23) or the Internet (see Chapter 24).

In short, your modem connects your computer (and therefore you) to the outside world. Without a modem, you can't do any of this, and it really is a whole different world out there.

Getting the right kind of modem

Once you decide to add a modem to your personal computer system, you're faced with a variety of choices. What kind of modem should you buy?

Inside or outside?

The first choice is simple—do you want an **internal modem** or an **external modem**?

An internal modem (see fig. 21.2) has to be installed inside your PC. It looks like any other board inside your PC and slides into any empty slot inside the PC case. It requires more technical knowledge to install, but—unlike an external modem—it doesn't take up any extra space on your desktop. Also, it doesn't use up one of the connections on the back of your PC. Stores that include a modem in a special computer package will usually give you an internal one because they cost less. (And if somebody else is going to do the technical work of installing it—great!)

Fig. 21.2
An internal modem, which hooks up inside your PC.

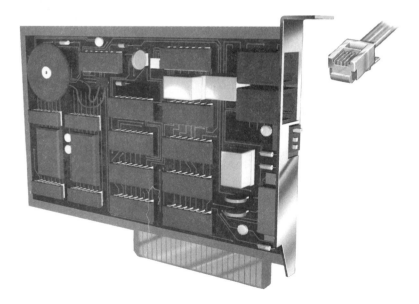

An external modem (see fig. 21.3) hooks up to the back of your PC. It's easy to install (just hook it up to an open connector on the back of your computer), but it has to be plugged into a separate power outlet and it takes up some desk space.

Fig. 21.3
An external modem, which hooks up to the back of your PC.

The information in table 21.1 can help you decide which type of modem you should buy.

Table 21.1   Do I need an internal or external modem?

Your computing needs	The type of modem you need
You don't want to mess around inside your PC.	External
You don't have an empty port (connector) on the back of your PC.	Internal
You don't have any adapter slots free inside your PC.	External
You need to move the modem from one PC to another.	External
You want to save a few bucks.	Internal
You want to know what your modem is doing by looking at a digital display.	External
You don't have extra room on your desk.	Internal

To fax or not to fax

Not only can you use a modem to communicate with other PCs, you can also use special **fax/modems** to send faxes to regular old fax machines. These modems work just like regular modems for normal communications, but also function as fax machines when you want to send or receive faxes. (Unless you have a printer, you'll have to view received faxes on your monitor. Fax/modems don't have any printing capabilities.)

Should you buy a fax/modem instead of a normal modem? Well, these days just about every modem on the market has fax capabilities. So as long as you're not paying extra for it, why not get a fax/modem? You never know when you might need to do some faxing—and using your PC is a pretty handy way to do it! There's a bonus too—faxes sent by a computer are usually of higher quality than those scanned by a regular fax machine.

To use your fax/modem for faxing, you'll need specific fax software or regular communications software that includes fax capabilities. Most fax/modems come with software that will work just fine, or you can buy a full-featured program like WinFax Pro from your local computer store. Windows 95 comes with built-in fax software that you can use to send faxes anywhere. The downside is that it doesn't include receive capabilities. For that, you have to subscribe to Microsoft's fax mailbox service. Just phone it once a day with your modem and pick up your faxes. (This is not really such a bad idea since using the same phone line for voice, data, and faxing gets a little complicated.)

How fast can you go?

The speed of your modem determines how much time you'll spend on-line. A faster modem transmits data faster, which cuts down the time you spend connected to a service. (And that can save you money since many places charge hourly rates for connect time.) Think of it like a garden hose. If you increase the water flow, you send more water through the hose in less time and get your lawn watered faster.

Modem speed is measured in **bits per second**, or **bps**. This describes the number of data bits that your modem can transmit in a single second. Obviously, the higher the bps, the faster the modem.

In addition to simple modem speed, you'll see some modems described with "V" numbers, which is an optional way to describe performance. For example, a V.32 modem communicates at 9,600 bps, a V.32bis communicates at 14,400 bps, and a V.34 modem communicates at 28,800 bps. You might also see modems rated as V.FC or V.FAST. They're pretty much the same as V.34. You don't need to worry too much about "V" numbers, however, because bps speed is almost always listed, too.

The only thing stopping you from buying the fastest modem available is the simple fact that *faster modems are more expensive*! So you probably want to balance speed with price, as shown in table 21.2.

Table 21.2   Benefits of different modem speeds

Speed	How good is it?
300 bps	Old and slow; not used anymore
1,200 bps	Still old, still slow; pretty much obsolete
2,400 bps	Tolerable; but still used by some older amateur BBSs
9,600 bps	Moderate performance and fairly inexpensive, but becoming hard to find
14,400 bps	Pretty zippy, but slightly more costly; necessary if you want to communicate with the Internet; pretty much the standard speed used today
28,800 bps	Best performance that approaches the limits of regular phone lines; wait for the price to come down before you buy

TIP   **When two modems are transferring information, they must be** running at the same speed. Don't worry about buying a modem that's *too* fast, though. If your fast modem phones an older slower modem, it will automatically slow down to whatever speed is required to achieve a connection.

Which is the right speed for you? I recommend a 14,400 bps modem; anything less just won't cut it on the Internet or if you're being charged hourly rates for access time. As for the new 28,800 bps modems, you'll probably want to wait until the price comes down a bit, especially since many BBSs and on-line services don't even operate at this speed yet.

Hooking it all up

When you get a new modem, you have to figure out how to hook it up and how to configure your system for the new modem.

The first part is pretty easy, especially if you have an external modem. See Chapter 2 for detailed connection instructions. If you have an internal modem, you'll need to take the top off of your CPU and follow the directions included with the modem. It's generally as easy as sliding the modem board into an empty slot, but you might want to check out the later sidebar, "Techie-talk about ports and IRQs."

If you're using Windows 95, there's a good chance that the installation of your internal modem will be a breeze. Windows 95 supports a new feature called **Plug-and-Play** that lets your PC do all the complicated work of configuring the modem. It works best if both your modem and the PC support Plug-and-Play as well. Look for the Windows 95 logo on the boxes they come in.

Don't pollute—telecommute!

Another wonderful word that has come into fashion is **telecommuting**, where workers use home computers to communicate with their coworkers at the office. They just phone in to the corporate network computers and do all their work through a keyboard on the kitchen table. Very handy for working parents with small children, plus it keeps a few extra cars off the expressways.

Don't expect to pull this off using a regular modem, though. Even the 28,800s aren't fast enough to make the flow of information instantaneous. This is actually the fault of the telephone line—not the modem. As you read in table 21.2, the 28,800 modem approaches the theoretical limits of what you can do over voice lines.

Serious telecommuters have the phone company install an **ISDN** line that gets connected to the PC with a special adapter. You don't need a modem to translate your data into sounds because you have something better: a direct digital link to the office. ISDN connections are often fast enough to let you transmit live video back and forth and see the people in your office.

You pay a fee for ISDN service and different telephone companies offer it in different qualities. (It's not even available in some places.) If you're seriously considering telecommuting, then ISDN is worth looking at. Besides, it keeps your real telephone line free for those personal calls.

How do I install a modem with Windows 95?

If both your PC and your modem say that they are Plug-and-Play compatible, you only have to insert the new modem and turn on the PC. Windows 95 will take care of the rest. If either your PC or your modem don't support Plug-and-Play (most don't as of this writing), then the job is just a little more complicated.

You still insert the modem and turn on the PC, but then you'll have to use the Add New Hardware Wizard. (It's an icon in Control Panel.) Just open the icon and follow the instructions. Windows 95 may tell you to change a setting on your modem to make it work, but this is easily done if you have the modem's installation manual.

Once your modem is in place, you need to install a communications software program. This program enables you to control your modem and get on-line. You'll probably have to tell it what kind of modem you have and where it's connected in your PC. Popular programs (discussed in Chapter 18) include ProComm Plus and WinComm Pro.

Once you have it all hooked up, it's time to get on-line! See Chapter 23 for help on finding and connecting to BBSs and other on-line services.

How to download a file

Downloading a file means you're copying it from another computer to your computer. **Uploading** a file means you're copying a file from your computer to another computer.

Today's communications programs (like ProComm Plus and WinComm Pro) make it easy to download files. In most cases, all you have to do is click a button or pull down a menu, and your software automatically downloads the file.

To properly download a file, however, both your computer and the **host computer** (the one sending you the file) must be speaking the same language, or **protocol**. There are several protocols for downloading files; they have names like Kermit, XMODEM, YMODEM, and ZMODEM. (If your software supports it, and if the host computer offers it, choose ZMODEM because it's faster and more error-free.) The Internet has its own protocol called File Transfer Protocol (FTP) and you won't get to choose.

Typical modem problems

- When I try to dial a number, my modem won't respond.

This problem is usually caused by an incorrect configuration, which occurs when you select the wrong port or IRQ. You'll probably need to reconfigure either your modem or your communications software.

- My modem disconnects in the middle of a call.

This can happen for a number of reasons. Do you have call waiting? If someone calls while you're on-line, the beeps will make the modem hang up. Call your phone company (or look in your telephone directory) to find out what your modem should dial to disable call waiting. Having someone pick up the extension in the kitchen will kill a modem too. I hang signs on all the extension phones that say, "Daddy's on the modem!" Another common cause is having a Windows screen saver activate during the call. Screen savers and modems don't mix, so disable your screen saver in Windows Control Panel before going on-line. Just a plain old noisy telephone line can also cause a disconnection. In that case, all you can do is try to reconnect and hope for a clearer line.

- When I use my modem I'm getting nothing but weird characters on my screen.

Garbage on your screen may result if your communications program isn't configured properly for the service you're dialing. Check the instructions for your on-line service and set up your software accordingly. (Look for references to Port Settings, Parity, and Data Bits.) This problem can also be caused by noisy phone lines; you may need to disconnect and retry another connection.

- When I try to download a file, parts of it are missing.

This can happen if your on-line session is prematurely interrupted or if you're plagued by a noisy phone line. You'll probably have to attempt the download again. Slower modem speeds are less susceptible to line noise, so try telling your software to use the next slower speed.

Techie-talk about ports and IRQs

Before you can use your modem, you have to configure it and your system for proper operation. For your modem to work properly, it has to be assigned to a particular **port** and **IRQ**. If you do this wrong, your modem won't work and it may cause other parts of your system to quit working, too! To do it right, you have to tell your software what port and IRQ the modem is using.

The average PC can have a maximum of four ports, labeled COM1, COM2, COM3, and COM4; but most only have COM1 and COM2 already installed. Only one piece of equipment can be assigned to each port; so if you have your mouse hooked up to COM1, you can connect an external modem to the remaining port COM2. If you're installing an internal modem, you will have to set it to act as COM3 or COM4 because your system already has the other two ports.

Describing what an IRQ (**interrupt request**) does is more technical than we need to get into. Just remember that IRQs are like COM ports—all the devices in your system must have their own IRQs. If your mouse and your modem wind up sharing the same IRQ, neither will work properly. If your trouble is with the IRQ, get a computer guru to help you out.

Part V: Connecting Your PC to the Rest of the World

22

Networks: Sharing Resources and E-Mail

● **In this chapter:**

- **What are networks and how can they help me?**

- **Teach your PC to share**

- **Get your mail electronically**

- **Server-based networks versus peer-to-peer networks**

Networks make it possible to quickly share ideas, information, gossip, and the location of the doughnuts from this morning's management seminar. . . . . ▶

S ports teams are more successful when the players work together
and divide the responsibilities according to each player's skills.
The more cohesive and organized the players are—and the better they
communicate—the more successful the team becomes. Networks turn a
bunch of individual computers into a "team" of computers that work coop-
eratively. Working together as a team brings the same benefits to a business
organization as to a sports team, and a computer network makes sure that
everyone in the office is on the same page of the "playbook."

Why use a network?

There are three primary reasons for using a network:

- You can easily share information with everyone on the network.

- Each person on the network can access expensive specialized hardware
  and software that they couldn't afford to purchase just for themselves.

- Communication is easier. In many offices, e-mail has become as important as the phone as a communications medium.

Sharing information

Networks make it easy to keep coworkers updated on important company
information. For example, with a network you could centrally store product
specification sheets so that any updates are instantly available to everyone
on the network. Or you could keep price lists on the network so that everyone is working with the same information. That way, no outdated information is mistakenly sent to a customer.

Everybody using the same software at the same time is no problem for a
network. Network operating systems allow companies to run **multiuser
software**, which is software that lets more than one person work with the
same application simultaneously.

 Plain English, please!

Multiuser systems let a whole bunch of people access the same data
at the same time, a capability that used to be available only with a
mainframe.

The most common multiuser programs are accounting programs. The data stored in accounting programs is usually divided into several files: customer, inventory, orders, accounts receivable, and accounts payable. These files are continually accessed by many different people. For example, order entry may be checking inventory to make sure they can fill a customer's order, while at the same time someone in accounting is performing a credit check on that customer. The network makes certain everyone gets the information they need and that all conflicting requests for information are handled in an orderly fashion.

Sharing equipment and software

The ability to share resources allows a company to let each computer, printer, modem, or other piece of equipment do what it does best—just as a coach decides which players play best at certain positions.

Within an organization, there are many different types of computers. Some are very large and can store lots of information; others are better at graphics,

What makes up a network?

There are three necessary components to any network: a network operating system, network cables, and network interface cards.

Getting all the computers to work together as a team requires a special operating system (see Chapter 1 for info on what an operating system is). A **network operating system** (**NOS**) can organize and control all the different computers attached to the network—think of this operating system as the network equivalent of a sports team's coach.

The next necessary item is the **network interface card** (**NIC**—pronounce it *nick*). A NIC is a device that is installed inside your PC and allows your PC to see, hear, and talk with all the other computers on the network. Just as a New York Knick might yell to other players on his team, "I'm open. Pass me the ball," your PC's NIC can yell to other computers on the network, "I'm ready. Pass me some data." The NIC lets your PC coordinate its efforts with other computers on the network.

The final necessary piece of the network team is the **network cable**. The NICs are only able to communicate across the network cable. Your computers, once networked, are basically on a very busy conference phone call, with every computer either receiving or yelling out instructions across the network cable.

and still others are speed demons that process information quickly. All of these qualities are seldom found in one computer.

Networks make sure that everyone in the office uses the maximum amount of available resources. A good example might involve three different employees with three different computers and a printer. Suppose Bob's computer is relatively slow, but it has a large amount of disk space. Your computer is fast and great at graphics, but has limited disk storage. Lori's computer is used mostly for printing color transparencies and is attached to a very fast, color laser printer.

Before being networked, you could only create smaller, less impressive graphics because you couldn't store the big files necessary for larger, more impressive graphics. You also had to carry your disk down to Lori's computer and wait for her to get out of your way so you could get printouts of your graphics.

If your company installed a network, you could "borrow" disk space from Bob's computer and you could also print to Lori's printer without carrying a disk to the other side of the office. By combining resources and playing off of each computer's strengths, a network results in a more flexible and productive team.

E-mail: passing notes to each other

Networks also allow coworkers to send memos and computer files to each other through popular **electronic mail programs** (**e-mail**). These days it seems like everybody's talking about e-mail. Why? Because it's changing the face of the world. Electronic mail and other computer-based communication methods are changing the way we work, communicate, and even socialize.

There are two basic types of e-mail: the kind you use on a regular network, and the kind you can send to people who aren't connected to your network (via "on-line" mail services). This section covers office e-mail, but many of the same principles apply to e-mail on CompuServe, America Online, the Internet, and other on-line services as well.

Most people are familiar with fax machines. You compose and print out your message, put it on your fax machine, dial a phone number, wait a few moments, and poof! The same message comes out on another fax machine miles away. E-mail programs work in a similar way. Like a fax machine, you can send messages, receive them, forward them to others, and more. There's one big difference, however: no paper! It's all done electronically through your office's computer network or over regular phone lines.

Another important difference is that e-mail is lightning-quick! Certainly much faster than the U.S. mail (often called **snail mail** by e-mail users) or your interoffice mail system. Your message is delivered as fast as the network can deliver it (which is usually *really* fast).

An electronic "mailbox"

When you start an office e-mail program, like Microsoft Mail or cc:Mail, you usually have to enter your user name and a password, just like you do for any other network function. Your user name usually works as your e-mail **address**. Like your mailbox at home, you usually have an electronic **mailbox**, or **Inbox**, where your mail is delivered and stays until you're done with it. If your office uses a program called cc:Mail, your screen will look a little like figure 22.1. This particular figure shows the remote version of the software in use—this user can read her e-mail from home!

Fig. 22.1
So how much of this is junk mail, and how much is important?

Double-click here to see what's in your mailbox.

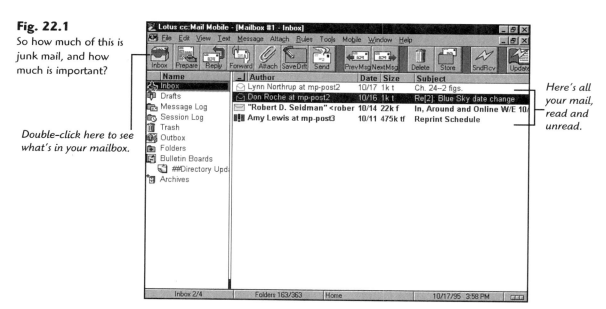

Here's all your mail, read and unread.

Q&A *I forgot my password. What do I do?*

The person in charge of your company's network (the system administrator) sets up the addresses and passwords for all e-mail users. That person can help you find out what your password is and even help you change it to something that's easier to remember.

How do I keep someone else from figuring out my password?

Be careful in choosing a password. Don't choose a number or phrase that's publicly available, such as your phone extension, your employee number, or your spouse's name. Choose something private like the name of the stray cat you adopted when you were 10.

Let's play post office: sending and receiving mail

All e-mail programs work differently, but the concept is the same no matter which package you have. And generally, they're pretty easy to use, at least for simple messages. For example, sending a message involves three basic steps:

1 Start a new message and address it. You can usually address a message to several people at once, or address it to a specific person and "cc" others, as shown in figure 22.2.

Enter the user's name here, or click it in the directory.

Fig. 22.2
The Address Message dialog box lists all the people on your cc:Mail network.

Address mode list

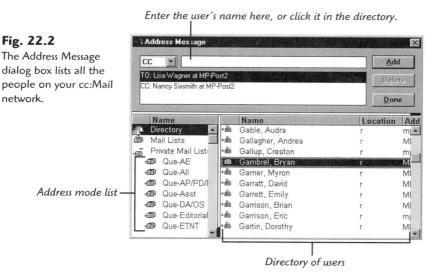

Directory of users

2 Type the text of your message. Most e-mail programs let you just type a message as you would in a word processor, edit the message, and even spell check to find mistakes.

3 Send the message. Your message is sent to each recipient's mailbox, no stamps required!

You can even send a file as a message

You can send just about any kind of document through the mail as long as it's in an envelope: checks, your resume, newspaper clippings from your Aunt Selma's wedding, or a catalog (and don't we all get enough of those?). Similarly, you can attach almost any file(s) to almost any message and send it along with the message, like we're doing in figure 22.3. Sending the file as an attachment to an e-mail message doesn't alter the file at all; it arrives in its recipient's mailbox completely intact.

Fig. 22.3
When you get a message that has an attachment and open the message to read it, use the Save As command from the File menu to save it to your hard drive.

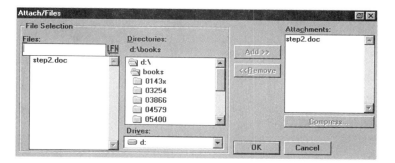

Sorting your mail electronically

When you want to read a message, you usually just click it and it opens up. Once you've read a message, you can discard it or file it to view or use later.

Most e-mail packages let you create file folders, or filing cabinets, to store and organize messages you've received (see fig. 22.4).

When you want to review a message you've filed in a folder, simply double-click the folder to display its contents, then double-click the message you want to read again.

Fig. 22.4
Create the folder, then just drag a message into the folder where you want to store it.

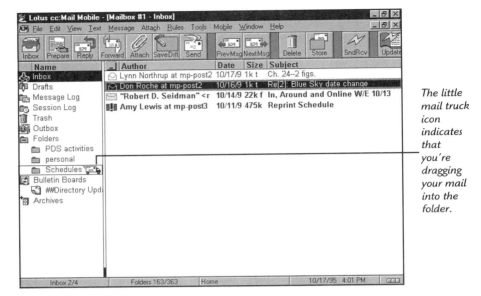

The little mail truck icon indicates that you're dragging your mail into the folder.

So which program should I use?

Generally, when you're working on a network, you have to use the e-mail program that's installed on that network. You really don't have a choice. Having all the users on one package ensures that the communications will work smoothly. It's also a lot less confusing!

Windows 95's Microsoft Exchange

Windows 95 users may have another e-mail option—Microsoft Exchange (see fig. 22.5). Microsoft is touting Exchange as a "universal" mailbox. In its initial incarnation, it isn't quite as sophisticated as the regular e-mail programs, but it has all the standard features plus the ability to connect to most of the various network e-mail systems in use. With Exchange, you can use the same program to access your local network e-mail system, Internet e-mail, on-line services such as CompuServe, and even a fax modem.

Server-based networks

Server-based networks are built around specialized computers, called **servers**, that run a network operating system (refer to the earlier sidebar, "What makes up a network?"). Servers contain information or computing resources that need to be shared. A server's resources may include disk space, shared files, printers, modems, or other specialized hardware.

Fig. 22.5
Microsoft
Exchange is the
universal e-mail
mailbox that
comes with
Windows 95.

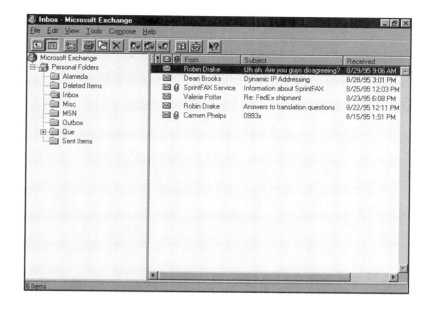

Once the servers are set up, the **workstations**, running normal PC operating
systems, access either information stored on the server or resources attached
to the server. In a server-based network, all the workstations can share the
resources of the server in a hub-and-spoke arrangement. Workstations can
communicate with each other only indirectly—through the server.

Do I need a server-based network?

What's so great about a server-based network? These networks are typically
faster, more secure, and better suited for use with multiuser applications.
What's not so hot? They aren't quite as flexible as peer-to-peer networks
(these are discussed on the following page) and may be overkill for smaller

What's with all this "client/server" talk?

A **client** (also called a workstation) is any computer accessing the services of another computer,
which is called (you guessed it) a **server**. With
some network operating systems, a computer
can be both a server and a client! That is, the

computer shares some of its resources and stored
information with other computers, but can
simultaneously use resources and information
stored on other computers.

organizations. Generally, a specially trained network administrator is required to keep the network operating properly.

Server-based products

The leading server-based network product is NetWare, produced by Novell, Inc. Competing products, such as Microsoft LAN Manager, Banyan Vines, and DEC PathWorks, have their strong points and ardent fans, but haven't made much of a dent in a market largely dominated by Novell. Someday, the server version of Microsoft Windows NT may become a contender, but it's still too early to tell.

NetWare is the industry's leading network operating system (NOS, remember?) software by a large margin. NetWare is supported by thousands of dealers and specially trained personnel worldwide.

NetWare is available in many different flavors and for many different-sized networks. Here is a partial list:

- *Personal NetWare.* This is a peer-to-peer product (see the next section) that is great for smaller networks.

- *NetWare 3.x.* Currently version 3.12, this is the most popular NOS. This product is great for medium-to-large networks.

- *NetWare 4.x.* This NOS is designed for very large networks, and includes special tools for organizing and managing the resources of a very large, or multi-location, network.

Peer-to-peer networks

Peer-to-peer networks aren't based around servers with specialized NOS software. With a peer-to-peer network, all the computers run some type of NOS and have the ability to share their information and resources (usually printers and disk space) with other computers on the network.

The great thing about peer-to-peer networks is their flexibility. Each user can make any part of their system available to other users on the network. If one day you suddenly feel like sharing your printer, you can set it so that everyone else can print to your printer. (You can do it yourself—no network administrator is required.) If it gets a little too noisy in your office, you can "disconnect" your printer from the network and have it all to yourself again. The same is true for any resource or data file on your system.

The downside of peer-to-peer networks is that they are tougher to manage and control because the resources are spread out and not centralized on one server. Also, they typically don't perform as quickly as server-based networks. This is especially true if your computer is being used heavily by others on the network. As a result, peer-to-peer networks that work well for small workgroups are often unsuited for larger, company-wide networking.

The best of both worlds

Fortunately, peer-to-peer and server-based networks aren't mutually exclusive. It's possible, and sometimes highly desirable, to run both systems simultaneously.

For instance, a large company will certainly want a server-based network. A department or team within the company might need to remain a part of the company-wide network. But they might also need the flexibility of sharing files and resources in the workgroup without going through the company-wide network (and getting the network administrator involved every time they need to make some small change).

The popular peer-to-peer networks let you do just that. It can be tricky to set up both kinds of networks on the same computers, but once it's done, they can work great.

The top two peer-to-peer networks are Windows by Microsoft and LANtastic from Artisoft, Inc. Both products can work either entirely on their own, or they can coexist with other server-based networks like NetWare.

Windows 95 and Windows for Workgroups

Microsoft Windows for Workgroups is a special version of Windows with peer-to-peer networking features. Windows 95 includes those same features, and more. Both Windows 95 and Windows for Workgroups let you share any of your local resources (disk space, printers, modems—you get the picture by now) with your coworkers. It even communicates with today's more complex and capable fax machines and photocopiers. Talk about connected!

With its Network Neighborhood, Windows 95 makes network resources as easy to use as the resources of your own computer. Each computer on the network appears as an icon, and double-clicking the icon gives you access to more icons for the disk drives, printers, and other shared resources. As you can see in figure 22.6, the icons look and act like the icons for the folders and printers on your own computer.

Fig. 22.6
The highlighted folder icon is really a shared disk drive on another computer on the network.

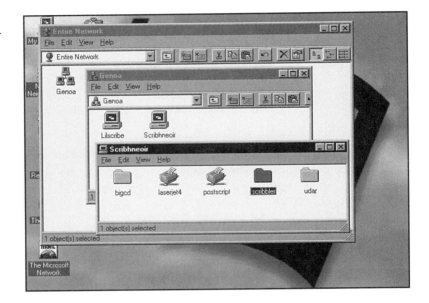

LANtastic

LANtastic (the current version is 6.0) is the other popular peer-to-peer network. Its main claim to fame is that it requires very little of your computer's memory to run.

LANtastic has a full suite of Windows and DOS applications that makes managing the network easier. Artisoft also makes a full range of hardware designed to work with LANtastic, but LANtastic will work with hardware built by other companies.

23

Bulletin Boards and On-Line Services

● **In this chapter:**

- ● **What do on-line services really offer?**

- ● **How to sign up for an on-line service**

- ● **Leading commercial services**

- ● **What's a BBS?**

- ● **Which type of service is best for me?**

Once you get started on-line, you'll find it hard to quit. After you're hooked, you might talk yourself into paying any price for the satisfaction of dialing up! . . . . ▸

O nce you have a modem installed on your PC, you can use it to join the global community of computer users. While it's possible to use your modem to contact another computer user directly, it's much more practical to exchange messages through an intermediary set up for that purpose—an on-line service or a bulletin board system (BBS).

On-line services are fun and informative

Browsing through an on-line service is kind of like walking through your hometown. You pass the post office, the newsstand, the video arcade, the library, and all sorts of small shops, stopping to chat with other passersby once in a while. When you connect to an on-line service, you find pretty much the same activities, only electronically.

Electronic mail

One of the prime uses of any on-line service is the ability for users to exchange electronic mail. E-mail is nothing more than a message sent electronically. No paper, no envelope, no stamp—just words and an address. Unlike regular mail, e-mail arrives where it's meant to, almost instantaneously. (See Chapter 22 for more on e-mail.)

Get the latest scoop

Most on-line services provide some sort of news service. This may range from a simple "top of the news" bulletin on a local **BBS** (**bulletin board system**), to a full Associated Press newsfeed on CompuServe or America Online. In any case, on-line is a great place to get up-to-the-minute news, weather, and sports information.

Chew the fat

If you've never done it, you might find it difficult to believe. But it's possible—and popular—to "talk" to other users of an on-line service. That is, you can use your computer keyboard to send **real-time messages** back and forth in what are called on-line **chat** sessions. Most services allow private (one-on-one) chats, as well as multiple-user conversations, often called **conferences**. Really, it's a great way to meet new people—even if you never get to look them in the face!

Plain English, please!

A **real-time** conversation is like the kind you have on the phone: you and the person on the other end of the line communicate back and forth with no delay. Contrast this with, say, playing "phone tag," where you and the other person are forced to leave detailed messages on each other's answering machines. E-mail messages are a sort of "phone tag" on the information superhighway.

Special interest groups

Imagine attending a party or club meeting where you can listen to and participate in just the conversations that interest you—and do so at your convenience. You can do just that in the areas (called **forums**, **roundtables**, **discussion groups**, and the like) that on-line services provide for people with similar interests to exchange messages. You can find groups discussing various professions, hobbies, lifestyles, and other topics. Participants exchange messages similar to e-mail except that they are public—anyone can drop in and read a message and the replies to that message.

Play games

If you like to play games—either by yourself or with a partner—you can't do better than a good on-line service. On-line, you can find lots of single-player games, as well as (on some services) the ability to engage other users in multiplayer action and adventure games. (It beats playing checkers at the barber shop!)

Bring home interesting files

One of the most popular parts of any on-line service is the file library area. This is where you can find files—pictures, lists, software programs, you name it—that you can download directly to your computer. It's like having a giant software giveaway at the end of your phone line!

Shopping, shopping, shopping!

In addition to all the free files you can download, many on-line services (particularly the commercial ones) provide on-line electronic shopping areas. From these services you can browse through and order all sorts of merchandise. It's like peeking inside your PC and finding the Home Shopping Network, complete with cubic zirconia!

Browse through electronic libraries

When you need to do some information research, you can head to your handy encyclopedia or down to your local library—or you can jump on-line. Commercial on-line services provide massive electronic libraries of information of just about any sort you can imagine. Want to check a company's performance? Look up incidence of repair for a particular make of toaster oven? Search through some old magazine articles? You can do all this—and more—on-line.

Get technical support

And if all that isn't enough, you can also use on-line services to find answers to any computer problems you might have. Most major software and hardware companies maintain a significant presence on the commercial on-line services. You can go on-line and talk directly to technical specialists who can help you solve software and hardware problems.

How much does it cost?

Okay, you're sold. You want to join an on-line service. But what's involved?

First, you need to decide which service (or services) to join. Depending on your needs, you may want to subscribe to a large, national, commercial service; or you may be satisfied with a local BBS. Either way, it'll probably cost you money.

While CompuServe, Prodigy, Microsoft Network, and America Online all offer a variety of pricing plans, the base rate is generally about $10 per month. For the monthly fee, you normally get several (typically five) hours of access. If you spend more time using the on-line service, you'll pay more—usually about $3 per hour. In addition, some services, or access at certain days and times, may cost considerably more. Expect to spend $20-30 per month for moderate use of a commercial on-line service—but beware, you can rack up a much larger bill if you let yourself get carried away.

The cost to access a local BBS is as variable as the purpose and character of the BBSs themselves. Some BBSs are operated by hobbyists and computer clubs, some by business associations and other groups, and some operate as for-profit enterprises. Most BBSs are free or charge a small fee ($10 or less) to partially offset their costs. Some specialized BBSs command an access fee significantly higher than the commercial on-line services.

All right, where do I sign?

The major commercial on-line services provide special communications software that you use to access their service. You'll need to get a membership kit that includes that software. Then, to join CompuServe or other on-line services, you simply install the new software and follow some on-screen instructions.

Getting the membership kit is easy. All you have to do is call the on-line service and request it. They'll usually provide the software free, or at a very modest cost. You can also buy a membership kit for the service of your choice at most software retailers. (They cost around $20-$30, but most of the services offset the cost of the kit with an equal amount of free on-line time.) You might also get a membership kit included in the package when you buy a new computer or modem or even as part of a promotional mailing. The access software for the Microsoft Network is included in Windows 95.

The first time you access the service, you'll need to supply information such as your name and address. You'll also need to furnish a credit card number for billing.

 Q&A *If I don't want to use my on-line service anymore, is it hard to quit?*

No, not really. Although it varies from service to service, you shouldn't have any problem canceling your subscription. In fact, several services offer 30-day trial memberships where you get to try them out before making a commitment. Even if the service you joined doesn't offer a trial membership period, it probably either offers a way to cancel your subscription on-line or via a quick phone call.

You'll use your own communications software, such as HyperTerminal or ProComm, to access a local BBS. Joining is normally as simple as having your modem dial the phone number of the BBS, and then typing the answers to a few questions. You normally have to pick an on-line nickname for yourself, as well as a secret password. (This is so no one else can log on using your name.) If the BBS charges an access fee, you'll probably have to send the BBS operator a check. Many local BBSs are small operations that aren't equipped to handle credit card payments.

The big services: commercial systems

When you go on-line with a major commercial service, it's like cruising the streets of a big city. You have access to *thousands* of shops and services, and you can run into an incredible variety of people on the street. The newspapers are big and comprehensive, and the libraries have a tremendous amount to offer.

TIP   **Electronic cafes are appearing in cities around the country. They** serve up computer terminals with access to the Internet for the cost of a latte. It's an interesting way to try out the on-line world.

Starting simple with Prodigy

The easiest commercial service to use is Prodigy. Prodigy was formed as a joint venture between IBM and Sears and designed to be accessible by all levels of computer users.

Prodigy features a jazzy-but-simple interface (see fig. 23.1), with large type and big navigation buttons. Among Prodigy's features are:

- News, weather, and sports coverage
- Business and finance information

Get on-line for free with community FreeNets

In addition to traditional BBSs (many of which have some sort of user fee) and commercial on-line systems (all of which cost money), there is one other way to get connected—and this way is free. FreeNets are community-based BBSs that provide a way for citizens to get on-line at no charge.

Communities provide FreeNet access to their citizens as a community service; it's like an electronic town hall. FreeNets are normally nonprofit organizations, funded by government sources and corporate donations.

Most FreeNets assemble information of specific interest to their communities. You might find local news items, community calendars, lists of public-service organizations, and other such information. In addition, many FreeNets now feature free access to the Internet.

- Entertainment news

- E-mail and messages

- On-line shopping

- On-line travel reservations

In addition, Prodigy provides access to the Internet newsgroups (sort of an electronic messaging and discussion center arranged by topic), as well as the ability to send and receive messages to and from the Internet. Recently, Prodigy added the ability to view World Wide Web pages, and even create a Web page of your own.

Fig. 23.1
It's easy to find your way around Prodigy. Kids particularly enjoy how easy it is to use.

Expanding your horizons with America Online

America Online (AOL) is the fastest-growing on-line service today. With millions of users, AOL provides a variety of services to the average computer user. AOL looks and feels a bit more sophisticated than Prodigy, but it's really just as easy to use (see fig. 23.2). Almost everything is done by clicking a button or selecting a menu item.

America Online offers the following types of services to users:

- News, weather, and sports

- A large selection of national newspapers and magazines in electronic format

- Stock market and financial services

- On-line shopping

- E-mail and messages

- A variety of **departments**, or on-line neighborhoods, for special interests

- Live on-line chat

In addition, AOL users enjoy several types of Internet access, including newsgroups, e-mail, and **Gopher**, an Internet searching tool. AOL was the first of the major commercial services to offer World Wide Web access to its members.

Even though AOL isn't my primary service, I do like it. It's probably the best place to get packaged information, especially periodicals. In addition, many companies are hooking up with AOL for exclusive services, including MTV, DC Comics, NBC, and the *New York Times*. It's definitely worth a look.

Fig. 23.2
Lots of options are available on America Online. You can even get up-to-the-minute weather information—faster than watching the local news!

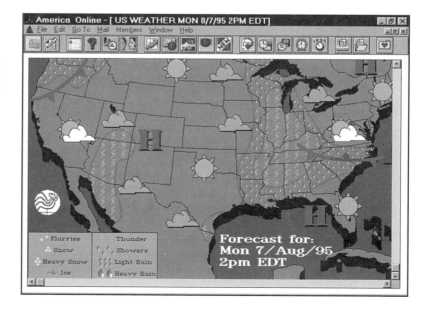

Going global with CompuServe

CompuServe is the oldest of the major commercial on-line services and is truly global. (You can get versions of the CompuServe operating software in German and French!) While CompuServe isn't hard to use, it does require a little more skill than Prodigy or America Online. But you'll be rewarded for your work by the largest selection of different services of any on-line service.

Here's what CompuServe offers:

- The largest number of special-interest forums of any commercial service

- News, weather, and sports

- Stock market and financial services

- A vast repository of information in searchable electronic databases

- On-line shopping

- E-mail and messages

- Live on-line chat

- Internet features, including newsgroups, e-mail, gopher, World Wide Web, and **FTP** (for file transfer protocol—a fancy term for a tool that lets you transfer files from one computer to another).

CompuServe is the only major commercial service that can be accessed in plain text mode using ordinary communications software such as HyperTerminal. You'll want to use a specialized access program such as WinCIM, though (see fig. 23.3). It makes CompuServe much easier to use.

For the slightly more experienced computer user, CompuServe could be the service of choice. The variety is much greater here, and the user traffic is livelier. In addition, CompuServe better serves research needs, while offering all the amenities of the other services.

Fig. 23.3
Think CompuServe is just for stodgy businesspeople? There's plenty of fun, too. For example, check out the Comics Publishers forum.

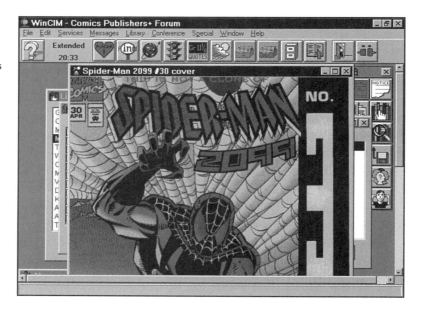

The new kid on the block: Microsoft Network

The Microsoft Network (MSN) is a new player in the commercial on-line service game (see fig. 23.4). Ordinarily, a new, unproven addition to a competitive field might be ignored at first. But coming as it does from Microsoft, the world's dominant software publisher, MSN arrives on the scene with considerable clout.

The Microsoft Network features:

- E-mail and messages

- Live on-line chat

- Special interest areas

- News, weather, and sports

- Technical support areas

- Internet features, including newsgroups, e-mail, and a very good World Wide Web browser

If you have Windows 95, you already have the access software for the Microsoft Network. To sign up, just double-click the MSN icon on your desktop and complete a simple sign-up process (supply your name, address, and a credit card number for billing). Once you get on-line, you'll find that getting around in MSN is much the same as navigating your own folders and documents with Windows 95.

Fig. 23.4
Some of the graphics on MSN are really impressive for an on-line service.

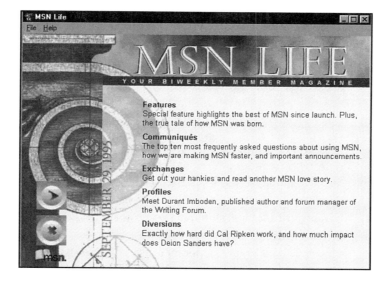

The jury is still out on whether MSN is truly a worthy contender among the on-line services, or if this youngster will fail to live up to its promise. Initially, MSN just doesn't have the depth and richness of the larger on-line services. Still, there's some interesting stuff going on, and it's growing every day. If you have Windows 95, MSN is definitely worth looking at.

The smallest services: bulletin board systems

Remember when I said cruising an on-line service was like walking through your hometown? Well, a BBS is more like a *small* town or neighborhood— not a lot of variety and with modest offerings of local interest only.

What you'll find on a typical BBS

Most BBSs offer the following features:

- Bulletin boards for notices of local events

- E-mail and messaging

- File libraries for downloading

- Games

In addition, many local BBSs also offer connections to larger national networks. Some BBSs are even providing access to the **Internet** (see Chapter 24 for more information about the Internet). BBSs that offer these features enable their users to connect with users across the nation.

In general, though, most BBSs stay local in their focus. Usually, that focus is defined by a geographic locality. Some BBSs have users scattered over a larger regional or national area, but they remain "local" in the sense that they appeal to a small community of people with similar interests such as a club, a hobby, or membership in a professional organization. Many companies operate BBSs for the people who use their products. If you want a broader, more national or global perspective, you need to join one of the commercial services or get on the Internet.

On the plus side, however, the best place to meet local users and find out items of local interest is on your local BBS. I find myself logging onto several local BBSs (see fig. 23.5), even though I subscribe to the national services— for the same reason I read both my local newspaper and *The Wall Street Journal*. I need local *and* national news.

Fig. 23.5
Some BBSs offer games
you can play on-line;
others provide infor-
mation or programs
you can download.
More advanced services
even have graphical
interfaces that work
much like Windows.

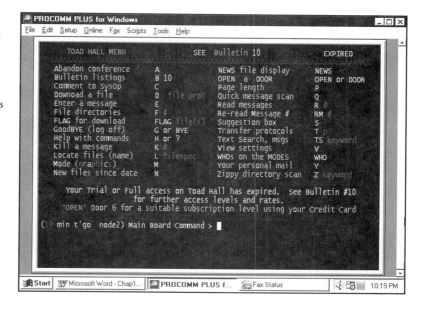

Finding the best BBSs

There are literally tens of thousands of BBSs in the United States. How do
you find the one that has the features you need? One of the best sources of
information about different BBSs is Que's *BBS Directory*. Here's a short list
of some of the country's best BBSs.

TIP   **To find a BBS near you, dial the User Group Locator at**
914-876-6678 (using your voice phone).

BBS	Location	Number	Comments
Burn This Flag	San Jose, CA	408-363-9766	Devoted to controversial subjects.
CT Adult Connections	Farmington, CT	203-889-0735	Lots of adult pictures and chat.

continues

BBS	Location	Number	Comments
CD-ROM Specialty	Thousand Oaks, CA	805-373-2965	Tens of thousands of shareware, freeware, and public domain programs via CD-ROM.
Desert Nights	Camp Pendleton, CA	619-430-7734	Information and files of interest to military personnel.
Dissociation Network	Albany, NY	518-462-6134	Devoted to social work, mental health, mutual support, and the medical profession.
GIFt Shop	Concord, CA	510-689-4686	Lots and lots of graphics files (in GIF format), including adult graphics images.
Japanese Network	Brooklyn, NY	718-833-5949	Specializing in Asian issues—it even has an option for Japanese language text!
Public Brand	Indianapolis, IN	317-856-2087	The premier source for shareware software.
Sports Club	Pasadena, CA	818-792-4752	Devoted to sports fans of all types.
The WELL	San Francisco, CA	415-332-6106	One of the nation's oldest and most impressive BBSs. Always worth checking out.

 Plain English, please!

The files and programs you'll find on-line are either **shareware** or **freeware**. Shareware authors ask that you pay them a modest registration fee if you decide to keep and use their programs. By paying this fee, you'll usually receive documentation and information on future versions of the program. Since shareware registration payments are based solely on "the honor system," it's up to you to make sure you pay for any shareware you find useful. Freeware authors, on the other hand, don't ask for any fees for use of their programs.

Which service is for you?

Let's wrap this up with a table that will hopefully direct you to the type of service best suited to your needs.

Your computing needs	Type of service
Adult interests	Local BBS (specializing in adult graphics and chat)
E-mail	America Online, CompuServe
Entertainment news	America Online, Prodigy, CompuServe
Family use	Prodigy
Games	Local BBS (specializing in games), CompuServe
Graphics files	Local BBS (specializing in graphics), CompuServe
Learning the on-line ropes	Prodigy
Local interests	Local BBS
Internet access	America Online, CompuServe, Microsoft Network
On-line chat (with local users)	Local BBS
On-line chat (not limited to local)	America Online, CompuServe
On-line news and magazines	America Online
On-line research	CompuServe
On-line shopping	Prodigy, America Online, CompuServe
Software files	Local BBS (specializing in shareware), CompuServe
Special interest forums	America Online, CompuServe

continues

Your computing needs	Type of service
Stock market and financial services	America Online, CompuServe
Technical support	CompuServe, Microsoft Network
Travel reservations	CompuServe, America Online, Prodigy

24

What Exactly Is the Internet?

● **In this chapter:**

- **Why is everyone talking about the Internet?**

- **What do you like? It's out there**

- **Getting to know the World Wide Web (WWW)**

- **What can the Internet do for me?**

- **Getting connected to the Internet**

The Internet may be the hottest topic to come along since the telephone. But will the Net live up to its hype? . . . . ➤

Did you know that Internet users are part of a revolution? That may seem like a strong statement, but the Internet *is* a revolution, or at least part of one. It's the Communications Revolution: an age in which a large percentage of our daily activities (entertainment, education, news, financial transactions, shopping, and communication) occur via electronic communications.

TIP **The Internet is a many-tentacled beast whose workings are much** too complex to cover in this space. The information in this chapter will give you some idea of what the Internet is and some of the information available on it. To actually use the Internet, however, you'll need more information. Many books are available on the subject of the Internet; one we highly recommend is Que's *Using the Internet*.

Everybody's talking about the Internet

The Internet has caught the attention of the mass media. Everywhere you turn, you see references to and reports on the Internet. Consider this:

- Most of the major newspapers and news magazines have run feature articles on the Internet and "the Net" continues to figure prominently in their coverage.

 Plain English, please!

Those in the know refer to the **Internet** as simply the **Net**.

- Major motion pictures have been released in which the Net is a key part of the story line.

- Characters on popular TV shows are depicted using the Net. There's even a nationally syndicated cable TV show devoted to covering the Net.

- Local and national TV news and talk shows often show their Internet address on-screen and encourage viewers to contact them.

- Internet e-mail addresses commonly appear alongside fax numbers on company letterheads and business cards.

- Companies large and small are rushing to set up World Wide Web sites to market to the rapidly growing population of Net users.

What is the Internet?

The Internet is not a super BBS or on-line service. It's not even a nationwide network (although that description comes closer to fitting than most others). Perhaps the best description of the Internet is a network of networks.

It's all made possible by a set of specifications and procedures for linking computer systems. Of course, there are some wires and phone lines required to physically link the computers. But it's those all-important specifications that let different networks using different kinds of computers and operating systems communicate with each other. The key elements are a network protocol (called **TCP/IP**) and a system of assigning addresses to each computer on the Net (kind of like the standardized formats for telephone numbers or ZIP codes).

 Plain English, please!

In case you want to impress your friends, **TCP/IP** stands for Transmission Control Protocol/Internet Protocol. You don't need to know how it works—just that your computer will need to use TCP/IP to communicate on the Net.

The Internet started as a way to link the computers at military installations and university research facilities to facilitate military research. However, the Internet is no longer under government control.

Now, no single person, company, or government owns the Internet. The Internet is an affiliation of hundreds of thousands of private, commercial, academic, and government-supported networks that exist in countries around the world. It's a collaboration among many different computer systems and millions of people.

What can the Internet do for me?

Simply put, when you connect your personal computer with the Internet, you can share data and information with any of the millions of other people who are connected.

That's a simple concept, but the implications are staggering. Think about it. With an Internet connection, your computer can reach out over a wire and connect to another computer that might be on the other side of town, across the country, or around the globe. The physical location of the other computer makes very little difference—all you need to know is the address.

Among the millions of computers connected to the Net, there are a great many computers set up to provide public access to all sorts of information:

- News

- Weather

- Research materials and results

- Scholarly writing

- Amateur writing

- Health and lifestyle information

- Shopping

- Product information

- Freeware and shareware computer programs

- Information of interest to professional groups

- Discussion groups on thousands of topics

- Information on government programs

- The congressional record

- Information on political parties and candidates

- Information on hobbies, pastimes, special interests, and even the activities of local clubs and organizations

Enterprising Net users have developed an assortment of specialized software to make it easier to access the plentitude of information you can find on the Net. They have names such as WinGopher, Free Agent, Eudora, Pegasus, WS FTP, Mosaic, and Netscape. (We'll show examples of some of them later in this chapter.)

Universal e-mail

Perhaps the most significant impact that the Internet has on most users is that it makes it possible to exchange e-mail with nearly everyone who has an e-mail address. It wasn't always that way.

Imagine being able to use the telephone only to talk with other telephone users within your local exchange. You could call your neighbors, but you couldn't call a business in another part of the city, much less a friend who lives in another state.

Until fairly recently, that's the way it was with e-mail on most networks and on-line services. You could exchange messages with other users on the same network or service, but sending a message to a user on another system was difficult or impossible.

The Internet changes that. Your e-mail program can now call long distance. Generally, any user with an e-mail account on a network or on-line service that's connected to the Net can exchange messages with any e-mail user on any other network or on-line service that's also connected to the Net.

What does this mean to you? Well, for instance, you might subscribe to CompuServe and use its e-mail feature to send messages to a friend who has an account with America Online, to your daughter who has an e-mail account on the college computer system, to a colleague using his company's computer network, or to a customer in Greece.

Dangers inherent in the Internet

The Internet is often described as a "wild and woolly" place and compared to the lawless Old West. In fact, the Internet (actually the people who use the Net) merely reflects society as a whole—the good, the bad, and the "different."

Just as you can find serious ethical discussions and zealous religious comments on the Internet, you can also find candid discussions of some bizarre sexual activity (complete with pictures). But don't worry, you won't have your sensibilities assaulted by either extreme unless you seek them out. If you stumble across something unpleasant by mistake, you can always just leave.

Children should be properly supervised when they use a computer to access the Internet just as they should be supervised when wandering about in a big city. Make sure they visit the Net's equivalent of the public library and game arcade and don't turn down the wrong street and enter an XXX-rated movie theater.

Finding the cool stuff

The amount and variety of information available on the Internet is truly astounding. No matter what your profession, weekend pastime, or personal hobby, you can find valuable (and fun!) resources and people who share your interests. The following examples give you just a glimpse of some of the possibilities.

TIP   **Don't be alarmed by all these bold letters and symbols. They're all** different types of Internet addresses, and as you become familiar with the Internet you'll understand Internet addressing as well as you understand how to address and mail a letter to Aunt Harriet.

Use Gopher to find information

- You are interested in the rights and welfare of children.

Try a Gopher search to find a computer that stores the information you want. For example, at the UNICEF Internet Gopher computer, you can browse through newsletters, press releases, legislative issues, and

Privacy on the Net

There is good reason for concern about the privacy of messages sent through the Net. An e-mail message or other information traveling through the Internet doesn't follow a direct path—everything is forwarded from computer to computer like links in a chain. A message might be intercepted and read at any stop along the way. As a result, an Internet e-mail message is about as private as a post card.

The sheer volume of Internet e-mail makes it highly unlikely that anyone other than the intended recipient will take the time to read the e-mail message you send. However, you must consider the possibility that it could happen.

As a result, you should think twice before putting sensitive information—such as credit card numbers—in an e-mail message.

To combat the lack of privacy in Internet messages, you can use encryption software to transform your message into unintelligible babble. Even if the message is intercepted, it's meaningless. Only the intended recipient can read the message by deciphering it with a special digital key. The Netscape World Wide Web browser includes automatic encryption technology. A program called PGP (Pretty Good Protection) is the most popular encryption utility for e-mail messages.

speeches that deal with the rights and conditions of children around the world. To find this information, you can search for the word UNICEF (see fig. 24.1).

Fig. 24.1
This gopher search located a number of listings for UNICEF. Only a few will fit on the screen, but you can browse through the list, and then select the one you want to see.

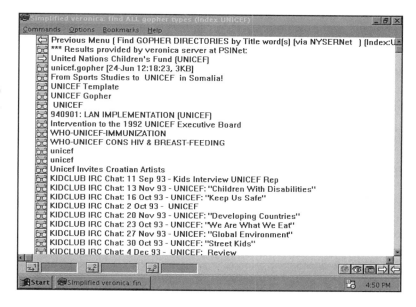

Gopher software makes it easy to locate and access all kinds of information. All you have to do is make a selection from a simple menu. When you select an item from the menu, Gopher takes you to the associated file, document, or another menu with more choices.

UseNet and mailing lists— discussions on almost everything

- You need to know what's going on in the world.

  Join a newsgroup like **nashville general**—you'll get all kinds of information relevant to the newsgroup you selected, as shown in figure 24.2.

A UseNet Newsgroup is a collection of messages (called **articles**) about a specific topic. The last time I checked, there were well over 10,000 newsgroups and the number grows every day. Although newsgroup articles are a form of e-mail, you'll need to use a special program called a **news reader** to post, read, and reply to newsgroup articles.

Fig. 24.2
One of the postings in this newsgroup is a catalog of special interest videos you can order on-line. WinVN is the news reader software program shown.

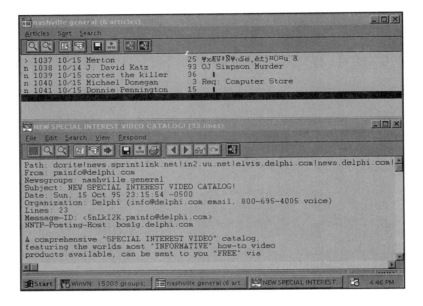

- You always wanted a hot red sports car.

  Subscribe to the exotic cars mail list (**exotic-cars-request@sol.asl. hitachi.com**) to get into regular discussions about exotic and rare automobiles, including maintenance and what it's like to drive these cars.

By subscribing to a mailing list, you get to "listen in" on e-mail conversations on a particular topic. Mailing lists are similar to UseNet Newsgroups, except that you don't need any special software other than your normal e-mail program. Subscribers to a mailing list use e-mail to discuss a topic of mutual interest by sending messages to the computer hosting the list. Software on the host computer forwards copies of the messages to everyone on the mailing list, who can then read and reply to the messages if they want.

Files everywhere with FTP

- You need some more software programs for your computer.

Connect with computers at the University of Michigan, Washington University, and Indiana University (see fig. 24.3)—all have programs that you can bring to your computer.

Fig. 24.3
You can find thousands of software programs and other files available for down-loading. The software program shown is WS_FTP.

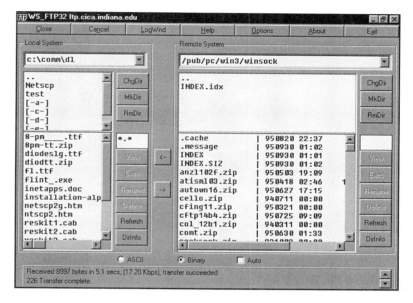

FTP (**File Transfer Protocol**) is the Internet's standard for copying files over the Net. Several programs can transfer files using the FTP protocol. WS_FTP is a Windows program designed specifically for FTP file transfers. Some software companies supply bug-fix patches and other supplemental files to Internet users via FTP, and several sites serve as vast storehouses of freeware and shareware software.

Netscape, Mosaic, and the World Wide Web

- You'd like to see a list of books on computer topics that you can buy.

Visit the Macmillan SuperLibrary site on the World Wide Web at **http://www.mcp.com** (see fig. 24.4). You can even review outlines and see sample chapters or articles containing great tips and tricks on your favorite software programs.

Fig. 24.4

This figure shows the SuperLibrary, using Netscape as the browser for the World Wide Web. Depending on your computer and the site you're visiting, you can view pictures, hear sounds, and even see "movies."

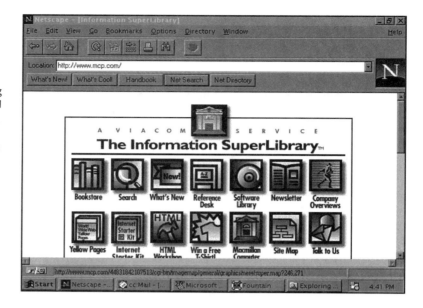

- Your son or daughter wants to know exactly how tall a Tyrannosaurus rex really was.

  Try an interactive museum of dinosaurs located on a computer at the Honolulu Community College in Hawaii (**http://www.hcc.hawaii.edu/ dinos/dinos.1.html**). View drawings of dinosaurs and photos of fossils of these prehistoric creatures—oh, and you'll learn that old T. rex stood 13 feet tall (check out fig. 24.5).

The **World Wide Web** (known as **WWW** or the **Web** for short) is perhaps getting more attention than any other aspect of the Internet. And no wonder! The Web is exciting, easy to use, and has lots of great graphics.

The Web works by using browser software such as Netscape and NCSA Mosaic to view documents containing special **HTML** codes (**HTML** stands for HyperText Markup Language) that indicate the size and position of text, display graphics on-screen, and provide **hypertext** links to other documents. The hypertext links can connect a Web document (or page, as it's called) to a multitude of other Web pages and files—like the threads of a spider's web.

Fig. 24.5

Come face-to-face with T. rex at this interactive multimedia display about dinosaurs that's on a computer in Hawaii.

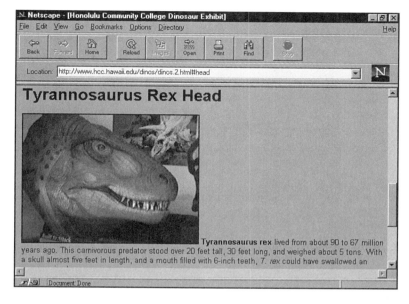

> ❝❝ *Plain English, please!*
>
> **Hypertext** is a system by which you can click a key word in one document and jump to or view another linked document or file. For instance, if this book was a hypertext document, clicking the word "hypertext" in bold type in the paragraph above would display this definition. ❞❞

The Web is a graphically-rich medium. What's more, there are provisions for on-screen forms that let you send information back to the host computer. This makes possible on-line petitions, marketing surveys, and catalogs with automatic order entry for on-line shopping.

The WWW already includes multimedia capabilities with sounds and animation. In addition, some people are experimenting with enhanced versions of HTML with virtual reality capabilities. The possibilities are endless.

How to get connected

Not long ago, getting connected to the Internet required the help of a computer professional with sophisticated networking experience—not to mention some expensive hardware and communication lines. These days you have several options for easy, economical access to the Net.

Just because you have an Internet connection doesn't mean you can take advantage of all the Net has to offer. There are different levels of Internet access, beginning with e-mail only and progressing up through the direct Net connections that support graphical World Wide Web browsing. Also, you'll need special software for Web browsing and other advanced Net features.

Is your network on the Net?

If your computer is connected to a network, you should check with your network administrator to see if the network is connected to the Internet. If so, you're in luck. You have an Internet connection and your network administrator should be able to help you learn to send e-mail to Internet addresses and use the other features that are available through your network.

Connecting to the Net through an on-line service

All the major on-line services are connected to the Internet and offer Internet access to their subscribers. Basically, all you need is a modem and a subscription to the on-line service. (See Chapter 23 for more about on-line services.) After joining the on-line service, you may need to install some additional software and change some settings to use the Internet access features. If so, you'll find all the software you need and plenty of help available on-line.

TIP   **Joining an on-line service such as America Online, CompuServe,** Prodigy, or the Microsoft Network *is by far the quickest and simplest way to get connected to the Internet.*

Internet service providers

Another option for Internet access is an Internet Service Provider (ISP). An ISP is similar to an on-line service or BBS, except that the ISP specializes in Internet access and offers few, if any, other services. Normally, you connect to the ISP via your modem.

Some larger Internet Service Providers such as Netcom and Pipeline have membership kits and custom software that you use to access their service, just as you would an on-line service. Ordinarily, however, you'll use your own software and one of the two general types of Net connections available through most ISPs: shell accounts and SLIP/PPP accounts.

Using a shell account

A **shell account** (sometimes called a **dial-up account**) is usually the simplest and least expensive form of Internet access available through an ISP. You use your own communications software program (see Chapter 18) to dial the ISP and log into their computer. Once you log in, your computer becomes a simple terminal linked by modem to the ISP's host computer. You can type commands at your keyboard that will be executed by the host computer and the results are displayed on your screen.

Normally, a shell account is limited to handling text information. Therefore, you can use it to exchange e-mail, read newsgroup articles and access information with Gopher. But a shell account can't take full advantage of the graphical features of the World Wide Web.

What does SLIP/PPP mean?

A **SLIP** or **PPP** account with an Internet Service Provider gives you the most robust connection to the Net. When you connect to the Internet with a SLIP or PPP account, your computer becomes a full-fledged member of the Internet network with its own Internet address—a peer to every other computer on the Net. The full range of Internet services are available, including FTP file transfers and all the graphics of the World Wide Web.

 Plain English, please!

SLIP stands for Serial Line Internet Protocol and **PPP** stands for Point to Point Protocol. Both protocols do the same thing—they allow an Internet connection to work over a modem instead of a hardwired network.

Unfortunately, a SLIP/PPP connection is complicated and difficult to set up. You need to install the TCP/IP software on your computer, plus you'll need special software to dial in to the ISP. Then you'll need separate software for each thing you want to do on the Net. You'll need an e-mail program, a news reader, a program for Gopher access, and one for FTP file transfers. For the World Wide Web, you'll need a Web browser.

Prepackaged Internet software kits make things easier. Windows 95 includes TCP/IP and the dialer you need to contact your ISP. However, for now at least, getting all the parts to work together properly is still a job best left to experienced computer users.

Part VI: Appendixes

What to Do When You Need Help

It's ten o'clock at night and you're just putting the finishing touches on the report you need for a meeting first thing in the morning. The spell-check is done, the figures and graphs are positioned correctly, and you've selected that *perfect* typeface for the words. Humming to yourself, you click the little printer button at the top of the screen. Nothing happens. You click the button again and still, your printer just stares at you. No flickering lights, no whirring. Help!

Who you gonna call? You'd be surprised at how many options you have in this time of crisis. Think of this section of the book as your Yellow Pages listings for "I'm Really Stuck!"

Windows 95 probably has the answer

When Microsoft decided to write Windows 95, they spent a lot of time experimenting with the **user interface**, or the way a user talks to the computer. They tested innovations on average people like you and me, then conducted surveys to see how everyone liked the changes. These tests were not just to see if people liked pressing a Start button with the mouse. A large amount of time was spent researching improvements to the Help facility.

Plain English, please!

The **Help facility** is a sort of user's manual on disk. With a couple of keystrokes or mouse clicks, it pops up on your screen offering, well, help. Because it is ready and waiting for your questions, it is often called **on-line Help**. Almost every program ever written offers some kind of help for users who get lost or need a quick answer. Many come complete with a table of contents and an index.

One thing that surprised the researchers was that most people didn't want more information in the Help screens. (This is the exact opposite of most trends in on-line Help.) Instead, everyone said, "Give us exactly what we need to know and stop cluttering our minds with things we don't care about." That made sense. Then the replies went further, "And stop making us always look up problems in a table of contents. If we don't know what the problem is, how can we look it up?" That made sense, too.

So Microsoft set out to redesign the Help facility. At the same time, they wanted to keep as many of the good things as possible from past versions of Windows Help. Let's take a tour of what Windows 95 Help has to offer.

Browsing through the Help topics

If you run into a problem with Windows 95, you can access Help instantly because it's right there on the Start button's menu. When you click Start and select Help, a window of available Help topics appears on your screen (see fig. A.1).

Fig. A.1
The Help window lists only a few general topics, but allows access to a wealth of information.

Q&A   *What do the icons mean in the Help screens?*

There are two basic icons that you'll find here. The icon that looks like a sheet of paper with a question mark is a Help topic. If you double-click it, you'll see a screen of information about that topic. The book icons are like volumes of information. When you double-click one of them, the icon actually changes to an open book, showing a list of topics (or maybe more books) that it contains.

The first topic in Help is a ten-minute tour of Windows 95 that shows you the main features. Think of it as a "ten cities in five days" kind of tour. It's just enough to get you on your feet and poking around for yourself. Directly beneath it is a Help topic for people who are already familiar with Windows 3.11. There are sufficient differences between the two programs that this topic will save users a lot of searching around.

The book called *Introducing Windows* is designed to help you register the software (in case you haven't already), and also tells you how to load and use any of the accessory programs, such as the calculator, Paint, and WordPad. In fact, it will load the program for you, so you can start learning hands-on right away.

If you called up Help because you wanted to know how to do something, like load a program or copy a file, you should open the *How To...* book (see fig. A.2). You can even learn how to use Help here if you want!

Fig. A.2
Most of your questions that start with, "How do I..." can be answered in this Help section.

Double-click here to find out how to run a program.

Double-click here to find out how to copy a file.

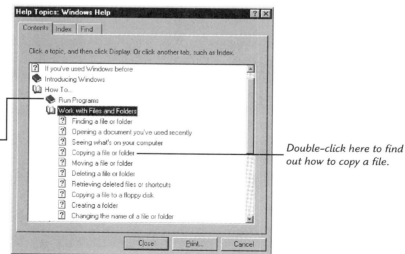

Help has something for everybody! Even after you're comfortable with the software, you might want to look in the *Tips and Tricks* section. It's chock-full of time savers and all those answers to niggly questions you never bothered to ask about.

TIP **The Help windows can be stretched to any size you like, just like** any other window. If there's more information on a topic than will fit in the window, just drag the left border out a bit. All the paragraphs will rearrange themselves to fit the new window shape.

What is Troubleshooting?

The *Troubleshooting* book, at the bottom of the list, is the one you use when your printer fails to budge at ten o'clock at night and there's no one else around to help. It's a compiled list of the most common PC problems and their solutions, and it even guides you through a step-by-step process to find the trouble. You'll be asked to pick from a list of symptoms and then given the most likely cause of the problem (see fig. A.3).

Fig. A.3
The Troubleshooter is easy to use: just pick your problem from a list and answer the questions on the screen.

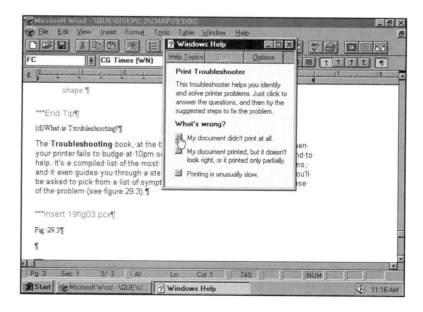

TIP **You can print out a copy of any Help topic to keep for future** reference. If the <u>P</u>rint button is displayed at the bottom of the window, just click it with your mouse (refer to fig. A.1). Otherwise, there's a second Print command located under the <u>O</u>ptions button in any window (refer to fig. A.3).

How to find the topic you want

Windows 95 has two ways to let you find a particular Help topic that may be hiding from you. The first is to use the index. Just click the Index tab at the top of the Help Topics window. Suppose you want to find out how to add a new printer to your computer. Just begin typing the first few letters of "Add a new printer." The topic you want (or one that's close to it) appears in the bottom window (see fig. A.4).

Fig. A.4
When the topic you're looking for appears in the window, select it with your mouse and then click the Display button.

As you start typing here...

...the topics appear here.

Click this tab to access the index.

Sometimes, you might try searching for a topic, but you won't be using the same terminology as the Help index. (After all, if you knew everything about it, you wouldn't need help!) In this case, Windows 95 lets you search all of the Help topics for any occurrences of a certain word. You are shown a list of all the topics that contain the word you typed.

You access this feature by clicking the Find tab at the top of the Help Topics window. Before you can use it the first time, you must tell Help to build the **database**. Just follow the instructions that appear on the Help screen. This preliminary work takes a couple of minutes, but you won't have to do it again.

Q&A *What's a database and why does Help have to build one?*

A **database** is simply a long list of computerized information, organized in a way that it can be easily searched. When you tell Help to build the Find database, it creates a huge listing of all the important words in all the Help topics. You wouldn't be able to search for words like *the* or *and*, but you could search it for words like *mouse, icon, monitor,* and so on.

You are given a choice of sizes for your Find database before you create it, and Help recommends that you take the small one. That's because the database is stored on your disk as a huge file. The more detailed the database, the bigger the file. For people with hard disks that are almost full, the large database might take up all the space that's left.

TIP **You can even add your own comments to Help by attaching** personal notes to any topic. If personal experience has taught you something, open the appropriate Help topic and then choose <u>O</u>ptions, <u>A</u>nnotate from the menu. You can now type a short note and save it inside Help. The next time you open that topic, you'll see a paper clip next to the title. Click the paper clip and your note is displayed.

What exactly is context-sensitive Help?

You don't have to go searching through Help every time you have a question. Windows allows you to get "mini-help" to guide you through tasks while you're performing them. Many windows and dialog boxes have a button in the top right corner that contains a question mark. This is known as the **What's This button**. Any time you see a selection you don't understand, click the What's This button, then click once on the selection you're curious about (see fig. A.5).

Not all dialog boxes come with the What's This button, but that doesn't mean you can't still use context-sensitive Help. If you're wondering what an object on your screen does, try clicking it once and then press the function key F1 at the top of your keyboard. A Help screen usually pops up, telling you about what you clicked.

Fig. A.5
Context-sensitive Help tells you about what you're doing right now. No need to go searching through the Help facility!

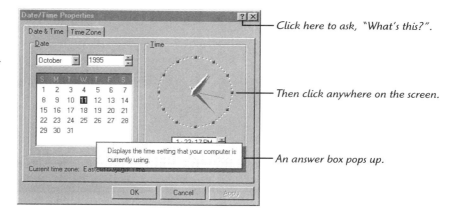

Click here to ask, "What's this?".

Then click anywhere on the screen.

An answer box pops up.

What exactly is the resource kit?

Even though the Help topics usually contain enough information to get you up and running again, sometimes you want to know the whole scoop about why certain things happen in your PC. Microsoft has written the ultimate technical reference on Windows 95 and called it the *Windows 95 Resource Kit.* You'll find a special Help file for the resource kit on the CD-ROM version of Windows 95.

The resource kit contains technical background on memory management, printer operations, and lots of things that the average person shudders to even think about. Still, if you have a thirst for knowledge and you're not afraid of a few technical buzzwords, take a peek at the resource kit.

I didn't buy the compact disc

If your copy of Windows 95 came on floppy disks, you won't have the resource kit available. You can buy the resource kit in book form at most computer stores. Many people would rather have a real book that they can flip through anyway, so even CD-ROM users may want to get this volume.

Don't just run out and buy the book because we told you to. When you see it in a store, glance over the chapter headings and poke around inside. If it seems to have the kind of information you can easily understand, then get out your wallet. If not, don't worry about it.

Getting help in any application

The Windows 95 Help facility won't tell you how to enter a formula in Excel, or how to change the margins in WordPerfect. For that, you have to ask the application itself for help. Different programs implement Help facilities with different degrees of success, but if you follow the guidelines that we discuss next, you'll probably find what you're looking for.

You can always try F1

Years ago, somebody decided that function key F1 would be a good way to access Help. Once the bandwagon started rolling along, almost everybody jumped on. Today, you can probably press that first function key in just about any program and you'll see some kind of Help screen. (A notable exception to this rule is the original WordPerfect for DOS. Help was keyed to F3 in this program, but was moved back to F1 when the Windows versions arrived.)

The best software programs make their Help screens context-sensitive too. If you're entering a formula in a Lotus 1-2-3 spreadsheet, for example, the Help screen that comes up talks all about formulas. You might say that context-sensitive Help knows where you are and has a good idea of where you're trying to go.

Did you read the manual?

Software companies don't give you a manual with your program just because they want to kill a few trees. They expect you to read it cover to cover and memorize all the major headings. Okay, not really. Let's face it—learning a new program from the manual is a little like learning a new language from a dictionary.

Still, the manual that comes with your program usually has the answer to almost any question—as long as you know where to look. Again, you're probably back to the old table of contents and index searches, but patience is a virtue. If you've never even opened the manual for your favorite software package, give it a try. You'll probably find all kinds of new features that you never even knew existed.

Can't find the manuals? Many offices today buy their software on a **licensing agreement**. That means they are allowed to copy the same program to a certain number of machines, but they only get one set of books. This saves money, but does nothing for the end users. Ask around to see who has the books. Often, they're long forgotten at the bottom of someone's desk drawer.

What's this "readme" thing?

If a new program has just been installed on your computer, you should take a few seconds to examine the directory (or folder) where that program was placed. You can view the files using Explorer, File Manager, or even the good old DOS DIR command. It's very common to find a file there named Readme.doc, Readme.txt, or Readme.*something*. In Windows-based programs, the readme file might even appear as an icon that you can click.

So what's in this readme file? Usually, a lot of last-minute tips and changes that didn't make it into the manual before it was sent to the printer. Most software publishers prefer to stick a readme file in the disks because it's cheaper than reprinting a 200-page book. The next time your software program refuses to operate the way the book says it should, look for a readme file.

Q&A *How do I see the contents of a readme file?*

If you use one of the many flavors of Windows, you probably only have to double-click the file name in the Explorer or File Manager. Whatever program the file needs will be loaded into memory and you'll be able to see the file's contents. If your computer uses only DOS, then you should try retrieving the readme file in your word processing program. Most readme files are stored in a **text-only** format so they can be displayed by just about any program.

Finding help in DOS

For years, DOS was known as the operating system for the cold-hearted. You really had to know what you were doing and your only resource was the "User's Manual from Hell." Thankfully, DOS's last couple of incarnations feature Help screens. They're not too pretty to look at, but hey, we're talking about DOS!

Starting with DOS 6.0, Microsoft actually went so far as to put the entire DOS manual on disk. What used to be a thick tome was reduced to a booklet and DOS technical support was now a few keystrokes away.

Just ask for it

To get general information-type Help while you're in DOS, just type **help** at the DOS prompt. DOS shows you a table of contents that looks like the one in figure A.6. This screen lists all the DOS commands. Press PgDn on your keyboard to see more.

CAUTION If you're connected to a network, typing the word **help** may bring up the network's Help feature instead of DOS. Oops. Try pressing Esc to make the screen go away, or choose File, Exit at the top of the screen. If neither of these work, scream for the network administrator. On these types of systems, you can only get DOS Help by typing the command word followed by **/?**.

Fig. A.6
DOS can give you help on any command.

```
 File  Search                                              Help
                   MS-DOS Help: Command Reference
 Use the scroll bars to see more commands. Or, press the PAGE DOWN key. For
 more information about using MS-DOS Help, choose How to Use MS-DOS Help
 from the Help menu, or press F1. To exit MS-DOS Help, press ALT, F, X.

 <What's New in MS-DOS 6.2?>

 <ANSI.SYS>              <Erase>               <Nlsfunc>
 <Append>               <Exit>                <Numlock>
 <Attrib>               <Expand>              <Path>
 <Batch commands>       <Fasthelp>            <Pause>
 <Break>                <Fastopen>            <Power>
 <Buffers>              <Fc>                  <POWER.EXE>
 <Call>                 <Fcbs>                <Print>
 <Cd>                   <Fdisk>               <Prompt>
 <Chcp>                 <Files>               <Qbasic>
 <Chdir>                <Find>                <RAMDRIVE.SYS>
 <Chkdsk>               <For>                 <Rd>
 <CHKSTATE.SYS>         <Format>              <Rem>
 <Choice>               <Goto>                <Ren>
 <Cls>                  <Graphics>            <Rename>
 <Command>              <Help>                <Replace>
 <Alt+C=Contents> <Alt+N=Next> <Alt+B=Back>            00006:002
```

To find out more about a command, press the arrow keys to move the blinking cursor to the command, then press Enter. To move across the columns from left to right, press Tab. You can move the other way by pressing Shift+Tab. DOS Help even supports a mouse if you have one; just click the command you want help with. DOS displays a whole screen full of notes explaining how to use the command. In figure A.7, DOS fully describes the FORMAT command.

To see the command in action, highlight Examples, then press Enter.

Fig. A.7
Here's the DOS Help screen for the FORMAT command. If the text doesn't fit on your screen, press PgDn to see the hidden parts.

To see some explanatory notes, highlight Notes, then press Enter.

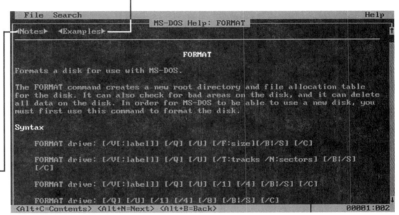

How to get Help on a command that won't work

You know the command exists. You've typed it twice and you still get an error message. If you've just about given up on trying to format that floppy disk, you can go directly to the proper Help screen. Just type the word **help** followed by a space and the command you're having trouble with, like this:

```
help format
```

You'll instantly be whisked to the correct Help topic, complete with notes and examples.

If you want a quick reminder on the syntax of the command (that is, you know the command but you're not sure of the order of all of its parts), you can type the command at the prompt, followed by **/?**, like this:

```
copy /?
```

This gives you a quick peek at the proper entry of the command, without all the bells and whistles of regular DOS Help.

 TIP **If you're using DOS 5, the /? switch is the only way to get any Help** at all. That means you already have to know the command exists and how to spell it. Plus, you only get the concise "type it like this" screen. At least with DOS 5, you get one of those nice thick manuals to fill in the gaps!

How do I get out of Help?

If you obtained Help the short way—using the /? switch after the command—you don't have to do anything at all. DOS fits all the help it figures you need onto one screen and returns you directly to the DOS prompt at the bottom of the screen. You can just type the command according to the instructions appearing on the screen above the DOS prompt.

If you accessed the more detailed Help by typing **help** at the command prompt, you must give a real *exit* command to get back to DOS. If your computer has a mouse, click the menu command Eile at the top of the screen. From the pull-down menu that appears, select Exit. You're back at DOS where you can try out what you've learned.

No mouse? You can still get into the menus by holding down the Alt key and then pressing the *underlined* letter of your menu choice. To select Eile, hold down Alt and press "F." Once the menu is opened, you can let go of the Alt key. To select Exit, press the letter "X."

What to do if Help doesn't help

You've rummaged around in every Help screen you could find. You even read the manual from cover to cover. What's left? You can always try to call the company that created the product that's giving you trouble.

Calling for technical support

Look in the manual that came with the product. Almost every company that sells computer products supports them with a **hot line**. The good ones are open from 8:00 a.m. to 8:00 p.m. local time. (Check to see if they're on the other side of the continent.) The best offer toll-free 800 numbers. Unfortunately, many companies are realizing that people will still buy their products even if they don't advertise their 800 numbers.

If you believe in Murphy's Law, the chances of you having trouble with your computer are directly proportional to the long-distance charges you'll incur. And the farther away that company is located, the longer you'll be placed on hold.

Things to know BEFORE you call

The last thing you want is to be put on hold for 15 minutes and then have the support person ask you a question you can't answer without dismantling your computer. You just *know* they'll tell you to call back with the answer, and that always means another 15 minutes on hold. When people talk about how office automation saves money, they never consider long-distance telephone charges.

Here are some things you should have on hand before you call for support:

- Your operating system version. If you use Windows 95, say so. Otherwise, tell them what version of DOS you use and any version of Windows that's present as well.

- Tell them what application program(s) is giving you trouble. If the problem occurs in more than one application, your problem is with the operating system or the hardware.

- How much free disk space do you have? In Windows 95, check the **Properties** for your hard drive. (Right-click the My Computer icon.) In DOS, a simple DIR will tell you how much is free.

- How much RAM is installed in your PC? (See Chapter 5 to find out if you don't already know.)

- What type of computer are you using? If you're using a clone bought at a local computer store, you'll get a hint by looking at the screen as soon as you turn on your PC. Look for *AMIBIOS*, *Phoenix*, or other words that might give some clue about the underlying hardware in the box.

They say they'll call back. Now what?

Most technical support centers will promise to call you back after one of two things happens: they have tried a certain number of predetermined experiments and no solution was found, or you exceeded the maximum number of minutes that the support person is allowed on the phone.

Whatever you do, don't let this person hang up! It's entirely possible that this problem is suitable for **escalation to second level**, but you have to make sure the support person knows you're serious about solving the problem.

 Plain English, please!

Most Help Centers use a hierarchy scheme where the person who answers the phone is **first level**. If he or she can't solve the problem, it will be **escalated to second level**, or sent to a specialist technician. Some organizations even have a third level for serious cases.

Before you hang up, ask the support person to repeat his name. (He said it once at the beginning of your conversation, but everyone forgets.) Then ask him for a specific date and time that you can expect a callback.

Don't hang up yet! You still have to make sure you don't get lost in the system! The last piece of information you need from the support person is a **tracking number** that you can use in case you have to call him back. (This almost guarantees that he will call you first.) Every major Help Center uses computer software to track every call, so ask for the number of your particular trouble ticket. Even if they don't call you back first, and even if the last person you spoke to was fired, you guarantee that your problem is on their "To be fixed" list. Who knows? Maybe they already found an answer!

Other sources for help

Here's the Number One rule for help (and we're sorry we took this long to say it): *You are never the first person to experience the problem.* No matter what command doesn't work, or what hardware conflict your PC is having, it happened to somebody else before. Believe it. You are no different from anyone else.

Ask around. If there's no one to ask, then go on-line (see Chapter 23) with your modem and ask a *world* full of competent users. Services like Compu-Serve have special areas for each of the major computer products companies. Send a question to the service you use and three hours later, if you didn't get an answer from the company whose product created the problem, you get an answer from another concerned user. (Most people remember their roots and are very willing to help out.)

If you haven't subscribed to one of the major commercial on-line services yet, maybe you have connected to a local bulletin board service (typically, some guy with a big computer and a modem in his basement). The **Sysop** (short for **system operator**) is usually a really keen hobbyist who either knows the answer or knows someone who does. Remember, you're never the first, so *ask around.*

What's on the CD?

The software programs included on the CD in the back of this book are useful and even fun! What you decide to install on your computer depends on how much hard disk space you have available (some programs take very little space, while others require more), and what particular features of the various programs you like. Each category offers several programs from which you can choose—but you may want to load all of the games!

Many of the programs on this disk are **shareware**. If you try a shareware program and would like to continue using it, please contact the manufacturer at the address or phone number listed in this appendix and register the software. **Freeware** programs, of course, are yours to keep and enjoy.

Installing the CD programs

The installation program on the *Using Your PC*, Second Edition CD is easy to use; in general, you can just follow the on-screen instructions. You don't have to install all the programs on the first go-round. Feel free to peruse this appendix, look over the program descriptions on the CD, and install whatever you like. You can add more programs later, if you prefer. The complete installation, using all the programs, requires more than 20M of disk space. If necessary, you can interrupt the installation to clear old stuff off your disk to make room for these new programs.

It's important to note that each program has its own installation routine, and the programs may install in a number of different folders on your hard disk, depending on how the software manufacturer set up the program. If you later decide to remove the software, be sure to clean up all the files that were placed on your system by the installation.

The installation process for Snake Chase and Easy Icons is a little different. In Explorer, open the folder for the program and double-click SETUP.EXE. Snake Chase is in the ENTERTN folder, in the SNAKE subfolder. Easy Icons is in the ICONS folder, in the EASYICON subfolder.

Running the CD for the first time

The very first time you put the CD in to use it, follow these steps:

1 Close any open application programs before beginning the installation. (This step isn't required but may be helpful.) Then open the CD-ROM folder in Explorer or My Computer.

2 Double-click the INSTALL.EXE file to start the installation.

The installation program copies essential system files to your hard disk, adds a Using Your PC entry to the Programs menu in Windows, and displays the installation screen shown in figure B.1.

Fig. B.1
The default installation will use drive C:\.

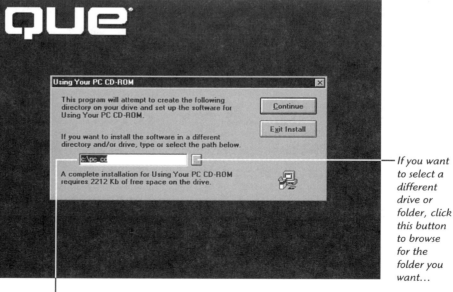

If you want to select a different drive or folder, click this button to browse for the folder you want...

...or type the desired path in this box.

3 If you prefer to install the programs in a different drive or folder, change the path in the text box or click the button to open another dialog box, where you can browse for the folder you want (see fig. B.2). Note that you may need to create special folders or specify the appropriate folder for each program as it installs.

Fig. B.2
Select the appropriate drive and folder in this dialog box and click OK.

4 When the path in the Using Your PC CD-ROM dialog box is correct, click Continue. If you decide not to install any programs at this time, choose Exit Install.

If you get a message that one of the Windows system files can't be copied, an application program may be using the file. Press Alt+Tab or use the taskbar to switch to any open programs, close those programs, and then click Retry.

5 The installation program asks whether it can create a Using Your PC program item in your Windows 95 Programs folder (see fig. B.3). If this is OK with you, click Create. If not, click the drop-down arrow and select the desired folder and then click Create.

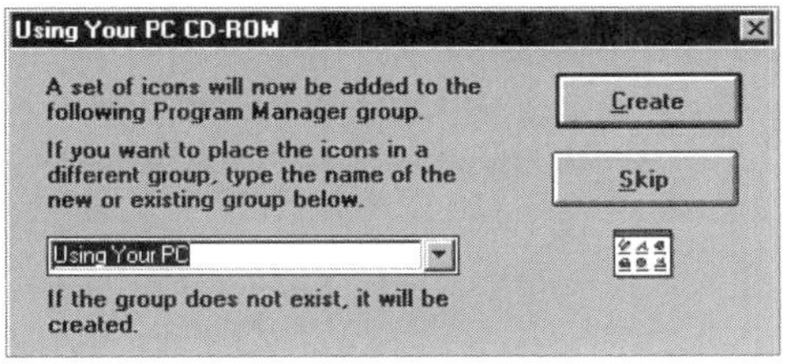

Fig. B.3
Creating the program item allows you to access the CD at a later date by clicking Start, Programs, and selecting the Using Your PC entry.

6 When the installation program has installed the Using Your PC CD software, a dialog box appears (see fig. B.4). Click OK to continue. The installation program closes and displays a window with the Using Your PC icon in it (see fig. B.5).

Note that if you use Alt+Tab or the taskbar to switch to a program in a maximized window during the installation process, you may need to minimize the program to return to the installation dialog box.

Fig. B.4
This dialog box tells you that the CD installation is complete.

Fig. B.5
You don't have to leave this window open; you can close it or continue with the installation.

If you want to install the programs now, double-click the Using Your PC icon and continue on to the next section. If you prefer to install the programs later, don't forget to remove the CD and store it in a safe place; then put it back in the drive when you're ready to install programs.

Installing the programs

Double-clicking the Using Your PC icon displays the Using Your PC CD-ROM dialog box (see fig. B.6). You can go ahead and install some or all of the programs you want, or exit the installation and come back to it later.

Fig. B.6
If you don't want to install anything now, choose Exit.

To install a program:

1 Click the category button for the program you want.

2 Click the program you want to install (see fig. B.7).

Fig. B.7
When you click the button for a program, its description appears in the middle of this dialog box.

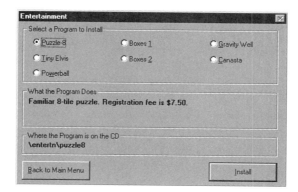

3 Click Install. The installation program may group some of the programs in a Using Your PC CD-ROM entry on the Start menu. If this happens, a dialog box will appear to get your approval. Change the menu location (if desired), and then click Create.

4 Repeat steps 2 and 3 for each program in this category you want to install. Several programs on the CD-ROM have their own installation routines. Follow the instructions on-screen for each program, changing folder locations if desired.

5 Click the <u>B</u>ack to Main Menu button.

6 Repeat steps 1 through 5 for each category of program you want to install.

Trouble installing? Exit the installation program and start again. If the problems continue, restart Windows and try again. If you still can't get a program to install, contact your computer guru for help, or call the software manufacturer (listed later in this appendix). You may need a registered version of the program to get it to run correctly for your particular setup.

7 When you're finished installing programs, click the E<u>x</u>it button. A dialog box tells you that you are leaving the installation program. Click <u>Y</u>es to continue or <u>N</u>o to return to installing programs.

Capture programs

It can be handy to "capture" a screen shot that displays the information on your screen, then save the screen shot as a graphics file that you can send to another computer or save on your hard drive or a disk. A screen shot can illustrate important information, such as what the screen should look like at a certain point in a process that you're trying to explain to someone.

 CAUTION **The more colors you use, the more realistic the screen shot will** look, but the longer the capture will take and the bigger the resulting file will be.

Clip'nSave 2.0 for Windows 95

Peter Krnjevic
Dynalink Technologies, Inc.
P.O. Box 593
Beaconsfield, Quebec
Canada H9W 5V3

E-mail address: 72220,2276 (CompuServe)

Phone: (514) 489-3007

Registration fee: $49.95

Clip'nSave 2.0 for Windows 95, shown in figure B.8, can capture a picture of the whole screen or just a portion of it, include menus and the mouse pointer, and capture the screen in monochrome (black/white/shades of gray) or in various color modes (16 colors, 256 colors, or 16.7 million colors). You can capture to a variety of popular graphics file formats, including TIFF, BMP, DIB, RLE, PCX, GIF, and EPS. Or you can capture directly to the Windows 95 Clipboard, so you can paste the result into a document.

Fig. B.8
Ever wish you could prove that you won that game of Windows Solitaire? Clip'nSave can capture your moment of triumph!

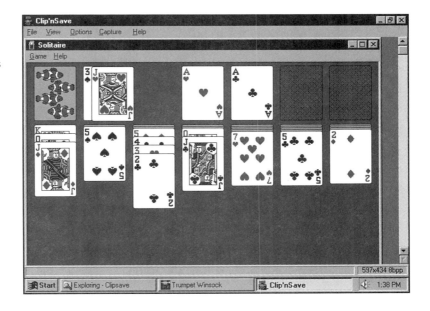

GrabIt Pro 5.0 for Windows 95

Software Excellence by Design, Inc.
14801 North 12th Street
Phoenix, AZ 85022-2515

E-mail address: 72200,576 (CompuServe)

Phone: (602) 375-9928
Fax: (602) 375-9928

Registration fee: $39.95

GrabIt Pro can capture a screen, a single window on the screen, or a rectangular portion of the screen that you define (see fig. B.9). You have the option of capturing the screen including menus, and with or without the mouse pointer.

Fig. B.9

Here, GrabIt Pro captures a screen shot of the entire Windows desktop. Once you have captured the screen, you can save the screen in one of several popular file formats.

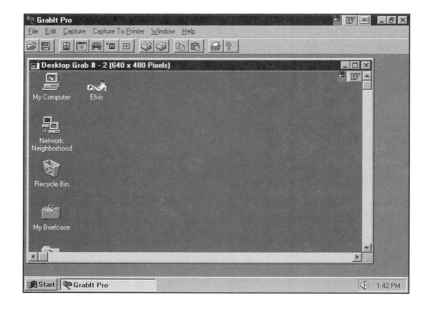

SnapShot/32 for Windows 95/ Windows NT

Greg Kochaniak
3146 Chestnut Street
Murrysville, PA 15668

E-mail address: 71461,631 (CompuServe)
gregko@kagi.com (Internet—preferred)

Phone: (412) 325-4001 (evenings)

Registration fee: $20.00

SnapShot/32 can capture the entire desktop, just the active window, or an arbitrary rectangular area that you define (see fig. B.10). You can even capture a screen shot with menus pulled down. Print a copy of the screen right away, or place the screen shot on the Clipboard for pasting into a graphics program. You can save the screen shot as a graphics file in BMP or GIF format.

Fig. B.10

SnapShot/32 is shown here capturing the Windows Calculator open on the desktop. You can even view the graphic in a special viewer window built into the program.

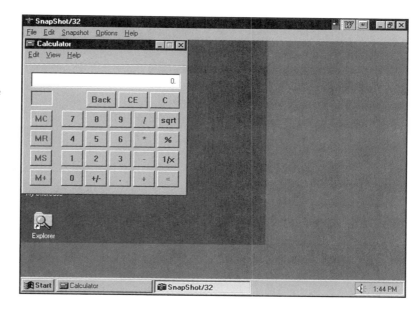

Clocks

Computers are great at keeping time—they have more clocks in them than a Swiss chalet. However, except for the clock in the corner of the taskbar at the bottom of the screen, none of the built-in clocks are especially visible or useful (or fun!). The clocks on this CD can do more than just provide the date and time; they can also work as stopwatches, sound alarms when you've got to run off to a meeting, and more.

Several of the clock programs on this CD can track Windows resources (a special area of memory used to hold things like menus and icons) and hard disk space for you. As you add more programs to your computer, you use up hard drive space. As you run more concurrent programs, you use up available memory. It's a good idea to monitor memory and Windows resources, because your computer can start to act strange (and even crash) if either of these quantities gets too low.

Stopwatch 2

Pocket-Sized Software
8547 E. Arapahoe Road, Suite J-147
Greenwood Village, CO 80112

E-mail address: 73667,3517 (CompuServe)

Registration fee: $7.50

Stopwatch 2 has a digital timer that lets you use your computer as a $1,500
stopwatch! You can save intermediate times as the stopwatch runs, thus
enabling you to record "lap" times for posterity. Figure B.11 shows the
Stopwatch program open on the desktop.

Fig. B.11
Stopwatch 2 can
record times for you
down to hundredths
of a second.

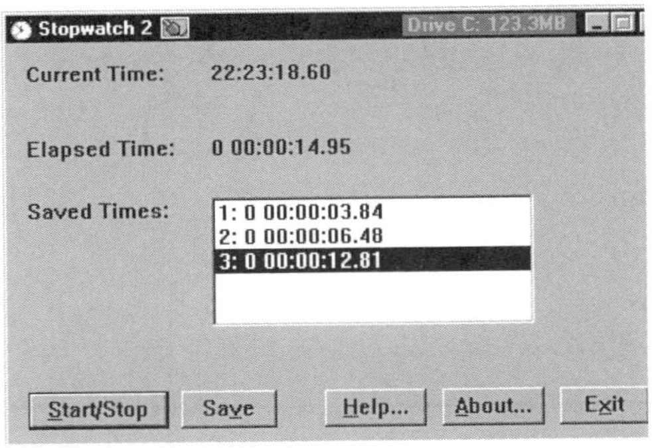

Talking Clock 2

Pocket-Sized Software
8547 E. Arapahoe Road, Suite J-147
Greenwood Village, CO 80112

E-mail address: 73667,3517 (CompuServe)

Registration fee: $7.50

Talking Clock 2 can display the time in a variety of formats that you
choose—and even speak the time for you if you have a sound card and a
set of speakers. Check out figure B.12 to see how it looks.

Fig. B.12
How big do you like
your clocks? Here's
Talking Clock 2.

Voice Clock 2.02

Erwin Koonce
P.O. Box 308
Jacksonville, AR 72078

E-mail address: 72610,1375 (CompuServe)

Registration fee: $10.00

Voice Clock can live in the title bar of a window or right on the desktop (see
fig. B.13). Using either a male or female voice, Voice Clock can announce the
time every 1 (sure to drive you crazy), 15, 30, or 60 minutes.

Fig. B.13
You can view the time,
hear it, or both with
Voice Clock.

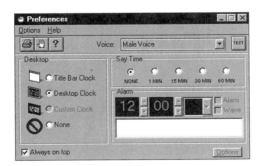

Win Bar Clock 4.1A

G.L. Liadis & Associates
5167½ Saling Court
Columbus, OH 43229

G.L. Liadis Software Inc.
Agali Beach Resort
Kardamyla
83100 Chios, Greece

E-mail address: 72274,3252 (CompuServe)
GL Liadis (America Online)
BBS phone: 614-888-4749

Registration fee: $10.00

This clock can display the time, amount of free hard drive space, memory, system resources, date, and any text message you want. You can set alarms and use timers to time various tasks. You can even set up a list of phone numbers, and then choose a phone number and dial it right from your computer (provided you have a modem installed). It can even be a simple time display, as shown in figure B.14.

Fig. B.14
Notice the tiny time display on the taskbar at the bottom of the screen? Win Bar Clock—shown at the top right here—is certainly more readable! You can also display virtually every piece of information about your system that you want.

Entertainment/games

If nothing else, computers are *great* for playing games! Here's a group of fun games and entertaining programs that you may find more than a bit addictive.

BOXES from DynoTech for Windows 95

DynoTech Software
1105 Home Avenue
Waynesville, MO 65583-2231

E-mail address: 71373,572 (CompuServe)
DTGames (America Online)
DynoTech (Microsoft Network)

Phone: (314) 774-5001
Fax: (314) 774-3052
Order line: 800-396-6832

Registration fee: $20.00

BOXES is a strategy game that requires brain power instead of speedy fingers, and is a welcome break from a day of work on your PC. The object: eliminate colored crates from the playing area by maneuvering and dropping boxes. Figure B.15 gives you an idea of how crazy this can be!

Fig. B.15
To complicate things, you need to watch for falling stones, bombs, power failures, and antigravity boxes!

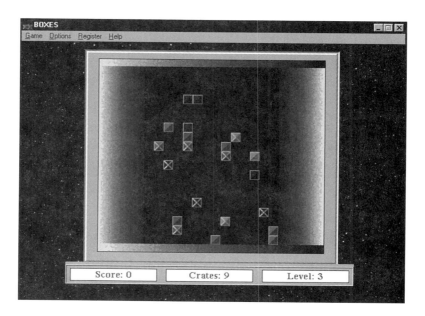

BOXES II from DynoTech for Windows 95

DynoTech Software
1105 Home Avenue
Waynesville, MO 65583-2231

E-mail address: 71373,572 (CompuServe)
DTGames (America Online)
DynoTech (Microsoft Network)

Phone: (314) 774-5001
Fax: (314) 774-3052
Order line: 800-396-6832

Registration fee: $20.00

So you think you've mastered all the levels in BOXES? Well, those devilish
folks at DynoTech are ready to challenge you with BOXES II (see fig. B.16).

Fig. B.16
The object is the same,
but the levels are
harder on your brain,
and the obstacles are
different in BOXES II.

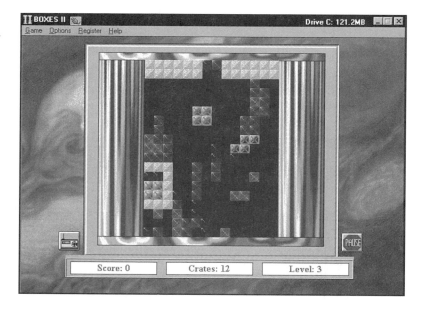

Canasta for Windows 1.4

W. Lottermoser
Public Software Library
P.O. Box 35705
Houston, TX 77235

E-mail address: 100517,3313 (CompuServe)

Phone: (800) 242-4775
Fax: (713) 524-6398

Registration fee: Contact Public Software Library

The popular Canasta card game is loads of feature-packed fun in this Windows version (see fig. B.17), with WAV sounds and MIDI music, many options and variations, and even animated card movements.

Fig. B.17
Try to beat the electronic card sharks in this Windows version of Canasta.

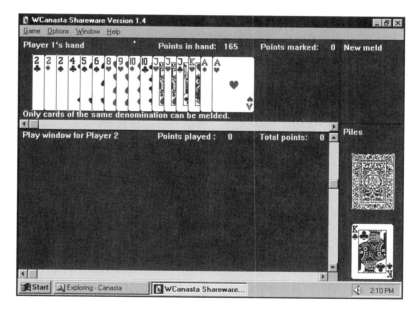

Gravity Well for Win32

David Hoeft
Software Engineering, Inc.
8352 S. Sunnyside Place
Highlands Ranch, CO 80126

E-mail address: 102330,474 (CompuServe)
DaveH@FreeHome.com

Phone: (303) 470-7142

Registration fee: $29.95

Gravity Well is a fast-paced action/strategy game (check out fig. B.18). You must pilot a spaceship between planets, leading your empire to expand. Planets orbit stars and exert gravity upon your ship. Three computer opponents compete for the same region of space.

Fig. B.18
Careful piloting is needed, but you can spend lots of time conquering the universe in Gravity Well!

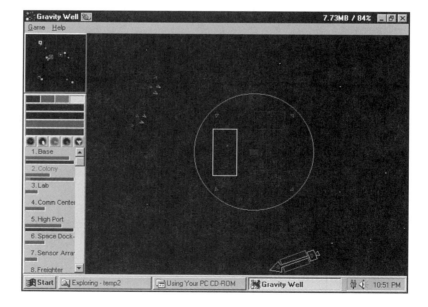

PowerBall

Peter Hoggan
Indi Software
Auchenlodment Road
Ederslie, Renfrewshire
Scotland, PA5 9NY UK

E-mail address: 100553,2112 (CompuServe)

Registration fee: £15 Sterling

PowerBall is a breakout-style game, where you use a paddle to bounce a ball and destroy bricks arranged in a pattern in the playing field (see fig. B.19).

Fig. B.19
PowerBall features lots of special effects, including "destroy everything" balls, extra lives, and a plasma gun. With registration, you receive Munchman, Defence, Table Tennis, and Space Invasion.

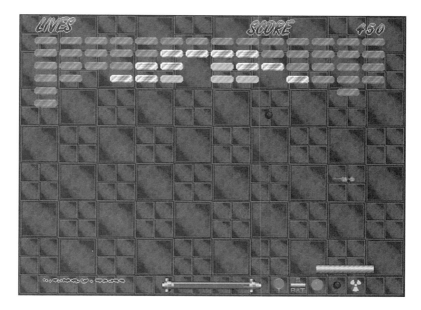

Puzzle-8 2 for Windows 95/Windows NT/ Win32s

Pocket-Sized Software
8547 E. Arapahoe Road, Suite J-147
Greenwood Village, CO 80112

E-mail address: 73667,3517 (CompuServe)

Registration fee: $7.50

One of the earliest computer games (it was even included on the original Macintosh) is the classic 8-tile puzzle. This puzzle has eight tiles, each with a number. These tiles are held in a three-by-three grid, and the object is to slide the tiles around until you have them in order (see fig. B.20).

Fig. B.20
Puzzle-8 2 isn't nearly as easy as it looks.

Snake Chase by Matco V1.0 for Windows 95

Matt Anderson
1413 Cora Street
Des Plaines, IL 60018

E-mail address: 71620,1552 (CompuServe)
Matco@ix.netcom.com (Internet)

Registration fee: $10.00

In Snake Chase, you are a snake in a maze and your goal is to collect all nine blue boxes on every level. Every time you grab a blue box, you are awarded points, and the length of your snake grows. If you run into yourself, or a maze wall, you lose a life. Figure B.21 gives you an idea of how it looks, but you should definitely try this one.

(This program requires a special installation process. See page 364 for details.)

Fig. B.21
If you register Snake Chase, you get 20 levels, sound effects, and a two-player simultaneous option.

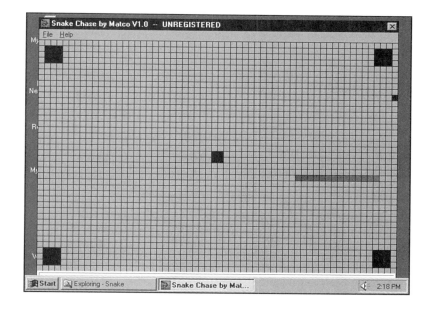

Tiny Elvis 1.5 for Windows

Matthew Smith
Pegasus Development
St. Louis, MI

E-mail address: 70661,3235 (CompuServe)

Registration fee: None

Is Elvis really dead? Just for the fun of it, Tiny Elvis sits on your Windows desktop, pops to his feet to comment on your "huge" icons and cursors; accompanied by gestures and Vegas-style posturing, as shown in figure B.22.

Fig. B.22
Tiny Elvis isn't very
useful—but he's a great
conversation starter.

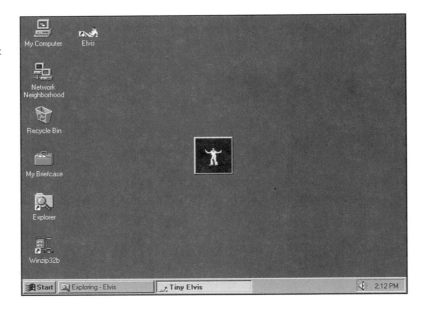

File and icon management

Although Windows 95 offers a lot of power when it comes to file and folder
management, the way the software is set up can complicate things. Sometimes, a collection of simple utilities can make your computer life easier. The
file management utilities on the CD can help you get your programs running,
find the files you need, substitute icons that are easier for you to recognize,
and generally become more efficient when using your computer.

Drag And Zip for Windows 95

Canyon Software
1537 Fourth St., Suite 131
San Rafael, CA 94901

E-mail address: 74774,554 (CompuServe)

Phone: (415) 382-7999
Fax: (415) 382-7998

Registration fee: $30.00

Many of the files you may encounter in Windows 95 are compressed to save space. Although several different ways of compressing files are used, the most popular is the ZIP format. Before you can use one of these compressed files, you must decompress (or **unzip**) the file. Drag And Zip for Windows 95, shown in figure B.23, makes it easy to unzip files.

Fig. B.23
You can even use Drag And Zip to create your own ZIP files to send to friends.

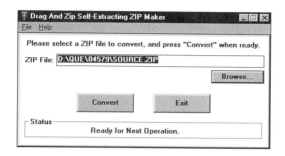

Easy Icons 95—Icon Management V3.1c

Paul Traver
P.O. Box 998
Bishop, CA 93514

E-mail address: 72144,422 (CompuServe)

Phone: (619) 873-8754

Registration fee: $19.00

Easy Icons 95 lets you look at the icon graphic stored in a file, extract the icon, and save it as an icon file (ICO) or a standard graphics (BMP) file. You can group these icons into libraries, and move icons around between libraries (see fig. B.24).

(This program requires a special installation process. See page 364 for details.)

Fig. B.24

Once you have an icon saved as an Easy Icons 95 ICO file, you can associate the icon with any file you wish—even overriding the icon that the file normally uses.

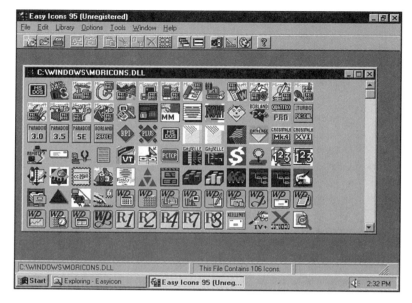

WinZip 6.0 for Windows 95

Niko Mak Computing
P.O. Box 919
Bristol, CT 06011

E-mail address: 70056,241 (CompuServe)

Registration fee: Contact Niko Mak

With WinZip, you can unzip files without leaving the Windows Explorer (see fig. B.25). You can open and view the list of files that have been compressed into the ZIP file, and easily extract any or all of the files—even running a program automatically once it has been unzipped.

Fig. B.25
A toolbar provides fast access to commonly used actions in WinZip.

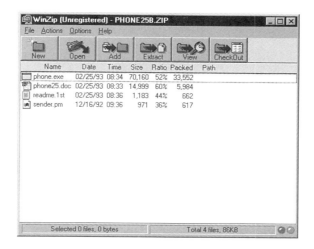

Media players

If you have a sound card and a set of speakers connected to your computer, you can play music and sounds. Music and sound files can be in one of two formats: MIDI or wave (WAV). A MIDI file stores music in a compact format, while a WAV file stores digitized sound—which can sound quite accurate, but these files can get very large. You can get MIDI or WAV files from disks, CD-ROMs, or an on-line service such as CompuServe or America Online.

HyperCD

Creative Pacific Pty. Ltd.
26/25 Devonshire Street
Chatswood, Sydney
N.S.W. 2067
Australia

E-mail address: 76702,1774 (CompuServe)

Registration fee: None

If your Windows 95 computer has a CD player, HyperCD lets you play audio CDs. You can control the playing CD, including moving from track to track, and fast forwarding or "rewinding" through the music (see fig. B.26).

Fig. B.26
HyperCD's buttons
work much like those
on your tape player.

MIDI JukeBox 2

Pocket-Sized Software

8547 E. Arapahoe Road, Suite J-147
Greenwood Village, CO 80112

E-mail address: 73667,3517 (CompuServe)

Registration fee: $10.00

MIDI JukeBox 2 lets you play WAV or MIDI files, and choose whether to play
the sound(s) once or in a continuous loop. Figure B.27 shows this player.

Fig. B.27
Even without a sound
card, you may be able
to use your computer's
internal speaker if you
have a speaker driver.
Ask your computer
dealer for help.

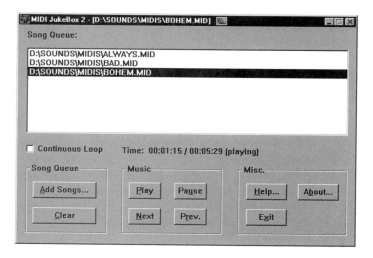

Miscellaneous utilities

These programs enhance Windows 95 in a number of ways, making it easier
to get your programs running, find the files you need, control your printer,
and even protect your computer with passwords.

BananaPC V1.6 for Windows 95/ Windows NT

Chris Scott
8850 Teakwood Court
Manassas, VA 22110

E-mail address: 74155,466 (CompuServe)

Registration fee: $10.00

BananaPC makes it easier to use the programs in your computer by letting you launch selected programs with a single click of the mouse. It also displays the time, and provides a pair of eyes that follow the cursor and a convenient list of the programs that you have running (see fig. B.28).

Fig. B.28
BananaPC lets you hide some of the running programs if your computer screen gets too "busy." From this list, you can quickly switch to another program.

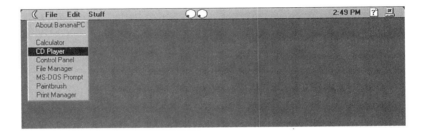

The Barry Press Utilities

Barry Press
2494 East Cheshire Drive
Sandy, UT 84093-1849

E-mail address: 72467,2353 (CompuServe)

Registration fee: $20.00

The Barry Press Utilities for Windows 95 include some very useful programs:

- A simple monthly calendar shows you any month between 1980 and 2037.

- The CodeList program can print a text file (a file that doesn't contain anything but plain text). You can customize the font, set the printer orientation, and more.

- The Match program compares two text files and displays the differences between the files in a window (see fig. B.29).

- The Flipper program lets you quickly switch the direction of printing in your printer between portrait and landscape by double-clicking the Flipper icon.

- If you want to play multimedia files—files that include animation and sound—at random times, Waver is for you. You can set the minimum and maximum time interval for interrupting your work with a multimedia snippet!

Fig. B.29
The Barry Press Utilities include many other programs that you'll find useful.

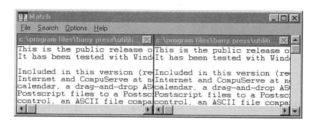

Plug-In for Windows 2.60

Plannet Crafters
P.O. Box 450
Alpharetta, GA 30239-0450

E-mail address: 73040,334 (CompuServe)
DMandell (America Online)
VSFB48A (Prodigy)
PlanCraft (Microsoft Network)

Registration fee: $20.00

Plug-In for Windows provides many enhancements for users of Windows 95 (see fig. B.30). Place the date, time, and amount of available Windows resources on the title bar of the active window. With a sound card, add a talking clock that announces the time whenever you want, as well as chimes. And more!

Fig. B.30
Specify a screen saver, set up alarms, keep your schedule handy, and have lots of other fun with Plug-In for Windows.

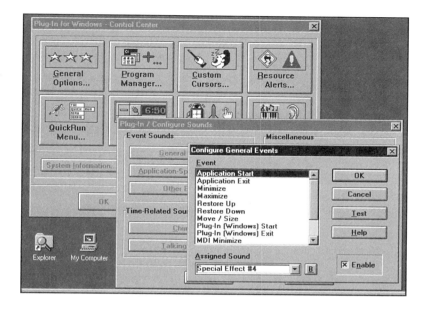

PSA Cards 2.5

William L. Rogers
PSA Software
1319 Silk Oak Drive
Fort Collins, CO 80525

E-mail address: 72064,1437 (CompuServe)

Registration fee: $25.00

PSA Cards looks and works like a card file (see fig. B.31). Just click a divider tab or card to open or close it. Enter name and address information on a card, and group cards together for organizing various lists—Christmas cards, invitations, or addresses to use with your word processing software. Print Rolodex cards, envelopes, mailing and shipping labels, and address booklets.

Fig. B.31
You can dial any phone number, provided you have a modem. PSA Cards can pop up reminders for birthdays, anniversaries, and appointments.

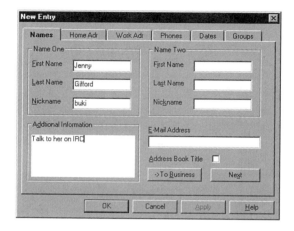

QuickTutors 95

E-Ticket, Inc.
Attention: Mail Order Sales
2118 Wilshire Blvd., Suite 1118
Santa Monica, CA 90403-5784

E-mail address: rgibson@eticket.com (Internet)
esales@eticket.com (Internet)

Phone: (520) 577-2221
Fax: (520) 577-2896

Registration fee: $19.95–$24.95

QuickTutors 95 consists of 40 minitutorials (five in this demo version) that cover topics ranging from how to use the Windows 95 Explorer to how to activate a new modem (see fig. B.32).

The full version of QuickTutors 95 can be purchased at your local computer software retail store, via the Internet Shopping Network (http://www.internet.net), or via e-mail (esales@eticket.com). Send written correspondence or an order form (which can be printed from within the Sampler version) to the address above.

Fig. B.32
QuickTutors are interactive, self-paced minitutorials that walk you through a particular task in Windows 95 and then allow you to perform it while the lesson is fresh in your memory.

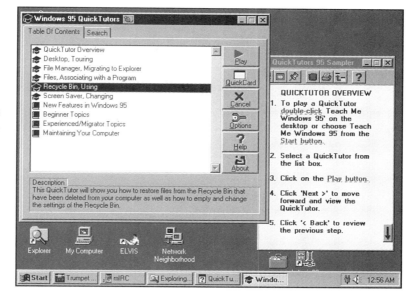

Win Calendar for Windows 3.11/ Windows 95

G.L. Liadis & Associates
5167½ Saling Court
Columbus, OH 43229

G.L. Liadis Software Inc.
Agali Beach Resort
Kardamyla
83100 Chios, Greece

E-mail address: 72274,3252 (CompuServe)
GL Liadis (America Online)
BBS phone: 614-888-4749

Registration fee: None

This small 3D calendar is handy for checking past or future dates (see fig. B.33).

Fig. B.33
The Win Calendar
program is free—enjoy!

WinU

Data Outlet
P.O. Box 37278
Richmond, VA 23234

E-mail address: 72340,375 (CompuServe)

Phone: (804) 768-0424
Orders only: (800) 242-4775

Registration fee: $29.95

You probably have many interesting programs on your computer—perhaps
some that you don't want everyone to use. It wouldn't do for someone to use
your account to download a large file, or mess around with your financial
records. WinU can help limit the programs that a casual user of your PC can
get to. WinU allows you to specify a list of programs that can only be reached
by specifying a password, thus limiting access to those programs (see fig.
B.34).

Fig. B.34

A handy feature of WinU is that you can set a time limit for running any particular program (like a game!). When the time limit is up, the program ends (with an appropriate warning first).

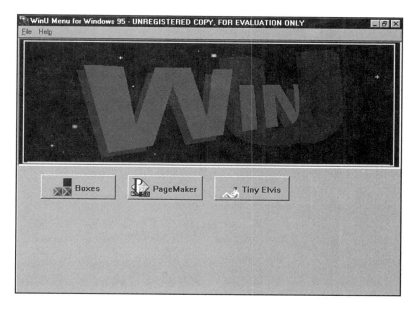

Screen savers/wallpaper

A screen saver places a varying pattern on the screen if no one touches the mouse or a key on the keyboard for a predetermined length of time. These programs were invented to prevent burn-in on older monitors, and they're not really necessary anymore—but they're still fun to play with and watch. And wallpaper? It's just plain interesting to look at!

Screen Saver Pack V1.00 for Windows 95/ Windows NT

Pocket-Sized Software

8547 E. Arapahoe Road, Suite J-147
Greenwood Village, CO 80112

E-mail address: 73667,3517 (CompuServe)

Registration fee: $7.50

The Windows 95 Screen Saver Pack has a whole bunch of colorful screen savers, including Clock, Dancing Lines, HyperCycloids, Life, Snakes, Zoom, and Spheres (shown in fig. B.35).

Fig. B.35
Spheres is just one of
the fun screen savers in
the Windows 95 Screen
Saver Pack.

Wallpaper Manager Plus for Windows

Curtis Marx
Noble Dog Software
52 Highland Ave.
Arlington, VA 02174

E-mail address: 72560,1110 (CompuServe)

Phone: (617) 648-8919
Fax: (617) 648-8921

Registration fee: $20.00

Wallpaper Manager Plus turns a variety of common formats of graphics files
into Windows wallpaper files. These formats include BMP, RLE, and PCX
(if you register, you can use the popular GIF and GLZ formats as well). This
program lets you organize your wallpaper into different galleries, and display
the wallpaper in random or programmable order (see fig. B.36). (Note that
some of the built-in wallpapers show classic works of art that may not be
suitable for viewing by young children.)

Fig. B.36
If you have access to a scanner, you can create your own wallpaper from photographs, as shown in this figure.

Viewers

One of the neatest things you can do with your computer is display full-color graphics on the screen. You can obtain these graphics on disks, via CD-ROM, from the Internet, or even from an on-line service such as CompuServe or America Online. These graphics files can be in many different formats, and special programs must be used to view the different graphics files. Fortunately, this CD provides several viewers for you to choose from!

ACDSee V1.25

ACD Systems
2201 North Collins, Suite 230
Arlington, TX 76011

E-mail address: dvan@pinc.com (Internet)

Registration fee: $15.00 (without disk) or $30.00 (with disk)

ACDSee is a graphics viewer that can display most of the popular file formats for graphics, including BMP, GIF, JPEG, PCX, Photo-CD, PiNG, TGA, and TIFF. You can view the images as they are decompressed, and use all the colors that your computer can handle. Figure B.37 shows the ACDSee viewer.

Fig. B.37
The ACDSee viewer
can even create a slide
show that switches
graphics automatically
or under manual
control.

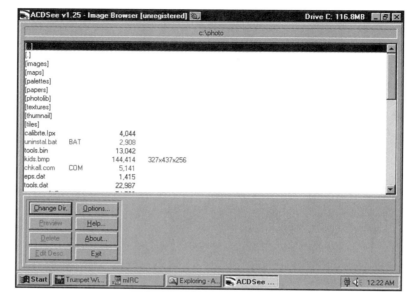

BmpView 1.0 for Windows 95

Daniel Brum
3219 Yonge St., Office 226
Toronto, Ontario
Canada M4N-2L3

E-mail address: 74762,315 (CompuServe)

Registration fee: None

BmpView lets you see only one of type of graphics format—a bitmap file
(BMP). You can get a quick preview of any BMP file on your hard drive.
Check out the tartan bitmap file that comes with Windows 95 in figure B.38.

Fig. B.38
Once you've found the file you want, you can automatically launch your favorite graphics editor (including Paint, which comes with Windows 95) directly from BmpView.

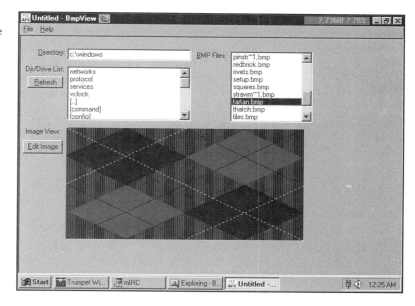

Drag And View for Windows 95

Canyon Software
1537 Fourth St., Suite 131
San Rafael, CA 94901

E-mail address: 74774,554 (CompuServe)

Phone: (415) 382-7999
Fax: (415) 382-7998

Registration fee: $35.00

You may have noticed in Windows Explorer that some kinds of files have the option for QuickView in the shortcut menu that appears when you right-click the file. Drag And View gives you more options: you can display most of the popular file types, including graphics, word processing, spreadsheet, and database files (see fig. B.39). The option to use Drag And View appears in the shortcut menu, just like QuickView.

Fig. B.39
Nine additional file types are available with the registered version of Drag And View, including CorelDRAW!, computer graphics metafile (CGM), and WordPerfect.

PolyView 2.16 for Windows 95/ Windows NT

Polybytes
3427 Bever Avenue S.E.
Cedar Rapids, IA 52403

E-mail address: PolyView (America Online)
Polybytes@kagi.com (Internet)

Registration fee: $20.00

PolyView has the ability to view the most popular file formats, including JPEG (JPG), GIF, BMP, and Photo-CD (PCD). You can display multiple graphics in separate windows, or display a single file in a full-screen mode. You can even set up a "slide show"—displaying the graphics you choose in the order you select (see fig. B.40).

Fig. B.40

You can adjust how the image looks in PolyView by changing the brightness and contrast of the image.

What If I Have an Earlier Version of Windows?

If your computer doesn't have Windows 95 installed on it, the odds are pretty good that you use an earlier version—Windows 3.1, Windows 3.11, or Windows for Workgroups 3.11. The computer community refers to these versions by the moniker 3.x (where the x can stand for either 1 or 11). Like Windows 95, Windows 3.x lets you accomplish the same things as in DOS by manipulating pictures and objects with your mouse. But because some areas in the two versions are quite different, this appendix shows some major things you'll want to do with Windows 3.x and how to do them, if:

- You're not yet using Windows 95.

- You have one version at home and another at work.

- You need to be able to use Windows 3.x occasionally.

How to get Windows 3.x up and running

Some PCs are set up so that Windows 3.x starts by itself. If so, you're all set. If you find yourself staring at the DOS prompt after turning on the equipment, you can probably start Windows by typing **win** and pressing Enter. If that doesn't work, try changing to the Windows directory first (use the command **cd\windows**). Then type **win** again.

If you've tried both methods and you're still staring at DOS, either Windows isn't really installed on your computer, it's been installed incorrectly, or some other error has occurred. If you have the original disks and you know how to do it, go ahead and reinstall the software yourself. Otherwise contact your computer guru or the store where you bought your PC. While you're at it, tell them to fix it so Windows loads automatically for you.

Program Manager manages your programs

When Windows starts, you probably see the Program Manager window on the screen (see fig. C.1). The Program Manager window contains smaller windows called **program groups**. Your programs are found inside these groups. Remember, a window is just a rectangular area with something in it. Think of the window as a border that keeps the things inside from getting out. Your programs run in windows, and it's possible to open several windows with a different program running in each one.

Fig. C.1
Double-click the little Program Manager icon at the bottom of the screen to open the Program Manager window.

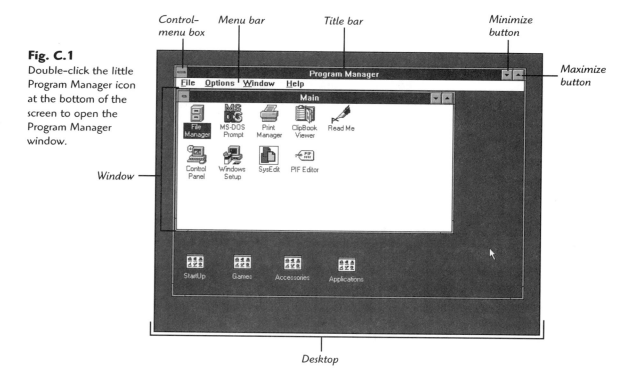

Program Manager is the main access point for all the programs you use in Windows. The square pictures at the bottom of the box are called **icons**. An icon is the term for a small graphics object that actually represents something much bigger. If you look closely at these icons, you'll see that they look like little windows themselves and that they each contain their own groups of icons. (At least they're *supposed* to look like that.) These icons at the bottom of Program Manager go by the special name of **program group icons**.

A program group is nothing more than a way of organizing your programs into categories that are easy to find. Windows automatically gives you programs divided into the following groups: Main, Accessories, Games, Startup, and Applications. You probably have other groups as well, depending on what programs are installed in your computer.

Finding your programs

Since your programs are all hidden within the group icons at the bottom of the screen, you have to open the icons to see what they contain. With a little practice, you get used to which groups contain which programs—just like you know which filing cabinet drawers contain which files at the office.

To open a group icon and see its contents, you point to it with the mouse pointer and double-click the left mouse button. (Press and release the left mouse button very quickly two times.) Try this now with the group icon named Accessories. The icon should open on the screen, as it turns into a small window full of icons (see fig. C.2).

Fig. C.2
When you double-click a program group icon, it turns into a window full of icons. Each icon represents a program you can run.

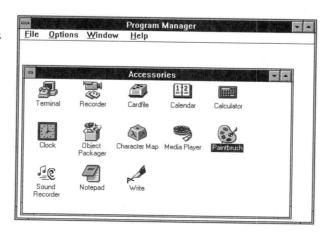

It takes a little practice to double-click successfully. Try holding the mouse very still during the clicking. If you still have trouble, there are other ways to open an icon:

- Click the icon once. A menu pops up next to the icon. Point to the word Restore with the tip of the mouse pointer and click the left button one time.

- Click the icon once to select it, then press the Enter key on your keyboard.

- Use the menu in the Program Manager window to open a group. Point to the word Window in the menu and click once. A **pull-down menu** appears that contains the names of all your groups listed in a single column. Click the name of the group you want to open.

How do I start a program?

You run a program pretty much the same way as you open a program group—by double-clicking its icon. Let's say you want to do a few quick operations on your Windows Calculator. Just double-click its icon, and the calculator pops up on your screen (see fig. C.3).

Fig. C.3

The calculator works just like the one you have on your desk—except you press the little buttons by pointing and clicking with your mouse. Hint: The asterisk is for multiplying and the slash is for dividing.

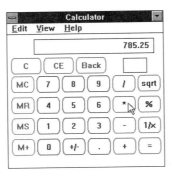

If you tend to work more with logarithms and cosines, try the Scientific version of the calculator. See the menu option called View at the top of the calculator's window? Click it to open the menu; then click the Scientific option.

All done? Close it up

Whenever you're finished using a program, you put it away to clear some space on your desktop for the next program you want to use. Just as there are lots of ways to open an icon, there's more than one way to close an open window. I like to use the **Control-menu box**, which is the little gray box in the top left corner of every window (refer to fig. C.1).

Click this box once with your mouse, and a menu drops out of the box. Click once on the menu selection Close and the program disappears. You can also close a window by double-clicking the Control-menu box. Try it!

I like the keyboard better

If you'd rather not use the mouse—and sometimes the mouse isn't the quickest method—you can use the keyboard for many menu operations in Windows 3.x. For example, you can open any menu by pressing the Alt key. Then you can use the arrow keys to jump from menu to menu, or press the underlined letter (called the **hot key** or **accelerator key**) in the menu name to drop down the menu. To choose an option on the menu, use its hot key. For example, you can close most programs by opening the File menu and choosing Exit. To do this with the hot keys, you'd press Alt to open the menu, *f* to drop down the File menu, and *x* to choose Exit.

For really fast access, try the **keyboard shortcuts**. Whenever you click a pull-down menu, if that menu selection has a shortcut, it will be shown next to the command. For example, the shortcut to close an open program window is to press the Alt and F4 keys. If the shortcut requires a key combination like this, you'll see a plus sign (+) between the names of the two keys: Alt+F4. Hold down the first key, press the second key, and then release both keys.

Hopping from group to group

In Windows, you don't necessarily have to close a window before you can open another one. (It's neater if you do, but not always convenient.) Just as you might have two or three file folders open on your desk at the same time, you can have two or three groups or program windows open simultaneously.

You should still have the Accessories group open on your screen. If you want to see what's hidden in the Main group, just double-click the Main icon, or select it from the Window menu in Program Manager. The Main window opens on top of the Accessories window.

Q&A *The Accessories window is hiding the Main group icon. How can I double-click it?*

You can drag the Accessories window out of the way with your mouse. Position the mouse pointer anywhere within the window's **title bar** at the top of the Accessories window (take another look at figure C.1 if you're not sure where the title bar is). Press and hold down the left mouse button, then move the mouse pointer elsewhere on the screen. The window will **drag** with the mouse pointer to the new location you specify. When you release the mouse button, the window will **drop** into place. (If this window–dragging has you stumped, check out Chapter 10. Just about everything you can do with Windows 95 can also be done with Windows 3.x.)

Now that the Main group is lying on top of the Accessories group, you have a hard time seeing the Accessories window. To return to Accessories, just click your mouse anywhere within an exposed area of the Accessories window. Main and Accessories will appear to switch positions as Accessories comes to the top of the pile. (You can go back to Main by simply clicking anywhere within its window, too.) Think of it as paper-shuffling on your desktop. Whatever's on the bottom of the pile can be brought to the top with a single click of the mouse.

Want to close the open windows and start all over again? Each group window has a Control-menu box in the top left corner, just like the Calculator did. You can either double-click the box for the window you want to close, or click it once, then choose Close from the menu. Either way, the group windows will instantly shrink back down to icon size again.

On the other hand, if you want all those windows open, but need to be able to see their contents, open the <u>W</u>indow menu and choose <u>T</u>ile or <u>C</u>ascade. **Tiling** the windows displays them all next to each other, like floor tiles. **Cascading** sets them up like a waterfall, bouncing down from one window to the next. Can't see all the icons in each one? Use the scroll bars to find the icon you need, or click the window to select it and choose <u>W</u>indow, <u>A</u>rrange Icons to straighten them up.

Making Windows 3.x look the way you want

Most people decorate their work places to suit their personalities and help them feel more relaxed. Since Windows is where so many computer users spend their days, it stands to reason that you can decorate it a bit, too. The controls that let you start interior decorating with Windows are located in a special program called **Control Panel**. You will find it inside the Main group. Just double-click Main to open it (unless it's already open), then double-click the icon named Control Panel. A new window opens, resembling the one shown in figure C.4.

Fig. C.4
Control Panel lets you customize the way Windows looks and works. Your Control Panel icons may be slightly different because your computer may have different features that need controlling.

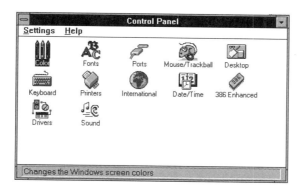

Changing the screen colors

Feel like repainting your Windows desktop? Just double-click the icon labeled Color. A dialog box appears, just like the ones in Windows 95. It contains the controls you need to repaint all the parts of your screen.

At the top of the Color dialog box is a section named Color Schemes. In the middle is a mock-up of some windows, menus, and buttons that allow you to preview how your color scheme will look (see fig. C.5). Click the arrow button next to Color Schemes to see the ready-to-go color schemes. Click one of the schemes to make it active and you'll see a preview of your choice. When you find a color scheme you like, click the OK button at the bottom of the dialog box and your Windows colors will change to the scheme you chose.

 Plain English, please!

Windows uses dialog boxes to give you options or messages. Dialog boxes can't be shuffled underneath other windows, but you can usually drag them out of the way if you need to see something underneath. To get rid of the dialog box, though, you must click OK, Cancel, or whatever is appropriate.

If you get tired of your selected colors, you can change them again anytime. Open the Color icon in Control Panel whenever you feel the urge to redecorate. If you prefer the colors that were there before you started experimenting, just choose the scheme named Windows Default at the top of the list.

Fig. C.5
Hot-Dog Stand is pretty flashy, while Wingtips is conservative. There are lots of choices in between, so feel free to experiment.

Click here when you have something you like.

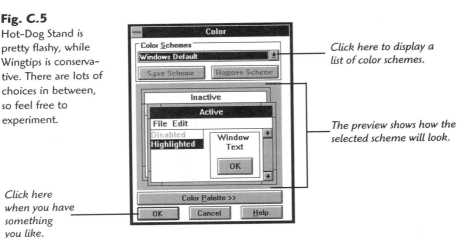

Click here to display a list of color schemes.

The preview shows how the selected scheme will look.

Just for fun—wallpapers, patterns, and screen savers

Wallpaper is an image or design that appears in the background behind Program Manager. You don't see it unless Program Manager is minimized or sized to be smaller than full-screen. (See Chapter 10 for details on resizing windows.) Windows comes with a wide selection of wallpaper designs—from tasteful and neat to busy and ostentatious.

Windows also comes with a number of built-in **patterns**, or you can build your own. Patterns are combinations of black-and-white pixels that create interesting little shapes. You can combine patterns with wallpaper to make your screen completely unreadable! Seriously, the pattern you choose appears behind program icons that are minimized, so try to find a combination that won't create eyeball wars, or don't use both a pattern and a wallpaper.

Screen savers are special programs that automatically take over the display when a computer is idle for a certain amount of time (see the monitors information in Chapter 6 for an explanation of how this works). Although Windows doesn't come with screen savers as fancy as those you can buy at the store, it does give you a few flashy choices.

To add a wallpaper, pattern, or screen saver, double-click the Desktop icon in Control Panel to see the available choices (see fig. C.6).

Fig. C.6
The Desktop dialog box lets you change several aspects of your Windows desktop.

Click here to create a new pattern from the one you've chosen.

Click here to select a built-in pattern.

Click here to see a list of wallpapers.

Click here to choose from available screen savers.

Click here to test the screen saver you've selected.

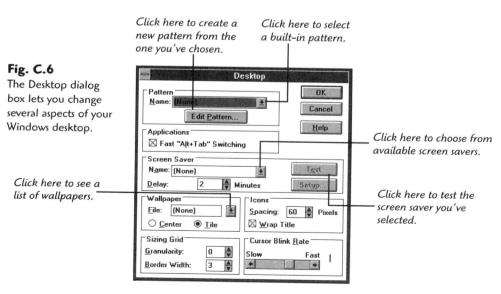

If the wallpaper you choose is fairly large, click the button marked Center in the Wallpaper section of the Desktop dialog box. This gives one large, centered image on your screen. Most of the wallpapers that come with Windows require that the setting be changed to Tile. This fills the screen with multiple copies of an image that has been saved at a small size.

To set the amount of time the computer must be idle before the screen saver appears, click the arrows next to the Delay box. Some screen savers have settings you can change, like personalized messages or colors. You can access these options by clicking the Setup button. When the screen saver is running, move the mouse or press a key to get back to work. The safest key to press is the Ctrl key.

 TIP **All of these options take memory to display. If you turn on** wallpaper, patterns, or screen savers, and your computer seems to slow down, turn them back off.

Other Control Panel icons

The Mouse settings can help you resolve uncontrollable mouse twitches. There are settings in this dialog box that let you control the sensitivity of the mouse pointer and how fast you have to double-click for the double-click to work. (Most new users like to change this setting to *slow*.) Southpaws can even change the position of the mouse buttons so that the right one works instead of the left. Be careful with this one. If you reverse the mouse buttons, you have to select everything with the *right* mouse button to change the settings back again.

The Sound settings are fun, but you can't use sound without a sound card or a special file called a **speaker driver**. Two speaker drivers—SPEAK.EXE and SPEAKER.DRV—are generally available from both Microsoft and various bulletin boards. If your system has a sound card, or if you got a speaker driver from somewhere, you can control what noises or tunes you hear whenever Windows starts, shuts down, encounters an error, and so on. The system uses WAV (pronounced *wave*) files. Lots of people have WAV files available—for bits of movie dialogue, or funny sounds like "uh oh." Check with your computer dealer if you want more details on using sound.

Control Panel lets you play around with a lot of other settings, too. Unfortunately, some of these controls can really mess up parts of your system. Check for instructions in your Windows documentation or the Windows Help system. In general, don't change the settings without knowing what you're doing.

File Manager handles disks and files

File Manager is a handy program that does file and disk management tricks and comes free with Windows. Because it's considered fairly important, it's located in the Main group and sports an appropriate icon: a filing cabinet. Open the Main group with a double-click of your mouse and then give the File Manager icon a double-click, too.

The row of disk-drive icons near the top of the File Manager window is your connection to all the disk drives on your system, including CD-ROM drives and network drives if you happen to be connected to a network. Click these icons to switch from one drive to another. The drive window changes to show the files and directories on the disk. You know which drive is **active** (the C: drive, in most cases) because its icon will be surrounded by a rectangle. In figure C.7, File Manager displays the files and directories in drive C:, the active drive.

Fig. C.7
Depending on your equipment setup and your versions of Windows and DOS, your File Manager screen may look or operate slightly different than shown here.

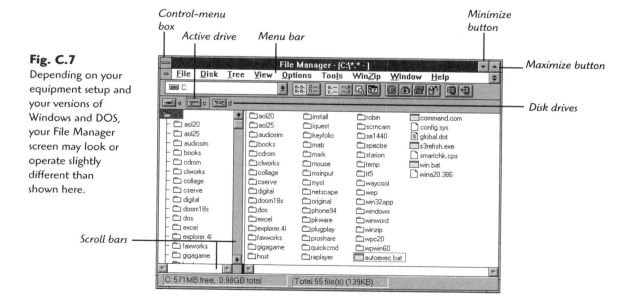

Finding files and searching directories

On the left side of the drive window, you see a column of yellow file folder icons with names next to them. Each file folder represents a directory on your disk. Each folder contains the files within that particular directory.

- To open a file folder and look inside, just click its icon. The file folder icon actually opens up.

- When a file folder is opened, the files and directories inside the file folder appear as names and icons in the right side of the window. For a full explanation of what the icons mean, turn to the section "How to peek into a file" later in this appendix.

- You can click up and down the column of folders and quickly see all the files inside any one of them.

- If there are other file folders (directories) inside the selected one, they are shown as yellow folders on the right side of the window along with the files. If you want to see them as part of the **tree structure** on the left, double-click the directory that they are stored in. The hidden **branch** of subdirectories is displayed (see fig. C.8), and you can click those subdirectories to see what they contain.

Fig. C.8
By double-clicking the directory name in the left window, its subdirectories appear as part of the tree so you can click them too.

Subdirectories

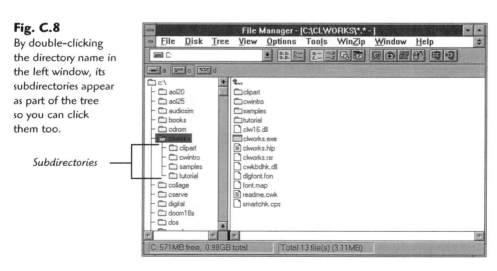

If you want to see all the subdirectories on a disk quickly, just select <u>T</u>ree, Expand <u>A</u>ll from the menu, and the complete directory tree unfolds magically before your eyes.

Of course, you can use File Manager to make your own directories or to get rid of directories you no longer want. To make a new directory, follow these steps:

1 Click the file folder that will hold the new directory. If you want a directory to be located directly off the root, click the top folder icon that has the backslash (for example, C:\).

2 Select <u>F</u>ile, Cr<u>e</u>ate Directory. The Create Directory dialog box appears.

3 Type the name of the new directory, then press Enter or click the dialog box's OK button.

Getting rid of a directory is almost as easy:

1 Select the directory you want to delete by clicking it with your mouse. Then press your keyboard's Delete key (or select the <u>F</u>ile menu's <u>D</u>elete command). A dialog box appears, showing the name of the selected directory. Click OK to delete the directory, or Cancel if you change your mind.

2 If you clicked OK, the Confirm Directory Delete dialog box appears. This is an extra step where File Manager asks, "Are you really sure?" If you click the <u>Y</u>es button, the directory is erased.

3 If there are any files in the directory, the Confirm File Delete dialog box appears. Click the <u>Y</u>es button to delete the file. If you know that there is more than one file in the directory and you want to delete all the files, click the Yes to <u>A</u>ll button.

You can even see more than one drive at a time

File Manager can show you more than one drive at one time. Just double-click the icon of the new drive you want to see. When you do, you get another drive window on top of the first. Can't see all of both windows? Use the <u>W</u>indow menu's <u>T</u>ile command, so you can see them both clearly (see fig. C.9).

In some versions of Windows 3.x, when File Manager tiles two windows, it places them one above the other. This is a little dumb because the directory tree listings in each drive run vertically and you never get to see much of the drive without scrolling. If this happens to you, when you select <u>W</u>indow, <u>T</u>ile, hold down the Shift key on your keyboard. The windows will appear side by side instead.

Fig. C.9
Use the Tile command to see two drives for the price of one!

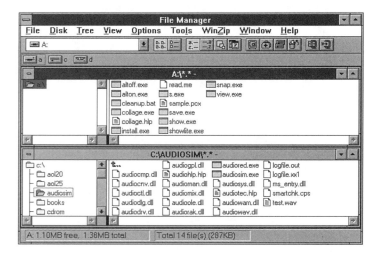

How to see more information

When you type the DIR command under DOS, you get more than a list of file names. The list includes extras such as the size of the file and when it was created. Many people like seeing this information and are disappointed when it doesn't show up in File Manager. It's not really missing: to see all file information, click File Manager's <u>V</u>iew menu, then select <u>A</u>ll File Details. After that, the file window looks something like figure C.10, with the files arranged in a single column. Each row in the window shows all the information for a file.

If you select the <u>V</u>iew menu's <u>P</u>artial Details option, you can choose which file info you want to see. Many people prefer to display simply the file sizes and dates.

Fig. C.10

File Manager can show you all the file details if you change the view options.

The icon in this column indicates what kind of file it is.

The file name is listed here.

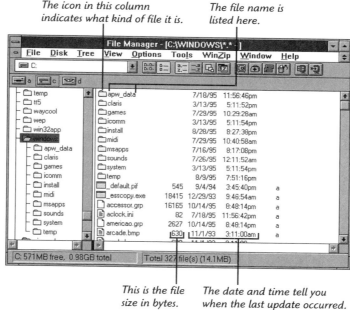

This is the file size in bytes.

The date and time tell you when the last update occurred.

File Manager lets you list your files in a number of different orders. In most cases, you'll probably want to arrange files alphabetically so you can quickly find them by name. On other occasions, however, you may want to see which files were modified most recently. Or maybe you want to see which files are hogging the most disk space. Because you have different needs at different times, File Manager lets you decide how to view your files: by name, by type, by size, or by date. Just pull down the <u>V</u>iew menu and choose one of the Sort options.

How to peek into a file

If you look closely at File Manager's file window, you'll see special icons next to each file name. These represent individual files, as explained in the following table.

Icon	What does it mean?
	These icons are files that Windows recognizes as programs. They all have the extension COM, EXE, PIF, or BAT. You can double-click these icons to run the program immediately.
	These icons are files that are associated with a certain Windows application program, such as Excel, WordPerfect, or Paintbrush. Windows knows which program saved this file on the disk. You can look at one of these files by simply double-clicking the file name. Windows gets the program, then the file, and loads them both into memory, giving you access to all the features of that file and that application.
	These icons are files that are not currently associated with any Windows application, which means you can't view them by double-clicking. (Try it. You get an error message, but it doesn't hurt anything.)

Copying, moving, and deleting files

File Manager lets you use your mouse to perform copies and moves. You simply drag the file name from one place in a window to another. Before you can start copying and moving files with File Manager, though, you need to know some of the assumptions it makes about your actions:

- If you drag a file from one place to another on the *same* disk, File Manager assumes you want to *move* that file rather than copy it.

- If you drag a file from one disk to another, File Manager assumes that you want to *copy* the file to the new location and keep the original wherever it was.

 TIP **If you always want your actions to be confirmed when copying,** moving, or deleting files in File Manager, choose Options, Confirmation and specify what you want to confirm. That way, you'll always get a pop-up dialog box requesting confirmation when you change a file. If you move or copy files a lot, you may find the confirmations annoying; just turn off the ones you don't want.

Copying a file

Because of the assumptions File Manager makes, there are two ways to copy a file using your mouse. To copy a file from one disk to another, first open a window for both disk drives by double-clicking the drive letter icon, and then tile the windows so you can see them both. Click the name of the file you want to copy. Hold down the mouse button and drag the file name from one window to the other. The mouse pointer changes to display a piece of paper with a plus sign (like the one here in the margin). Watch the rectangle that shows which directory is active—don't release the mouse button until you've selected the directory you want. (If you don't want the file in any directory, drag it to the root directory at the top of the directory tree.) When you release the mouse button, File Manager copies the file to the new location.

If you want to copy a file from one place to another on the *same disk*, the operation is a little different because File Manager assumes that you really want to move the file and not copy it. Hold down the Ctrl key and then drag the file with the mouse. The Ctrl key tells File Manager to copy the file rather than move it. (Just remember that Ctrl and Copy both start with the letter *C*.)

Moving a file

Moving files in File Manager is as easy as copying them, especially if you're moving from directory to directory on the same disk. To do this, just drag the file and drop it on the directory icon where you want it to go. The document icon attached to the mouse pointer doesn't contain a plus sign (check out the example in the margin); therefore, the document is being moved and not copied.

To move a file to another disk, open a window for both disks so you can see what you're doing. Hold down the Shift key, and then drag the file from one disk window to the other. The Shift key tells File Manager to move the file rather than copy it. (I try to remember this one by thinking that I want to *shift* the file over to another drive.)

Deleting a file

It's also easy to erase files with File Manager. Just click the file to select it and then press the Del key (or choose File, Delete). When the Delete dialog box appears, click the OK button, or click Cancel if you change your mind.

Q&A *It says* `This is a system, hidden, or read-only file.`

Files that are very important to the operation of your PC are usually marked with a special attribute that makes them system, hidden, or read-only. (You can see the attributes when you choose the View, All File Details option.) It's unusual to delete them, so Windows warns you first. You can delete them if you're sure you want to, but your system may not work properly afterwards.

Renaming a file

Sometimes, file names wear out their usefulness, and you need a fresh name to reflect what the file has evolved into. To rename a file, select it and choose File, Rename. A dialog box appears with the old name already filled in and an empty box where you can type the file's new name. Click the OK button when you're done, or Cancel to change your mind.

If you get the `Error renaming file` message, you're probably trying to use a name that has already been assigned to another file. (Or you might have tried to use a character that's illegal as part of the file name.)

Finding a lost file

When you get a lot of files and directories on a disk, it's easy to forget that special place where you put a file so it wouldn't get lost (ha!). To locate a specific file with File Manager, choose File, Search. You'll get the Search dialog box, as shown in figure C.11, in which you can type the name of the lost file and indicate which directory File Manager should look in first.

To search your entire hard disk, make sure this says `C:\`, and select the Search All Subdirectories option. When you select the Search All Sub-directories check box, File Manager searches not only the directory you typed in the Start From box, but every subdirectory inside that directory. If you deselect this check box, File Manager searches only in the named directory, ignoring all subdirectories.

File Manager uses the **criteria** you type in the Search dialog box to scan your disk for files that match the file name you requested. When it's done, File Manager displays the search results in a new window. The list in this window shows every occurrence of the requested file (there may be several with the same name in various directories). Look over the list for the location of the exact one you want.

Fig. C.11
Clicking OK starts the
search for the file.

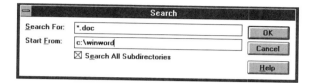

You can use DOS wild cards in the search. For example, you can tell File
Manager to search for the file *.DOC, in which case it would find every file
with a DOC extension. Never use *.* as a search criterion, because File
Manager will simply list every file on the disk, which doesn't help too much.

Dealing with groups of files

It's possible to select any group of files right in the file window and then
perform an action on that group. To select a group of files that are listed
together in a window, click the first file to highlight it. Hold down the Shift
key, then click the last file in the group. When you do, all the files between
the two clicked files are highlighted.

What if the files that make up your desired group are not listed together in
the window? No problem. Click the first file name, then add any number of
files to the group, one by one, by holding down the Ctrl key and clicking each
additional file name.

Once all the files are selected, you can drag the entire group to copy or move
them as desired. For example, you can drag the group to a new directory on
the same disk and the entire group of files will be moved. As you might
expect, you can drag the group to another drive, and the entire group will
be copied—very handy when you want a backup copy of important files! A
special version of the mouse pointer indicates that you are copying or moving
multiple files.

If you change your mind about doing anything with the group, click any
file name without holding down Shift or Ctrl, and your group is no longer
selected.

How do I get out of here?

When you're done with Windows and ready to turn off your machine, DON'T!
You must always exit Windows completely and return to the DOS prompt

before you turn off your PC. This is a cardinal rule. Windows and its programs always like to clean up after themselves by saving important files to the hard disk and deleting files they no longer need. If you just turn off the machine unexpectedly, they don't get a chance to do this. By properly exiting Windows, all of this housekeeping is automatic.

You exit Windows in much the same way as you exit any other Windows program. The Program Manager has a Control-menu box in the top left corner. You can double-click it to exit, or simply click it once and choose Close from the menu. Either way, a small dialog box appears in the middle of the screen. If you choose OK, you return to the DOS prompt where it's safe to turn off the computer. If you choose the other selection, Cancel, you stay in Windows so you can play around some more.

Index

PLUG YOURSELF INTO...

THE MACMILLAN INFORMATION SUPERLIBRARY™

Free information and vast computer resources from the world's leading computer book publisher—online!

FIND THE BOOKS THAT ARE RIGHT FOR YOU!

A complete online catalog, plus sample chapters and tables of contents!

- **STAY INFORMED** with the latest computer industry news through our online newsletter, press releases, and customized Information SuperLibrary Reports.

- **GET FAST ANSWERS** to your questions about QUE books.

- **VISIT** our online bookstore for the latest information and editions!

- **COMMUNICATE** with our expert authors through e-mail and conferences.

- **DOWNLOAD SOFTWARE** from the immense Macmillan Computer Publishing library:
    - Source code, shareware, freeware, and demos

- **DISCOVER HOT SPOTS** on other parts of the Internet.

- **WIN BOOKS** in ongoing contests and giveaways!

TO PLUG INTO QUE:

WORLD WIDE WEB: **http://www.mcp.com/que**

FTP: ftp.mcp.com

Que's *USING* Series

For the fastest access to the one best way to get things done, check out other *Using* books from Que! These user-friendly references give you just what you need to know to be productive—plus no-nonsense tips and shortcuts in plain English. Whatever the topic, there's a *Using* book to ensure computer confidence!

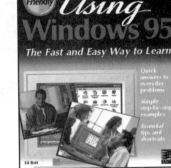

User Identification Level

| New | Casual | Accomplished | Expert |

Que's *SPECIAL EDITION USING* Series

For accomplished users who desire in-depth coverage, *Special Edition Using* books are the most comprehensive references. These books contain professional tips and advice—as well as valuable tools and software—to optimize results with all major hardware and software topics.

User Identification Level

| New | Casual | Accomplished | Expert |

*Look for **Using** books and **Special Edition Using** books at your favorite bookstore!*

Complete and Return this Card
for a *FREE* Computer Book Catalog

Thank you for purchasing this book! You have purchased a superior computer book written expressly for your needs. To continue to provide the kind of up-to-date, pertinent coverage you've come to expect from us, we need to hear from you. Please take a minute to complete and return this self-addressed, postage-paid form. In return, we'll send you a free catalog of all our computer books on topics ranging from word processing to programming and the internet.

.☐ Mrs.☐ Ms.☐ Dr.☐

me (first) [   ] (M.I.) [ ] (last) [   ]

dress [   ]

[   ]

y [   ] State [ ] Zip [   ] [   ]

one [ ] [   ] [   ] Fax [   ] [   ] [   ]

mpany Name [   ]

mail address [   ]

Please check at least (3) influencing factors for purchasing this book.

ont or back cover information on book .... ☐
ecial approach to the content .... ☐
mpleteness of content .... ☐
ithor's reputation .... ☐
blisher's reputation .... ☐
ook cover design or layout .... ☐
dex or table of contents of book .... ☐
ice of book .... ☐
ecial effects, graphics, illustrations .... ☐
her (Please specify): _____ ☐

How did you first learn about this book?

w in Macmillan Computer Publishing catalog .... ☐
commended by store personnel .... ☐
w the book on bookshelf at store .... ☐
commended by a friend .... ☐
ceived advertisement in the mail .... ☐
w an advertisement in: _____ ☐
ead book review in: _____ ☐
her (Please specify): _____ ☐

How many computer books have you purchased in the last six months?

is book only .... ☐   3 to 5 books...................... ☐
books .... ☐   More than 5 .... ☐

4. Where did you purchase this book?

Bookstore .... ☐
Computer Store .... ☐
Consumer Electronics Store .... ☐
Department Store .... ☐
Office Club .... ☐
Warehouse Club .... ☐
Mail Order .... ☐
Direct from Publisher .... ☐
Internet site .... ☐
Other (Please specify): _____ ☐

5. How long have you been using a computer?

☐ Less than 6 months   ☐ 6 months to a year
☐ 1 to 3 years   ☐ More than 3 years

6. What is your level of experience with personal computers and with the subject of this book?

	With PCs	With subject of book
New	☐	☐
Casual	☐	☐
Accomplished	☐	☐
Expert	☐	☐

Source Code ISBN: 0-7897-0637-7

7. Which of the following best describes your job title?

Administrative Assistant ☐
Coordinator ☐
Manager/Supervisor ☐
Director ☐
Vice President ☐
President/CEO/COO ☐
Lawyer/Doctor/Medical Professional ☐
Teacher/Educator/Trainer ☐
Engineer/Technician ☐
Consultant ☐
Not employed/Student/Retired ☐
Other (Please specify): _____ ☐

8. Which of the following best describes the area of the company your job title falls under?

Accounting ☐
Engineering ☐
Manufacturing ☐
Operations ☐
Marketing ☐
Sales ☐
Other (Please specify): _____ ☐

9. What is your age?

Under 20 ☐
21-29 ☐
30-39 ☐
40-49 ☐
50-59 ☐
60-over ☐

10. Are you:

Male ☐
Female ☐

11. Which computer publications do you read regularly? (Please list)

_____
_____
_____
_____
_____
_____
_____
_____
_____
_____

Comments: _____

Fold here and scotch-tape to mail.

This package contains one CD-ROM.

See Appendix B for a description of how to install the CD-ROM and the programs on the disk. Appendix B also includes descriptions of the individual programs and figures showing each program.

By opening this package you agree to be bound by the following: